BROKEN DREAMS

BROKEN DREAMS

AN INTIMATE HISTORY OF THE MIDLIFE CRISIS

MARK JACKSON

REAKTION BOOKS

For Siobhán

Your love, darling, impregnates my heart, touches it into calm, strongly beating
life so that when I am with you, I forget I am a dying man.

W.N.P. Barbellion, *The Journal of a Disappointed Man* (1919)

Published by Reaktion Books Ltd
Unit 32, Waterside
44–48 Wharf Road
London N1 7UX, UK

www.reaktionbooks.co.uk

First published 2021
Copyright © Mark Jackson 2021

Printed and bound in Great Britain
by TJ Books Ltd, Padstow, Cornwall

A catalogue record for this book is available from the British Library

ISBN 978 1 78914 395 9

CONTENTS

1
ANATOMY OF A CRISIS

'The paradox is that of entering the prime of life, the stage of
fulfilment, but at the same time the prime and fulfilment are dated.
Death lies beyond.'

ELLIOTT JAQUES, 1965[1]

Who – or what – killed Reginald Perrin?

Created by the comic brilliance of the English novelist and dramatist David Nobbs, Reggie Perrin figured as the protagonist in a series of
novels, the first of which, *The Death of Reginald Perrin*, was published
in 1975.[2] Reggie was 46 years old, lived with his wife Elizabeth and their
cat in a white neo-Georgian house in Surrey, and commuted to work
each day by train, which always arrived at Waterloo station precisely
eleven minutes behind time. As a beleaguered middle manager at
Sunshine Desserts, located in a 'shapeless, five-storey block' on the South
Bank of the Thames, Reggie was a slave both to the timeless rhythms of
the working day – the clock above the main entrance having been 'stuck
at three forty-six since 1967' – and to the idiosyncrasies of his imperious
boss, CJ. The Perrins's two children, Linda and Mark, had grown up and
moved out, leaving their parents living in a house that was no longer
a home.

Reggie's sense of midlife malaise is evident from the opening pages
of the novel. Visiting the company's doctor, who is suffering himself
from the insecurity and anxieties of middle age, Reggie admits to feeling
'listless and lazy', being unable to concentrate and having lost his 'zest
for living'.[3] Over subsequent days, his behaviour becomes impulsive
and unpredictable; he is tempted by thoughts of infidelity, argues with
his children, dictates abusive letters to clients, and compares himself
unfavourably with the self-assured solidity of younger men. While his
wife is visiting her mother in Worthing one day, Reggie begins to erase
the traces of what appears to him to have been an insignificant, now
spiritually bankrupt, life:

He threw the wedding photos on the fire. Hats curled and blackened. He threw the small-bore rifle team on the fire. Campbell-Lewiston, E. L., curled and blackened. His past went up in smoke, heat and little bits of ash.[4]

Burning the past was not an unfamiliar gesture for fictional middle-aged men. Joe Lampton, the 35-year-old working-class anti-hero of John Braine's *Life at the Top*, published in 1962, had harboured hopes that a spring bonfire would effectively obliterate the emotional and material baggage that had weighed him down during ten years of marriage and allow him to make 'some kind of fresh start'.[5] For Reggie Perrin, too, the seemingly trivial act of incinerating records from his youth constituted the seeds of a plan to convert his alienation from a meaningless, materialist world – 'I am not a mere tool of the capitalist society,' he writes on the crossword page of his daily newspaper – into self-affirming action.[6] Having written suicide notes to his manager at work, his fancied mistress and his wife, Reggie drives to the coast of Dorset, undresses and walks 'naked and hairy' into the sea.[7]

David Nobbs's ability to capture the multiple registers of middle-age disaffection becomes apparent not only in the last third of the novel, but in the iconic television series, *The Fall and Rise of Reginald Perrin* (1976–9), that followed.[8] Reggie Perrin does not drown. Instead, he swims back to shore, changes into new clothes, disguises himself with a wig and false beard, and drives away to start a freer life, unencumbered by anxieties about his capacity to perform satisfactorily either at work or at home. Reggie's midlife detour lasts no more than a few days. Nostalgia for his previous life leads him – in his new identity as Martin Wellbourne – to reconnect first with his daughter and then, at his own memorial service, with his wife and friends. By the closing scenes, Reggie (as Martin) is back working at Sunshine Desserts and on the verge of (re)marrying Elizabeth. Although the irony is evident, the outcome of Reggie's existential crisis is more hopeful than disheartening. Aware of Reggie's deceit, Elizabeth welcomes the opportunity that her husband's death and rebirth offers: 'Our marriage wasn't working all that well,' she explains to their daughter. 'Now it is going to work.'[9]

Suspects in the counterfeit death of Reginald Perrin are legion. It would be satisfyingly simple to explain his desertion in terms of a personal psychological breakdown, a form of para-suicide precipitated by the monotony of commuting to work – itself a metaphor for a fruitless journey – and his fear of ageing, fading virility and death. However convincing this emphasis on private anguish might seem – and there is much to commend it as a semi-plausible account of Reggie's demise – it pays insufficient attention to the social and cultural, and particularly the relational, factors that prescribed middle-age lives and pleasures in the post-war period. The boundaries and possibilities of adulthood, parenthood and family life after the Second World War – and the fall and rise of Reginald Perrin – were fashioned in part by longer life expectancies, most clearly visible in the extended period of time available to individuals and couples beyond the age of forty or fifty. The contours and inflection points of this protracted arc of life were marked by demonstrable physiological changes, particularly in women, whose biographies were often reduced to the calendar of menstruation, reproduction and menopause. But the seemingly natural biological boundaries that bookended adulthood in women, and to a lesser extent in men, were coloured by gendered expectations of self, family, work and home. It is not coincidental that Elizabeth – also of course at midlife – remains implausibly stable and dependable, the fixed domestic point around which characters in *The Death of Reginald Perrin* revolve in the face of her husband's crisis, her own agency flattened in the interests of family cohesion and narrative ease.

Reggie Perrin's rejection of home and work – an option not open to his wife – indicates that in men the stages of life were customarily measured not in terms of biological milestones but in relation to the onset, modulations and cessation of working life – that is, in terms of radically different perceptions and experiences of time and productivity. In the decades following the Second World War, the challenges of negotiating conflicting expectations across the life course, the uneven distribution of domestic responsibilities and contrasting opportunities for paid employment and leisure were thought to be the primary causes of post-marital unhappiness, the breakdown of families and accelerating levels of divorce.[10] As many contemporary studies of marital tensions indicated, these facets of midlife were not without economic, political and cultural, as well as conjugal, contexts. According to the British sociologist Ronald Fletcher, writing in 1962, stresses and strains in relationships were not the outcome of decaying family life, as some were suggesting, but the 'unforeseen consequences' of broader social transformations.[11] Reginald and Elizabeth Perrin were just one among countless couples struggling to cope with the political uncertainties and crises of the Cold War; with the accelerating pace of technological and cultural change that generated what the American writer Alvin Toffler referred to in 1970 as 'future shock';[12] with the boredom and monotony of work and domesticity; and with the atomizing imperatives of economic liberalism with its insistence on self-realization and self-fulfilment regardless of the impact on others.

Reggie's acting out of his midlife turmoil was therefore neither incidental nor unique. In spite of contemporary literary and scholarly preoccupations, nor was it confined to men. Passages of pain and self-reflection were demanded of everyone by a Western society – almost a world – in perpetual crisis, by imbalances of power and the disruption of social relations that blighted the middle decades of the twentieth century.[13] The propensity for happy young lovers to turn into sombre married couples, who had come to detest or fear each other during middle age, as Marie Stopes put it in 1928, emerged alongside fully realized fears of economic depression and fascism.[14] Attempts to resolve individual and marital tensions at midlife, or to heal fractured families, were devised by self-help authors, marriage guidance counsellors, divorce lawyers, psychoanalysts and politicians, who insisted that after the Second World War life could and must change – or at least return to some idealized impersonation of the past. Reginald Perrin's fretful, but ultimately fruitful, metamorphosis into Martin Wellbourne and the coincidental resolution of the crises imposed on his family were emblematic of the alternating dreams and despair of a world in disarray.

David Nobbs's comic optimism that Reggie could navigate his way successfully through midlife was not necessarily shared or replicated elsewhere. Longitudinal surveys and ethnographic studies carried out after the war suggested that some people blossomed in midlife, adjusting relatively comfortably to major life events. But many researchers emphasized how middle age was experienced as a period of anxiety and turmoil; as a phase of life in which physical and mental health, intimate relationships, families, career prospects and financial security fell irretrievably apart.[15] Shaping this bleak view was a long-held conviction, expressed in medical texts, novels and the media throughout the late nineteenth and early twentieth centuries, that middle age constituted at best a plateau period, and at worst a phase of steady decline, within the life course.[16] The forces of stagnation or involution were always personal, buried in the biology and psychology of everyday life. But they were also shaped by circumstances beyond the control of individuals

and families. During the late 1940s and '50s, the freedom and contentment of men, women and children were constrained by beliefs in an
ideal life course and an optimal family structure that were promoted
– most notably by the British prime minister, Winston Churchill, in
1943 – as one of the pillars of political promises to secure domestic and
social stability after the war.[17] Like so many middle-aged families living
through and beyond the Second World War, Reginald Iolanthe Perrin
(RIP) and his wife and children were derailed by uncomfortable com-
parisons between present achievements and past aspirations – leading
to fear of the future.

IN 1965 THE Canadian-born psychoanalyst and social scientist Elliott
Jaques introduced a term – the midlife crisis – that established the narrative parameters for David Nobbs's demotic portrayal of the revolt of
the middle-aged man.[18] Jaques's early work, carried out at the Tavistock
Institute of Human Relations in London during the 1940s and '50s, had
focused primarily on the ways in which social systems operated as
forms of 'defense against persecutory and depressive anxiety' among
their members, as well as a mechanism for protecting the integrity of
the system itself.[19] During the following decades, Jaques became an
influential figure in studies of bureaucracy, managerial accountability
and leadership, as well as human capacity, work and social justice,
introducing terms such as 'corporate culture', 'time-span of discretion'
and 'requisite organization' into professional and popular discussions of occupational hierarchies and working practices.[20] Jaques's
contributions bridged a number of academic disciplines – including
sociology, psychology and economics – but his theories of the interrelations between individual, institutional and social behaviour were
connected through his preoccupations with time, creativity and trust,
and his interest in the entangled determinants of psychic and social
equilibrium.[21]

Jaques's sociological and psychological writings were patterned
by his empirical studies of institutions such as factories, churches and
hospitals. They were also affected by his training and practice as a psychoanalyst and by the theories of Sigmund Freud and Wilfred Bion, as
well as Melanie Klein, with whom he had worked and published during
the 1950s.[22] These influences are particularly evident in his formulation
of the midlife crisis. Jaques had begun to think about the concept in

1952 – at the age of 35 – during a period of personal reflection on the challenges of midlife. His views were prompted not only by the conclusion of his own analytic sessions with Klein, but by Dante's account of a midlife journey into, and eventually through, darkness and depression in the *Inferno*, written in the late thirteenth century. When Jaques first presented his paper on death and the midlife crisis to the British Psychoanalytical Society in 1957, it generated only a muted response and it was not published in the *International Journal of Psycho-analysis* until eight years later.[23] In the paper, Jaques argued that during the middle years of life, when the 'first phase of adult life has been lived', adjustment to a new set of circumstances was necessary: work and family had been established; parents had grown old; and children were 'at the threshold of adulthood'. When combined with personal experience of ageing, the challenge of coping with these synchronous pressures generated awareness of approaching death: 'The paradox is that of entering the prime of life, the stage of fulfilment, but at the same time the prime and fulfilment are dated. Death lies beyond.'[24]

According to Jaques, those who had reached midlife without having successfully established themselves in terms of marriage and occupation, or who were emotionally immature, were 'badly prepared for meeting the demands of middle age'. As a result, they were likely to display what became the stereotypical or clichéd features of a midlife crisis, most notably dramatic transformations in identity and behaviour. Psychological immaturity, Jaques argued, provided the seeds for a depressive 'crisis of middle life' that emerged around the age of 35 and was energetically masked by a manic determination to thwart advancing years:

> The compulsive attempts, in many men and women reaching middle age, to remain young, the hypochondriacal concern over health and appearance, the emergence of sexual promiscuity in order to prove youth and potency, the hollowness and lack of genuine enjoyment of life, and the frequency of religious concern, are familiar patterns. They are attempts at a race against time.[25]

Without working carefully through the purgatorial anguish of midlife, Jaques warned, strategies intended to protect against the tragedy of death were unlikely to be successful: 'These defensive fantasies', he insisted, 'are just as persecuting, however, as the chaotic and hopeless internal situation they are meant to mitigate.'[26]

Jaques's portrayal of the midlife crisis was based only tangentially on his practice as an analyst; he outlined the features of merely one illustrative case of a middle-aged man (Mr N.), successful in his career and married with three children, whose 'unconscious depressive anxiety' had erupted into manifest feelings of loss and suicidal thoughts at the onset of the Christmas holiday one year. Psychoanalysis indicated that his 'phobic attitude to death and his escape into activity' to assuage his sense of panic could be traced to infantile fears of maternal abandonment, disappointment and persecution, now projected onto his wife and one of his children. Continued analysis allowed Jaques's patient to mobilize the 'positive factors in his personality' in order to address his emotional impoverishment, restore family relationships and overcome his midlife crisis.[27] The significance of this singular case has often been overlooked in assessments of Jaques's reflections on middle age, but in many ways it was his close analysis of the roots of Mr N.'s feelings about ageing and death that constituted a template for subsequent articulations of the causes, manifestations and treatment of the midlife crisis.

As Jaques acknowledged, one 'case history does not of course prove a general thesis'; it merely illustrated a theme.[28] He substantiated his argument about the perils and potentialities of midlife transitions with evidence drawn from studying what he referred to as 'a random sample' of over three hundred 'creative artists' – such as Mozart, Raphael, Rossini, Bach, Shakespeare, Dickens and Keats – who had either died in their mid- to late thirties or whose work had changed radically in volume or mode of expression during that period of their lives.[29] Accounts of the creative transformations experienced by composers, artists and writers as they attempted to resolve personal anxieties during middle age were not entirely new. The 'Gauguin syndrome', named after Paul Gauguin's surrender to his midlife eruption of artistic genius, was already being used to describe feelings of disappointment at the loss of youthful dreams, the burden of adult commitments and responsibilities, the renunciation of work and family, and the selfish pursuit of meaning and identity.[30] Gauguin's narcissistic – and deeply controversial – search for fulfilment at the expense of his wife and five children became a common trope in subsequent psychological discussions of the potential scale of midlife change and its impact on individual and family life courses.[31]

Stimulated by contemporary interest in the physical, psychological and spiritual dimensions of ageing, evident in the emergence of geriatrics or gerontology on both sides of the Atlantic, biographical and autobiographical studies of 'the curve of life', as well as reflections on patterns of productivity across the life course, were not unusual in the mid-twentieth century.[32] In the 1920s the American psychologist Granville Stanley Hall had substantiated his theory of a 'dangerous age' by recounting the emotional disturbances evident in the lives of middle-aged men as they faced the 'bankruptcy of some of their youthful hopes', referring at one point to 'the middle-age crisis' experienced by the German philosopher Friedrich Nietzsche in his thirties.[33] Carl Jung's concept of individuation, with its emphasis on integration of the self across the second half of life, was also assembled by juxtaposing case histories, notions of an archetypal life course and reflections on his own midlife struggles to assimilate conflicting facets of his personality.[34] In his reflections on 'the stages of life', Jung referred to the thirties and forties as a pivotal period of personal development comparable to Jaques's depiction of the crisis generated by the onset of middle age. 'We see that in this phase of life – between thirty-five and forty – an important change in human psyche is in preparation,' wrote Jung in 1933.

> At first it is not a conscious and striking change; it is rather a matter of indirect signs of a change which seems to take its rise from the unconscious. Often it is something like a slow change in a person's character; in another case certain traits may come to light which had disappeared in childhood; or again, inclinations and interests begin to weaken and others arise to take their places.[35]

What Jaques added to these earlier accounts of the creative transitions of middle age was a psychoanalytical framework that provided a basis not only for explaining, but for mitigating, the emotional turbulence and psychological imbalance characteristic of a midlife crisis.[36]

In Jaques's work, the midlife crisis was profoundly masculine. Although he acknowledged that women could experience a similar transition, he merely noted that it was often obscured 'by the proximity of the onset of changes associated with the menopause'.[37] This claim sat uneasily with his insistence that the midlife crisis occurred around the age of 35, a decade or so before most women experienced menopause. Jaques's disregard of gender as a mediating factor in midlife disturbances – or his implicit reduction of women's transitions to biology – was consistent with his earlier analyses of occupational and managerial practices. His studies of organizational cultures and remuneration rarely mentioned the paid work of women: in *Equitable Payment*, published in 1961, he referred in passing to 'the different needs of men as compared with those of women' in terms of 'socially necessary income'. But he excluded women from his analysis 'because of the complications in equating the value of men's and women's salaries owing to the undefined male-female pay differential'.[38] For Jaques, these issues were matters of government policy, not social scientific investigation.

There were broader drivers of Jaques's accent on men at midlife. Most post-war studies of psychological stress were concerned with the health and economic risks associated with overworked middle-aged business men, who were prone to stomach ulcers, diabetes, high cholesterol, hypertension and heart attacks – as well as stress-related psychological breakdowns.[39] The significance of stress in women was often downplayed. Examples of the tendency not just to ignore but also to denigrate the severity of women's midlife stresses are not difficult to identify. In 1961 the Canadian journalist Fred Kerner contrasted the competition and tension felt by working men forced to 'live up to a picture of masculinity' with women's less demanding roles as wives and homemakers. Men suffered more heart disease not because they were 'weaker', he insisted, but because they were overloaded by greater levels of stress than women:

> While nobody underestimates the job of being a housewife and mother, it has been found that men especially seem to have ailments which can most often be traced to prolonged tension. It seems that in spite of the many responsibilities involved, a woman's work at home apparently does not entail the same type of strain which most men undergo from day to day while working.[40]

Kerner's partiality was not unusual, but Jaques's reluctance to explore women at midlife and beyond – and indeed his dismissive collapsing of women's midlife crises into menopause – is still puzzling. There was clearly a literature on the psychological, as well as biological, experiences of women at midlife, a literature that was far more balanced in its treatment of ageing women and men and went well beyond simplistic accounts of the change of life on women's health. In the works of Dorothy Canfield Fisher and Marie Stopes on motherhood and marriage or in the writings of self-help authors and marriage guidance counsellors, the challenges facing women at midlife were regarded as no less common than those faced by men and similarly triggered by awareness of ageing and death. According to Fisher, for example, a woman – not unlike a man – could find that 'in middle life, in the prime of her powers, she is banished to the dismal ranks of the army of the unemployed'.[41] This is not to suggest that Elliott Jaques could or should have known about this literature, although some of it was indeed produced by former colleagues at the Tavistock. Rather it indicates the extent to which ideas about the multiple challenges faced by middle-aged women already held currency well before Jaques identified the midlife crisis as primarily the privilege of men.

Sociologists, psychologists, philosophers, historians and journalists, among others, have tended to regard the publication of Jaques's article in one of two ways. For some, 1965 constituted a pivotal moment at which understandings of midlife were radically transformed.[42] Certain evidence supports this reading. Already by the late 1960s, Jaques's account of the crises experienced at midlife was framing theoretical and professional attempts to understand and resolve the 'search for meaning' that was thought to typify the midlife identity crisis.[43] On both sides of the Atlantic, the midlife crisis became a prominent motif in research investigating the impact of life transitions on marriage trajectories, personal identity and health. It was used in the late 1960s, for example, by South African social scientists Rhona and Robert N. Rapoport in their work on the causes of overload in 'dual career families' at midlife.[44] In Britain, the notion of the midlife crisis framed understandings of the personal, familial and social causes and consequences of infidelity, separation and divorce. In particular, Jaques's work influenced the psychoanalytical approaches to resolving marital tensions adopted by Henry Dicks and his colleagues at the Tavistock Clinic in London.[45]

The multiple biological, psychological and social layers of midlife despair articulated by Jaques also figured in media discussions of life crises associated with male – and, less often, female – menopause.[46] 'The hormone-production levels are dropping,' wrote American journalist Martha Weinman Lear in 1973,

> the head is balding, the sexual vigor is diminishing, the stress is unending, the children are leaving, the parents are dying, the job horizons are narrowing, the friends are having their first heart attacks; the past floats by in the fog of hopes not realized,

opportunities not grasped, women not bedded, potentials not fulfilled, and the future is a confrontation with one's own mortality.[47]

In addition, the emotional turbulence of middle age provided the subject matter for post-war literary and cinematic explorations of the interrelations between personal, marital and social crises, some referring directly to the midlife crisis, others commenting more obliquely on the overlapping themes of love, infidelity and betrayal in middle age.[48] From these perspectives, Jaques's formulation of the midlife crisis in 1965 constituted a seminal contribution to scholarly and popular representations of adulthood.

There is an alternative literature, however, that has contested emphasis on 1965. According to Jaques's wife and co-researcher, Kathryn Cason, it took 25 years for her husband's 'work on midlife crisis to be accepted.'[49] There is some, admittedly rather raw, data to support Cason's view that usage of the term only reached a peak in the late 1980s and early '90s.[50] More critically, however, Susanne Schmidt has argued that it was only after the work of the American journalist Gail Sheehy in the mid-1970s that the notion of the midlife crisis became prevalent. It was through Sheehy's work, Schmidt suggests, that a more positive articulation of midlife possibilities, especially for women, became embedded in 'popular culture and social sciences in the United States and beyond.'[51] There have also been other historical contenders for the role of originator and popularizer of the term. In 1972 a journalist for *New York Magazine* claimed that it was the Yale psychologist Daniel Levinson – rather than Jaques – who had 'christened' the 'male midlife crisis.'[52] Whether Sheehy or Levinson is credited, this interpretation suggests that the concept of the midlife crisis was only fully recognized and widely embraced in America from the late 1970s and '80s onwards – that is, well after Jaques had set out what have since been regarded as the archetypal features of the male midlife crisis. Key to this later appropriation of the term was the growth of clinical interest in ageing, as well as feminist critiques of the double standard of ageing that denounced 'women with special severity', as Susan Sontag put it in 1972.[53] One striking feature of the literature following the 1974 publication of Sheehy's *Passages* in particular is certainly its strident rejection of negative connotations of midlife and its focus instead on the potential for growth and self-fulfilment – particularly for women – during the middle years.[54]

Although both interpretations of Jaques's publication offer significant insights into the history of the midlife crisis, they are incomplete. On the one hand, proponents of 1965 as the tipping point in the history of the midlife crisis have failed to acknowledge significant antecedents of Jaques's notion. The paradigmatic features of Jaques's midlife crisis – with its emphasis on dissatisfaction with work, disillusionment with life, desperation to postpone mental and physical decline, gradual detachment from family responsibilities and infidelity with a younger, more athletic accomplice – were well-established in self-help manuals, marriage guidance literature, novels and medical texts written during the interwar and immediate post-war years. Indeed, versions of the phrase itself had appeared in psychoanalytical literature in the years preceding Jaques's publication. In the early 1960s British marriage guidance counsellors and American proponents of Harry Stack Sullivan's theory of personality had already referred to the 'middle-age crisis' that could be generated by ill-health, external pressures and internal psychological struggles with the prospect of death.[55] Experiences and understandings of midlife in these terms were not independent of social context. Rather, they emerged against a backdrop of economic crisis and global instability during the interwar years and were brought to maturity by transitions in families, communities and societies generated by post-war reconstruction and the cultural revolutions of the 1950s and '60s.

On the other hand, scholars who have focused on the contributions of Sheehy, Levinson and others in the 1970s have tended to ignore Jaques's emphasis on the transformative potential of identity crises and the ways in which his psychoanalytical interpretation shaped psychotherapeutic practice. They have failed to recognize the extent to which Jaques's formulation of midlife transitions subverted the decline narrative that had been so prominent in early twentieth-century accounts of adulthood and continued to impact on models and experiences of middle age. While the midlife crisis depicted by Jaques could certainly trigger fears of fading imagination and declining energy, it could also be navigated successfully, leading to what he termed 'sculpted creativity' and serenity.[56] Alongside portrayals of the destructive behaviour that typified later accounts of the crises of middle age – evident in the fictitious death of Reginald Perrin – the germs of more optimistic accounts of the midlife crisis were already embedded in the work of Jaques and others in the 1960s, albeit obscured by images of anxiety-ridden middle-aged men determined to destroy themselves and those around them.

MIDDLE AGE, PERHAPS more than any other phase of the life course, defies straightforward definition. In Elliott Jaques's articulation, the midlife crisis was typically encountered by men and women in their mid-thirties at the onset of middle age, although the process of personal transition could run on for some years and varied between individuals.[57] Jaques's identification of 35 as the approximate age at which the future began to be eclipsed by the past and overshadowed by the spectre of death relied on a scriptural calibration of life expectancy: 'The simple fact of the situation', he wrote in 1965, 'is the arrival at the mid-point of life.'[58] In this sense, midlife – a term introduced in 1895 – consti-tuted merely a point midway along the normative biblical life span of three-score years and ten, the moment at which the 'half-time whistle' of life is blown, according to a relatively recent British account of the midlife crisis and male menopause.[59] Yet there was more to midlife than chronology. According to Jaques, the midlife crisis was primarily psychological and social, moulded not just by age but by the need to adjust to new family responsibilities and occupational conditions in order to achieve 'mature and independent adulthood'.[60] Midlife there-fore marked both entry into the multiple responsibilities of middle age and departure from the material and sensual aspirations of youth.[61]

In spite of Jaques's precision, it is clear that the frontiers of middle age – and by inference the timing of the midlife crisis – were fluid. In an article on 'America's Unknown Middle-agers' published in the *New York Times* in 1956, Thomas Desmond, chair of the Joint Legislative Committee on Problems of the Aging, explored what he referred to as the 'much misunderstood period' of middle age. Intent on promoting greater attention to health and well-being in adulthood and revers-ing contemporary emphases on 'decay and decline' through midlife, he advocated creating a distinct medical specialty of 'mediatrics' – analogous to paediatrics and geriatrics – to 'blossom forth to care for middle-aged folks'.[62] As Desmond and his peers recognized, however, there was a major challenge involved in establishing a dedicated field of scientific and clinical enquiry of this nature: there was no single definition or agreed meaning of the term 'middle age'.[63] For some of Desmond's contemporaries, middle age constituted a 'fixed period' between the ages of forty and sixty, a notion that had been promoted in the early twentieth century by the Canadian physician William Osler.[64] According to other mid-century writers, middle age in both men and women signified not a precise period of time, but a state of mind or set of life-course experiences – and often crises – related to balancing work, family and leisure and characterized by lassitude and boredom.[65] Mid-century measures of middle age related primarily to the life course of the professional classes. But ageing varied significantly according to socio-economic status: working-class men could be regarded as already old by their forties – that is, beyond conventional Western timings of midlife among the middle classes.[66]

The complexities and ambiguities of midlife and the relative invisibility of middle age, indicated in the post-war reflections of Desmond and others, have shaped histories of ageing. Historians have been particularly slow to understand middle age, which was perhaps the 'last portion of the life span to be discovered', on its own terms, rather than as a silent sequel to adolescence and early adulthood or merely as a prelude to old age.[67] Recently, however, a number of key studies have begun to expose the social, cultural and political determinants of shifting representations of midlife and to open up questions about the diversity of experiences of middle age according to socioeconomic status, race and gender across the nineteenth and twentieth centuries. Kay Heath, Patricia Cohen, John Benson, Steven Mintz and Ben Hutchinson have constructively directed scholarly attention to the middle years of life and exposed many of the myths of ageing through adulthood, in both the past and the present.[68] Similarly, anthropological and cultural studies by Margaret Lock and Margaret Morganroth Gullette have challenged beliefs in the biological inevitability of decline through the middle years, highlighting the ways in which narratives of ageing are themselves cultural fictions.[69] Indeed, Gullette's radical social constructionist approach explicitly targets the conventional Western ideology of midlife decline, or what she refers to as 'middle-ageism', by exposing the ways in which we are aged not primarily by biology, but by culture.[70]

By foregrounding the cultural determinants of ageing through midlife, historical, sociological and anthropological studies have revealed the ways in which middle age has been measured and experienced variably – but not mutually exclusively – in temporal, biological, psychosocial or cultural terms. Modern Western approaches to ageing have been defined by the ticking of a clock, distinguishing different life stages in terms of the number of years and decades lived. Age boundaries of this nature were mutable. In the late nineteenth century, censuses regarded thirty as the onset of middle age. As Benson has shown, however, by the 1920s increased life expectancy had served to elongate and recalibrate the life course, while growing cultural resistance to the inevitability of decline helped to raise the lower limit of middle age – at least among the affluent – from thirty to forty.[71] Across the middle decades of the twentieth century, advertising space in newspapers and magazines was increasingly dedicated to selling products aimed at countering the 'middle-aged spread' associated with complacency and self-indulgence and at alleviating fears of reaching forty, or what the manufacturers of tonics referred to as 'forty-phobia'.[72] At the same time, the upper limit of middle age was extended from fifty to sixty or sixty-five, reflecting longer lives, changing patterns of retirement, and attempts to promote economic growth by harnessing the financial resources and managerial capacities of privileged male 'middle-agers'. This mid-century framing of middle age as the years between forty and sixty-five paralleled, and perhaps implicitly informed, Jaques's chronology of life transitions: his prototypical midlife crisis occurred in the late thirties at the onset of middle age and was followed by another crisis at 'full maturity around the age of sixty-five'.[73]

The passing of time was not the only measure of ageing, although it was perhaps the most commonly used across the twentieth century. The perceived waning of midlife energy and productivity – with its associated psychological distress – was also read in physiological terms, particularly in women, whose middle years were reckoned by the rhythms of a biological clock and whose later years were thought to be dominated, and in some cases disrupted, by the hormonal imbalances, physical changes and emotional unsteadiness associated with menopause. Men were also thought to experience a male menopause or climacteric, typified by declining virility and a range of health-related challenges, but its more muted and extenuated character rendered it a less obvious determinant of existential crises. The timing and experiences of biological transitions across the life course were mediated by social norms. Margaret Lock, Judith Houck, Elizabeth Siegel Watkins and Hans-Georg Hofer have revealed how manifestations of ageing and the 'change of life' in women and men were medicalized and narrated in line with culturally specific gendered notions of domestic duties and occupational aspirations and achievements – that is, in terms of the contemporary values attached to the capacity of people to love and work.[74] In women, middle age was defined not merely by menstrual changes, but also by the departure of children from home to school, work or marriage, in some cultures by the transition from mother to grandmother, and increasingly by retirement from the workplace. Although men's experiences of ageing were undoubtedly transformed in the post-war period by expectations of companionate marriage and greater domestic responsibilities, the meanings and boundaries of male middle age continued to be understood largely in terms of patterns of work beyond the home, a practice dictated by patriarchal bureaucratic conveniences such as taxation, retirement and pension rights.

The writings of Gullette and others remind us that experiences of middle age were linked to a Western market economy that depended for its success on sustaining the spending power of individuals across the life course.[75] They also suggest that post-war conceptualizations of midlife as a time of crisis presupposed certain constructions of selfhood, of the relation between individuals and society, and of the performative nature of identity, notions that were recognized at the time by contemporary commentators.[76] Margaret Lock's comparative studies of menopause indicate that late twentieth-century Western accounts of ageing tended to prioritize self-empowerment and personal agency across the life course.[77] American and British models of the developmental stages – or seasons – of life and the transitions between them emphasized the ways in which periods of crisis could be harnessed to carve new identities, new healthier forms of self. But stressing the primacy of the individual generated fresh opportunities for conflict between partners and within families, making love 'more difficult than ever', according to some studies.[78] By contrast, Japanese models of socialization towards maturity focused traditionally not on 'learning how to maximize one's own interests', but on becoming 'social and moral beings'. At least before the encroachment of Western conjugal family structures and values and the rise of individualism, Japanese narratives of midlife conveyed an alternative model of the self, one that was 'created and recreated in daily life, beyond and within the confines of the body, through committed participation in social life and through self-reflection', rather than self-interest.[79] It was precisely the challenge of balancing the welfare of self and others, especially within the context of the family, which singled out middle age – and the middle decades of the twentieth century – as a time of crisis.

IN HIS EARLY twentieth-century studies of 'senescence', or the last half of life, Granville Stanley Hall cited the work of the Danish author Karin Michaëlis as the origin of the term 'a dangerous age', which Hall took to mean the point in life when men were 'prone to weigh themselves in the balance' as death approached.[80] What is interesting about Hall's appropriation of the term, given his almost exclusive emphasis on the creative crises of ageing men and the ways in which he drew on his own experiences during middle age and retirement in his seventies, is that Michaëlis's novel *The Dangerous Age* – first published in Danish in 1910 and translated the following year into English – comprised letters and fragments from the diary of a 42-year-old woman, Elsie Lindtner.[81] In narrating the emotional traumas of solitude and divorce in middle age, Michaëlis drew attention to the painful 'years of transition' in women between forty and fifty: 'The time is gone by,' Lindtner reflects in one journal entry. 'Life is over.'[82]

According to Michaëlis, *The Dangerous Age* – published in America as *The Critical Age* – generated 'storms of abuse from the ranks of the radicals all over Europe'. The text also attracted a combination of acclaim and disapproval from American journalists.[83] Contemporary outrage, particularly among suffragists, was partly triggered by Michaëlis's insistence that middle-aged women were unfit for office because of biological limitations. From Michaëlis's perspective, the 'distressing enigmas of feminine psychology', which included a propensity for women to lie more often than men, stemmed from physiological imbalances and crises dictated not by their social status but by nature.[84] There were, of course, alternative narratives of crises in the lives of women. In 1921, for example, the English novelist Rose Macaulay stressed the social, cultural and economic factors that shaped the capacity of women to cope across the whole life course, not just at midlife. In what was regarded at the time as a riposte to *The Critical Age*, one that challenged the biological determinism inherent in Michaëlis's work, Macaulay's account of the lives of four women at different stages of the life cycle – written when she was in her late thirties – suggested that the absence of full voting rights and the lack of financial or professional independence meant that all ages were dangerous for women.[85]

Nevertheless, it is clear that the notion that midlife – or entry into middle age – constituted a particularly critical stage of life gained considerable purchase immediately before and after the First World War. In men, crises were thought to be triggered by the tedium of working life. 'But when twenty years of toil have come and gone,' wrote the American pastor Newell Dwight Hillis in 1912, 'the work grows stale, the labor mechanical and meaningless, and the months become an endless round of hopeless repetition.' During this 'dangerous age', he continued, men turned to new sources of excitement such as gambling in order to combat the monotony of their lives.[86] In contemporary literature, male attempts to escape midlife ennui through over-indulgence were most clearly expressed in Sinclair Lewis's satirical novel *Babbitt* (1922), a work that gave birth to the term 'Babbitry' to describe the complacent materialism of middle-aged, middle-class American businessmen. Women were not excluded from accounts of midlife angst, but their crises were either triggered by their husbands' infidelity or inextricably linked to their roles as wives and mothers and portrayed in terms of fractured domestic relations. In *Midstream*, an autobiography published in 1914 when he was 35, the American author Will Levington Comfort referred to 'the restlessness and agony' experienced by women at midlife when they realized that they had become strangers to their husbands and children.[87]

The multivalent language of crisis was not only applied to personal transitions and family tensions. On the contrary, acceptance of midlife as a time of crisis depended on wider applications of the term, especially in relation to the chaos created by economic austerity, global and political conflict, environmental damage and rapid technological and cultural change. As optimism that peace would be restored after the First World War was swiftly shattered, Winston Churchill's model of 'the world crisis' infected political and popular imagination.[88] Citing H. G. Wells's prescription for salvaging Western civilization from the wreckage of the First World War, Hall suggested that the human race itself had 'passed its prime' and that a 'new social consciousness' was required to steer the world through a critical period of chaos into a healthier old age.[89] During subsequent decades of the twentieth century, the concept of 'crisis' was applied to describe the rising threat of communism and fascism; the disintegration of an imperialist world order that had been contemptuously established by the global North and West; the hardening of hostilities between West and East, epitomized by the Suez and Cuban Missile crises of the 1950s and early '6os; the disruption of gender relations and the recalibration of patterns of work and leisure; the perceived decline in ethical standards and cultural values;[90] and disillusionment with post-war promises of prosperity powered by the American dream.[91] Studies of crisis spread. According to some scholars, adoption of the term itself constituted a mentality to be probed and contested if the 'cataclysmic events' of the first half of the twentieth century were to be superseded by a 'post-crisis world', one in which global stability was to be achieved either through political negotiation or, perhaps paradoxically, through the 'inhibiting nuclear balance of terror'.[92]

Images and analyses of crises and catastrophes permeated the dystopian emotional and ecological landscapes imagined by contemporary writers. In *The Andromeda Strain*, first published in 1969, the American novelist Michael Crichton reflected on the generic nature of crises, defined in the novel as those situations in which a 'previously tolerable set of circumstances is suddenly, by the addition of another factor, rendered wholly intolerable'.[93] Crichton recognized that crises were the product of 'individuals and personalities, which are unique'. But he nonetheless suggested – in the apocryphal words of William Gladstone, who was confounded by multiple political crises throughout his parliamentary career – that 'all crises are the same'.[94] Although crises were 'made by men', similarities in their processes and structures rendered them predictable in retrospect, understandable through historical analysis. The origins and attributes of the midlife crisis can be seen in comparable terms. Like the biological, environmental and political crises of *The Andromeda Strain*, the midlife crisis, even when voiced in individual terms, was moulded by the specific preoccupations and prejudices of interwar and post-war populations.[95]

Crises appeared in other cultural and intellectual spaces, facilitating assimilation of the language of the midlife crisis into professional and popular discourses. Scholars described masculinity, middle-class families, parenthood and suburban working-class wives as either in crisis or vulnerable to crises.[96] Largely negative framings of midlife families failing to adapt to changing social pressures continued to shape interpretations and experiences of intimate relationships, especially in the context of rising levels of divorce across the second half of the twentieth century, not only in Western capitalist countries, but also for example in the German Democratic Republic and in Japan, where the prevalence of divorce had already traditionally been high.[97] Crises of identity in middle age, which were seen to undermine the stability and security of the nuclear family and to contravene conservative commitments to the sanctity of marriage, constituted a manifestation of the ways in which middle-aged men and women internalized and then acted out anxieties about the fault lines in modern societies, often to the detriment of partners and children. Rising levels of marital breakdown were driven by an ideological clash between nostalgia for a golden age of (heteronormative) marriage, in which social and domestic harmony were protected, and what Ulrich Beck and Elisabeth Beck-Gernsheim have termed an 'ego epidemic' characterized by the pursuit of individual, rather than shared, aspirations for self-fulfilment.[98]

A link between the individualizing imperatives of capitalist societies and the breakdown of families at midlife, understood by Beck and Beck-Gernsheim in terms of a 'collision of interests between love, family and personal freedom',[99] was expressed by other late twentieth-century commentators on social and cultural values. In an essay published in *New York Magazine* in 1976, the American novelist Tom Wolfe branded the 1970s the 'me' decade, a period in which the luxuries of self-expression and self-indulgence were democratized, made available for the first time to those outside the aristocratic, intellectual and artistic elite through a combination of sustained economic growth and the expansion of leisure time.[100] More recently, critiques of individualization and its consequences have been revived by the Polish sociologist Zygmunt Bauman. In a series of books published in the first decade of the twenty-first century, Bauman explored the 'temporariness of partnerships', as well as the transience and obsolescence of commodities, in terms of liquidity.[101] Within a liquid world of 'obsessive, compulsive, unstoppable change', Bauman argues, human bonds have become frail, power separated from politics and human identity transformed from a 'given' into a 'task', one dependent not on structural reform, but on individual endeavour.[102]

Historical sources only partially substantiate the critical position adopted by Bauman and others. Some post-war British commentators certainly regarded marital problems and divorce as products of 'the propensity to regard the assertion of one's own individuality as a right, and to pursue one's personal satisfaction, reckless of the consequences for others'.[103] But analyses of the relations between the politics of individualism and the avidity of individuals often lack historical specificity or cultural sensitivity. 'True observations about the human predicament', Bauman argues in *The Individualized Society*, 'stay true for a long time. Their truth is not affected by the trials of history.'[104] Universalist assertions of this nature should be contested. Jane Lewis has argued that the social impact of selfish individualism, supposedly manifest in women's increased employment outside the family and men's reluctance to commit to home and family, has been assumed rather than demonstrated in historical accounts of changing family structures and values.[105] Claims that families have been broken by the pursuit of instant gratification or by the commodification of parents, partners and children therefore need to be evaluated against the empirical record of how people have lived, loved and lost. Similarly, overly narrow portrayals of the midlife crisis as an individualistic search for self-satisfaction must be weighed against evidence that crises were not merely indications of the uncritical appropriation or internalization of the liquid values of modernity, but also paradoxically served as a means of rejecting its artifice and superficiality.

WHEN REGINALD PERRIN walked away from his life in order to sculpt a fresh identity, he became everyman, his wife and children everyday victims of a mid-century crisis of confidence in the capacity of previously trusted values and norms to reconcile individuals, families, societies and nations in conflict.[106] Articulation and propagation of the paradigmatic features of the midlife crisis in the second half of the twentieth century reflected contemporary reservations about whether bruised social relations could be effectively healed by the application of traditional salves – most notably the reinforcement of marital, gender, socio-economic and age-related hierarchies of power. The desire to acclimatize to unfamiliar social expectations without erasing old values was evident in moves to repatriate emotionally and physically wounded soldiers; to uphold the institution of marriage by modernizing divorce laws; to promote the economy through the consumption of leisure and goods; and to balance the capacity of women to work with the perceived need to restore domestic stability. Such efforts failed to satisfy demands for change because they served simply to reinforce outdated and divisive social norms and political structures. In this sense, understandings and experiences of the midlife crisis after the Second World War cannot be attributed merely to personal angst in the face of death, as Jaques insisted in 1965, or to an unequivocal manifestation of biological change. Rather, as Beck and Beck-Gernsheim have insisted, the midlife crisis must be understood as 'a *social*, not a natural event', a phenomenon shaped by newly complex and emergent interrelations between self and society.[107]

Across the late twentieth century and the early decades of the twenty-first, the midlife crisis featured in scholarly, literary, cinematic and media explorations of middle age, marriage, divorce and death. In some academic analyses, the midlife crisis was dismissed as a myth on the ground that crises in the middle years were by no means universal or inevitable, at least not in the stereotypical form evident in popular portrayals of midlife or in confessional and self-help literature on how to survive the biological and emotional challenges of 'middlescence'.[108] The notion of crisis was also contested by writers who stressed that the middle decades of life often constituted a period of growth and increased self-fulfilment and life satisfaction, rather than despair, and that the 'crisis model' of change across the life course was unsubstantiated.[109] In spite of disputes about its existence, however, the midlife crisis remained a 'media staple', as Elaine Wethington put it in 2000. Fuelled by concerns about the collapse of families and communities, the concept of crisis continued to inflect Western accounts of marital tensions, declining sexual prowess, the loss of reproductive capacity, occupational dissatisfaction and the search for personal meaning in a troubled world.[110]

Impulsive and destructive behaviours associated with the paradigmatic midlife crisis were mocked and satirized, or the term itself was applied disparagingly to crises in other domains of personal, social and political life.[111] In 1982 an American company produced a board game for two to six players 'in their prime'. Entitled 'Mid-life Crisis', the game was marketed with the slogan: 'Can you survive your mid-life crisis without cracking up, breaking up, or going broke?'[112] Although created and played in jest, 'Mid-life Crisis' captured the genuine difficulties experienced by middle-aged men and women in the decades after the Second World War. The 'Crisis Cards' and 'Zap Cards' that generated players' scores detailed the multiple obstacles to midlife happiness, as well as the personal, financial and family costs of failing to address them. More recently, *The Ladybird Book of the Mid-life Crisis* similarly reduced middle age to a series of clichéd vignettes of men and women behaving badly.[113] Not all popular treatments of midlife have been cynical. Joe Ollmann's graphic novel *Mid-life* – a book that he suggested should 'be taken with whiskey' – offers an honest, as well as humorous, account of a middle-aged man living uneasily at the halfway point between birth and death.[114]

In spite of tendencies to underestimate or trivialize the pressures of middle age, the personal and political resonance of the midlife crisis was apparent in the everyday lives of individuals, couples and families seen by marriage guidance counsellors and divorce lawyers or treated by psychologists and psychiatrists during the post-war decades. Indeed, recent attempts to dismiss the midlife crisis as a rare, or mythical, entity are contradicted by contemporary evidence from clinicians and counsellors. In 1981 the American physicians David and Beatrix Hamburg reported that over the previous two decades they had 'been consulted often by persons experiencing a mid-life crisis'. Rather than being infrequent occurrences, they claimed, crises in middle age constituted 'a significant portion of psychiatric practice in the United States'.[115] The experiences of marriage guidance counsellors in Britain after the war were similar. Every day they encountered distressed middle-agers, whose personal and professional lives had become painful and lonely as they faced the effects of marital conflict, the monotony of the workplace, ill-health and ageing – as well as the prospect of death.[116] As a notion that helped individuals and their families to articulate and address the stresses that overwhelmed them during middle age, the midlife crisis became not merely a fable or fantasy, but an observable social phenomenon.

In 1924 E. M. Forster had questioned whether anyone would want to read a novel about middle age.[117] As it happens, Forster was overly pessimistic about the appeal of the midlife novel. During the interwar and post-war years, the multiple crises of midlife – whether manifest in ill-health, the stagnation and collapse of relationships, or occupational frustrations – provided plots for novelists on both sides of the Atlantic. Writers such as Sloan Wilson, John Updike, Richard Yates, Simone de Beauvoir, Doris Lessing, Joseph Heller and Marilyn French explored the struggles of individuals and families at midlife as a mechanism for drawing out the drivers and impacts of major social, political and cultural transitions. In addition, television and film scriptwriters sought to exploit the physical and emotional turmoil of middle-agers for both tragic and comic purposes. With varying degrees of earnestness, films such as *Ikiru* (1952), *Journey to Italy* (1954), *The Seven Year Itch* (1955), *Scenes from a Marriage* (1973), *Middle Age Crazy* (1980) and *Shirley Valentine* (1989) betrayed the breadth and depth of post-Second World War obsessions with the crises of middle age. One result of such visible preoccupations with the perils of the middle years was that the midlife crisis became a model for understanding other personal transitions, such as the quarter-life crisis or retirement, as well as a device for conveying individual and collective experiences of ageing and health, love and work, peace and war, and life and death.[118]

THE FOLLOWING PAGES trace how the midlife crisis became a key feature of private lives and public debate across the middle decades of the twentieth century. Components of the crises of middle age were certainly identified and experienced during the interwar years. But, in the words of Joseph Heller in his fictional account of the gradual disintegration of an American middle-class family at midlife, 'something happened' after the Second World War to recalibrate the life course and reshape Western expectations of adulthood.[119] Family, social and gender relations were transformed; attitudes to love and work, as well as marriage and divorce, were re-orientated; and selfish aspirations for personal prosperity that had been awakened by the American dream and made possible by a gradual transition from austerity to affluence were amplified. Demographic shifts, economic necessity and emotional convenience restructured the habits and routines of everyday life during the 1950s and '60s, increasing the sense of separation between partners, between generations, between home and work, and between the various facets of personal identity as it evolved across the life course. It was the apparent alienation and fragmentation of individual and family lives after the war that created space and time for the midlife crisis to emerge and flourish.

2
LIFE BEGINS AT FORTY

'It is a mistake to think of life as a mere measure of time.'
GEORGE RYLEY SCOTT, 1953[1]

Delaying the onset or acceleration of age-related decline in physical ability and intellectual capacity – particularly after the age of forty – was a common aspiration of middle-class, middle-aged Britons and Americans during the interwar and post-war years. Stimulated in part by uncertainties about the political and economic stability of a world itself in crisis, preoccupations with looking younger and living longer – as the prominent American nutritionist Gayelord Hauser put it in 1950 – generated an expanding market for anti-ageing merchandise and medication, a phenomenon that was readily encouraged and exploited by the beauty and fashion industries, pharmaceutical companies and doctors, as well as self-help authors such as George Ryley Scott.[2] Between 1919 and 1979, Scott published over forty books on health, sex, prostitution, poultry farming, corporal and capital punishment, torture, birth control and marriage. One of Scott's well-known works was his 1953 study entitled *The Quest for Youth*, in which he explored a variety of techniques for 'retaining physical and mental vigour in old age' and for 'postponing or avoiding the coming of senescence', a term that denoted the deterioration in strength and ability that seemingly characterized the second half of the life course.[3]

According to Scott, scientists had been preoccupied for some years with addressing two key impediments to healthy ageing. First, they had attempted, in vain, to prolong the life span. While average life expectancy had increased across the first half of the twentieth century, largely as a result of falling rates of infant mortality, the upper limit of life had changed little. In spite of developments in the study of rejuvenation, very few people lived beyond the age of seventy – 'the period allotted to man by an omnipotent deity', in Scott's words.[4] Second, scientists

had focused far more effectively on extending the period between adolescence and senescence, allowing people to remain active during their
middle years. However, even here much remained to be achieved. While
rising standards of living had enabled a greater proportion of modern
Western populations to enjoy a more energetic and fulfilled middle
age, the majority of people continued to 'become old before they need',
according to Scott. Failing 'to get out of life all that they should' and
living in a 'mentally comatose state; impotent, moronic and cerebrally
exhausted', many men and women continued to give the impression that
they were 'prematurely tired of life'. Although slowing down in middle
age might be tempting, it could also develop into a dangerous habit.[5]

Scott's advice to readers wishing to avoid early ageing and senility
was undemanding. In the first instance, they were to avoid conceiving of
life merely in terms of age and numbers. Believing that it was a mistake
'to think of life as a mere measure of time', Scott argued that there was
no virtue in 'living to be a hundred if, during the final thirty years, one
merely exists as a useless, an inactive and an unintelligent organism'.
Rather, people should aim to prolong 'virility of thought and action'
without regard for their chronological age.[6] Second, readers should
look beyond simplistic rejuvenation techniques, however promising
those might appear, and focus instead on diverting destructive impulses
into more creative activities that would retain or extend intellectual
capacity across the life course. In line with psychoanalysts – including
Elliott Jaques – and counsellors reflecting on the skills required to attain
and maintain emotional maturity, Scott highlighted the importance of
sublimation, a term that captured the personal and social significance
of transforming damaging behaviours – some of which came to typify
the midlife crisis – into socially acceptable actions.[7] Betraying contemporary double standards in relation to gender and ageing, Scott
argued that sublimation came more easily to women, whose apparent
narcissism enabled them to develop interests that subverted disruptive
sexual instincts and enriched their intellectual and social lives.[8]

Scott spoke for – and to – a generation struggling to cope with the
sense that time was running out for the civilized world as much as for
individuals within it. But his admonition not to measure life in terms of
time alone was rarely incorporated into personal or political accounts of
ageing. Fears for the future were certainly not only triggered by awareness of the passing of years and decades. They were shaped also by
growing recognition that American dreams of economic and spiritual

affluence – dreams that had been forcefully re-articulated by James Truslow Adams in 1935 – were under threat amid the ruins of the Second World War and the hostilities of the Cold War.[9] Nevertheless, post-war researchers portrayed midlife not in terms of collective prosperity and shared values, as Adams and others had imagined, but explicitly in terms of personal time being wasted or lost amid the aimless routines and occupational pressures of middle age. According to the developmental psychologist Erik Erikson, the failure to mature effectively through midlife could leave people feeling that 'time is now short, too short for the attempt to start another life and to try out alternate roads to integrity'.[10] In 1963 psychotherapists Jane Pearce and Saul Newton explained the 'middle-age crisis' even more forcefully in terms of time mislaid or misspent.

> The secret illusion of eternal youth wears thin during the middle years. Time presses, the future has arrived. Promised projects can no longer be postponed – they are noted to have been already accomplished, imminently to be tackled or jettisoned. One can be a promising young man until one loses his hair. Now repressed needs clamor for satisfaction, and substitutes for them taste increasingly of ashes. One does not want to die without having lived.[11]

Novelists similarly painted middle age in terms of time squandered on meaningless pursuits. At the start of the final volume in the Rabbit series of novels by John Updike, Harry 'Rabbit' Angstrom – 56 years old, overweight and with a failing heart – is driving home having picked up his son, daughter-in-law and two grandchildren from the airport. "'Driving is boring,'' Rabbit pontificates, "but it's what we do. Most of American life is driving somewhere and then driving back wondering why the hell you went."[12] As Updike's novels suggest, the shifting dial between time past and time future remained the principal yardstick for gauging the utility or futility of life. Haunted by numbers, Western societies continued to demonstrate what Susan Sontag referred to in 1972 as 'an almost obsessional interest in keeping the score card of aging'.[13] It was within this emotional framework of temporal checks and balances that entry into middle age came to be seen as one of the specific 'punctuation marks' in the life cycle, as American psychologist Bernice Neugarten put it in 1976.[14] Midlife, Granville Stanley Hall had suggested in 1921, was 'the critical age when men are prone to weigh themselves in the balance' as their 'sense of superfluous time' is lost and the tide begins to 'turn again home'.[15] The tendency for men and women to take stock of their lives continued to be recognized as a peculiar feature of middle age across the post-war years.[16] Midlife was a time to measure achievements against the customary milestones of a standardized life course, re-evaluate work and relationships, recognize the bankruptcy of youthful hopes, and attempt to turn back the clock before it was too late.

A sense of time structured cinematic treatments of ageing, creativity and death during the middle years of the twentieth century. In *Ikiru* (1952), co-written and directed by the widely acclaimed Japanese director Akira Kurosawa, the central character, Mr Kanji Watanabe, is a middle-aged, widowed civil servant who begins to re-evaluate his life when he learns that he is unlikely to live more than a few months. Fearing that he is merely 'killing time', not 'really alive at all', Watanabe pledges to devote his remaining energies to ensuring that a local petition for a children's playground is no longer ignored by town hall bureaucrats.[17] 'It's not too late,' Watanabe realizes in the midst of his personal despair. 'It isn't impossible; I can do something if I want to.'[18] By reinvigorating the final months of his life, Watanabe converts his preoccupations with death into social activism, achieving in the process his own transformation or awakening. Watanabe was not the only fictional character to attempt to reverse the loss of creative productivity wrought by time. In Pinfold's angst-ridden awareness of ebbing creativity in Evelyn Waugh's *The Ordeal of Gilbert Pinfold* (1957) and Krapp's interweaving of his past, present and future – or adolescence, midlife and senescence – in Samuel Beckett's *Krapp's Last Tape* (1958), time appeared both as a measure of life (or being) and a metaphor for living (or doing).[19] The irony, recognized by the English novelist John Braine in 1957, was that by midlife time was a resource that was no longer available. 'Time, like a loan from the bank,' he wrote in *Room at the Top*, 'is something you're only given when you possess so much that you don't need it.'[20]

In spite of Scott's caution that contemplating life in merely chronological terms hampered the pursuit of happiness, post-war Western populations who had aged together through economic crisis and global warfare, but who now expected to live longer and more productive lives in conditions of relative affluence, identified with fearful images of emotional and temporal bankruptcy after midlife. Recovering lost time or appreciating time as a limited commodity in a world dictated by clocks became an obsession, particularly among the middle-aged, who felt themselves to be dying just as they had begun to live. Crises of chronology were never merely personal. Popular framings of middle age in terms of crises triggered by a sense of physical decline, family conflict and impending death drew heavily on political appraisals of the 1920s through to the 1960s as crisis decades marked by the collapse of economic security, political stability, social order and domestic cohesion. Individual reassessments of the meaning of life, manifest in prolonged periods of introspection and self-doubt, were therefore interwoven with Western attempts to establish what Adams had referred to as 'a new scale and basis for values'.[21] In theory, experience and imagination, the midlife crisis emerged at a moment when the socio-economic conditions that had made possible a relatively stable and clearly defined life course – structured around an extended middle age as the prime of life – collided with fresh anxieties about the difficulties of adjusting to cultural upheaval.

IN HER REFLECTIONS on the transition from middle age to old age, published in 1970, Bernice Neugarten – one of the most influential and politically active American scholars in the field of developmental psychology and gerontology – emphasized the manner in which individuals passed through a socially, as well as biologically, regulated life cycle. 'There exists a socially prescribed timetable,' she wrote, 'for the ordering of major life events: a time in the life-span when men and women are expected to marry, a time to raise children, a time to retire.'[22] This normative pattern, Neugarten continued, was 'adhered to, more or less consistently, by most persons within a given social group', providing a yardstick by which peers could measure their own progress through life.

> Men and women are aware not only of the social clocks that operate in various areas of their lives but also of their own timing; and they readily describe themselves as 'early,' 'late,' or 'on time' with regard to the major life events.[23]

Recognizing that life histories needed to be considered within their social and cultural contexts, which served to create norms and expectations regarding age-appropriate behaviour, Neugarten insisted that any

attempt to chart the course and stages of the life cycle should acknowledge the ways in which 'historical time, life time (or chronological age)
and social time' were all 'intricately intertwined'.[24]

As historical demographers and family historians have revealed,
the standardized life course described by Neugarten was a peculiarly
modern, middle-class, Western and, as it transpired, transient phenomenon. The modern life cycle – or the 'life course paradigm' as the
notable historian of ageing and family relations Tamara Hareven put it
in 1994 – emerged during the early twentieth century, reached its apogee
in the decades after the Second World War and was already beginning
to fragment by the 1980s as career choices and family structures began
to change again.[25] According to the historian Michael Anderson, a
number of features distinguished the life cycle followed by modern
British populations as opposed to their predecessors in the eighteenth
and nineteenth centuries: they generally lived longer, married and set
up home at a younger age, had fewer children clustered together earlier
in the marriage, and worked – often in the same job – for a standard
period of time set primarily by company and state pension schemes.[26]
This pattern and its implications, especially for post-war women, were
recognized by contemporaries. In his Reith Lectures, broadcast by the
Home Service in 1962, George Carstairs, Professor of Psychological
Medicine at the University of Edinburgh, pointed out that women's
domestic lives had been transformed by three key social transitions:
'men and women now tend to marry earlier, to have much smaller families, and complete their families in a much shorter space of time'.[27] The
result, as the British social scientist Richard Titmuss had suggested in
1958, was that women spent a far smaller proportion of their lives concerned with childbearing and maternal care than previous generations:
'by the time the typical mother of today has virtually completed the
cycle of motherhood', he wrote, 'she still has practically half her total
life expectancy to live.'[28]

An increasingly homogenous life course impacted on the boundaries,
experiences and challenges of midlife. In the first instance, the teasing
out of the life cycle created a longer period of adulthood and middle
age, not only for individuals but for nuclear families ageing together
through periods of childbirth, child-rearing and the eventual flight of
children from the parental home to enter the workplace, pursue further
education or marry. Second, smaller family sizes and the tendency for
children to be born earlier in the marriage and within a smaller number

of years meant that parents lived and worked longer after their children had been born and grown up than previous generations. By the early 1950s, for example, women on average were likely to live for a further 52 years after the birth of their last child, well beyond the menopause, their children's marriages and – if they worked – retirement. Interwar and post-war generations were the first to routinely know, and be able to care for, their grandchildren and sometimes great-grandchildren.[29]

Demographic changes and shifts in individual and family schedules also affected inheritance, contributing to mounting domestic pressures around midlife. Anderson's analysis shows that those born in 1891 could expect to inherit from their parents at the age of 37, while they still had children at home and when their oldest child was 'at best only just entering the labour force'. By contrast, those born in 1946 could expect to wait until 56 before both parents had died, that is, well after their children had left home, leaving the middle-aged vulnerable to economic constraints, particularly when they were sandwiched between caring for children and caring for parents.[30]

Standardization of the life course resulted in a large proportion of the population passing through these transitions – from single to married, through parenthood, into the period when children left home, and on to grandparenthood – in increasingly concentrated spaces of time. What had once been phases of gradual evolution, with significant overlap between life stages, became relatively sudden ruptures in life experiences, carrying the potential for personal and domestic crises. As Benita Eisler's study of everyday life in the 1950s indicates, in this sense the post-war generation, most of whom had married within four years of leaving school and had children shortly afterwards, constituted a unique cohort. Having grown up during the Depression, middle-class women of the 1950s and '60s were energized by shared expectations of reaching family milestones together and enjoying the confidence of companionate marriages and the friendship of neighbours. But they were soon disheartened by a society that continued to privilege the achievements of husbands over those of their wives.[31]

According to Howard Chudacoff, the growing homogeneity of experiences through the life course was one factor leading to greater 'age consciousness' in American culture.[32] The construction of age-related norms during the late nineteenth and early twentieth centuries was encouraged by transformations in the rhythms of education and the workplace, by new forms of classification and communication, and by mounting dependency on clocks in office, factories, schools and homes – clocks that not only measured time, but controlled it. Awareness of chronological milestones was promoted by a growing consumer economy with its renewed emphasis on the consumption of entertainment, home furnishings, cars, holidays, clothes, food and drink. In her study of envy in America during the early decades of the twentieth century, Susan Matt has argued that by the 1920s purchasing mass-produced goods was no longer condemned as immoral, but now heralded as a legitimate activity in the pursuit of happiness – one that also promoted further expansion of the consumer economy.[33] This transition created a challenge for those white, middle-class middle-agers who had sufficient income to purchase an expanding range of commodities, namely how to 'keep up with the Joneses', a notion that continued to inform American and British attitudes to family life through the post-war years.[34]

Customs relating to age and success were reinforced by the sales strategies of companies such as Hallmark Cards, which exploited growing preoccupations with age boundaries by producing birthday cards marking the successful passing of chronological milestones – decades as well as years.[35] Marketing techniques that played on age as a measure of achievement – or failure – were echoed in advertisements for age-defying tonics and creams that emphasized the need to resist the potential physical, emotional and domestic decay associated with reaching a threshold birthday. From the early twentieth century, it became commonplace not only to measure life in annual or decennial increments, but to evaluate individual and family progress against age-specific benchmarks of status and success, at home as much as at work. The emergence of uniform indicators of achievement during the first half of the twentieth century created a cohort of expectant middle-agers, children of a morbid interwar economy who were beginning to experience together greater opportunities for longer, healthier lives during the 1950s and '60s.[36] But standardization of the life course also increased the likelihood of people experiencing an assortment of personal disappointments, domestic tensions, occupational discontent and economic pressures as they struggled to keep pace with the demands of an individualistic capitalist society, in which the pursuit of self-fulfilment began to supplant commitments to family cohesion.

Demographic stability of the life cycle was not necessarily matched by greater family stability or equality within relationships.[37] Nor were improved life prospects, generated by the emergence of relatively well-defined and extended life stages alongside rising standards of living, distributed evenly or democratically across populations. Rather, opportunities for self-realization across a longer life course, particularly through the consumption of goods and leisure, varied widely according to economic and cultural circumstances.[38] In the first instance, it is evident that the modern Western life course, with its advantages and limitations, first appeared among the urban middle classes, who benefited earlier than their rural and working-class peers from reductions in mortality rates and improved standards of living. Retaining older traditional patterns and rhythms across the life course, which in some ways provided a buffer against rapid social change, working-class parents and their families aged more rapidly, as George Orwell pointed out in 1941: 'One of the few authentic class-differences, as opposed to class-distinctions', he wrote in an essay on Donald McGill's seaside postcards,

> still existing in England is that the working classes age very much earlier. They do not live less long, provided that they survive their childhood, nor do they lose their physical activity earlier, but they do lose very early their youthful appearance. This fact is observable everywhere, but can be most easily verified by watching one of the higher age groups registering for military service; the middle- and upper-class members look, on average, ten years younger than the others.[39]

Orwell's suggestion that the manifestations, and to some extent the meanings, of age were determined primarily by differences in attitude and opportunity between classes was echoed in studies that revealed how experiences of the life course varied according to cultural expectations and aspirations related to family structure and the distribution of financial and caring responsibilities.[40] In 1967 a comparative study of life cycle patterns suggested substantial differences in the timing, perception and consequences of major life events in Japan, China and the United States. Traditional Japanese stem families tended to pass through three stages defined in turn by the initial co-location of successive generations; the death of the father and transference of headship to the son; and the subsequent death of the mother with the creation of a new nuclear family. With its emphasis on family values, succession of the family line and support of ageing parents, this structure was thought to allow families to adjust effectively to economic pressures.[41] In contrast, Chinese joint families, in which all siblings stayed within the parental home, often dissolved because of tensions across and within generations. And the American nuclear family, the life course of which was defined in terms of the timings of work, marriage, childbearing, contraction of family size and old age, allowed the intrusion of critical transitions to fracture domestic stability.[42]

Cultural differences shaped individual and family life courses – and the experiences of adulthood and midlife – in other ways. Sudhir Kakar has argued that in India middle age only constituted a distinct life stage among the Westernized urban elite and that adulthood was measured primarily in terms of changing roles within the family – such as the marriage of the first child – rather than individual age. These differences from Western accounts of midlife did not mean that mature Indian adults did not experience transitions or crises; on the contrary, pressure to relinquish power to the next generation, to withdraw gradually from the outside world and to renounce sexuality could create an existential crisis not dissimilar to that described by Elliott Jaques.[43] Steven Mintz and Susan Kellogg's detailed study of American family life indicates how adulthood and ageing were also not uniform across America, where black families suffered disproportionately in terms of economic depression, unemployment and early widowhood, altering their experiences and expectations across the life course.[44] As Steven Mintz has argued elsewhere, differences in family structures across America, including the rates and timings of marriage and divorce, were not products of race alone. They were also the result of 'divergent social and economic circumstances' marked by 'deepening class differences' and contrasting occupational and educational opportunities.[45]

Studies of cultural variations in how the life course was constructed, represented and experienced suggest the need to be cautious in accepting uncritically the notion of a standardized, homogenous life course, or at least in applying the modern middle-class Western model indiscriminately to other times and places. While the contours of the life cycle, whatever its precise rhythm, flow and duration, constituted one mode of demographic reality, the meanings and boundaries of different life stages were always determined by local values and practices. Categories such as adolescence and midlife – and their associated identities and sense of temporality – 'do not arise in language and practice at random',

Thomas S. Weiner and Lucinda P. Bernheimer suggested in their study of midlife identity among children of the 1960s. Rather they become prominent in particular places at specific historical moments 'because they encode adaptive challenges and problems that emerge at certain times in life'.[46] Recognition of the cultural specificity of ageing, and the ways in which the sequence of stages of life can be read alternatively, but not exclusively, in individual, family or social terms, also indicates how experiences of the life course are always relational, never entirely personal. Midlife and its crises were shaped by conjugal and intergenerational relationships as well as by personality and circumstances – a set of conditions that explains why not all families or individuals responded in the same way to major life events.

Alternative iconographies of the life course emerged during the twentieth century as the complete life cycle and its stages were imbued with different symbolic meanings. Ancient, medieval and early modern representations of the life cycle had been dominated by literary and visual images of a journey or pilgrimage through the stages of life, with middle age understood as a period of power and privilege before the predictable waning of physical vigour.[47] Stripped of their religious significance, similar notions of rise and fall – sometimes expressed in the form of a staircase – certainly populated modern discussions of ageing. In 1921, for example, Granville Stanley Hall referred to the 'binomial curve' of life, 'rising from a baseline at birth and sinking into it at death'.[48] But at the same time, the older circle of life, with its cosmological resonance, was being gradually broken by the secular, individualizing imperatives of the Western world, the journey now shadowed by anticipation of its destination – personal death. Attempts to recast images of decay and death in softer, more organic terms failed to dispel the sense of desolation that was generated by the seeming inevitability of bodily decline and spiritual dissolution during later life. References to the seasons of life, or to safe passages between them, did not fully eradicate fears of crisis, particularly in middle and old age. From Thomas Cole's *The Voyage of Life* (1842), to the series of paintings by Phoebe Anna Traquair titled *The Progress of a Soul* (1893–1902), and Jasper Johns's *The Seasons* (1986–7), mature middle age – depicted as autumn or fall – was regularly represented as a phase marked by emotional turbulence and fractured identity.[49] Although the final canvases by Traquair and Johns implied the potential for restoration of the self and victory over despair in later years – suggesting that the life course was sometimes imagined more as a sine wave than a binomial curve – feelings of emptiness and loss often remained.

Historical studies of the life cycle – and particularly those that focus on middle age – are limited. But increasing political resistance to 'ageism', a term introduced in 1968, has led scholars to challenge reductive stereotypes of the life course and to recognize the complexity of experiences across space and time.[50] This process has demanded analysis of new sources, most notably literary and cinematic treatments, as well as personal accounts, of ageing. In 1988 Margaret Morganroth Gullette explored the emergence of a new revisionist genre of American fiction – led by Saul Bellow, Margaret Drabble, Anne Tyler and John Updike – in which narratives of resilience and progress helped to dispel earlier fatalistic accounts of decline during and beyond the middle years.[51] In her analysis of novels written about – and often at – midlife, Gullette teases out how cultural contexts collided with the authors' personal lives to make possible freshly optimistic visions of the life course. Gullette's analysis of the first three novels in the Rabbit series by Updike – the fourth in the series was completed after the publication of Gullette's work – is particularly pertinent. The complete cycle of novels, published at approximately ten-year intervals between 1960 and 1990, set out the life of Rabbit Angstrom at the ages of 26, 36, 46 and 56. Gullette is surely right to read the third novel as a commentary on the potential for midlife reconciliation with past failings, acknowledgement of present fortunes, and hopes for personal and family stability in the future.[52] After all, it is in *Rabbit Is Rich* (1981) that Angstrom articulates the sense of freedom and indulgence made possible by reaching the middle years: 'Middle age is a wonderful country, all the things you thought would never happen are happening.'[53] But there is another key feature displayed in successive decades of Angstrom's life: namely that any stage of the life course could be scarred by crises, by subtly shifting tensions between individual desires, family demands and social expectations.

Notwithstanding the late twentieth-century works of Margaret Drabble, Anne Tyler, Doris Lessing, Simone de Beauvoir, Angus Wilson and others, who exposed the obstacles navigated and possibilities harnessed by women through their middle years, midlife novels and films exploring the new landscapes of adulthood were usually written by men and populated by male protagonists, male narcissistic fantasies of sexual and political power, and male fears of waning virility and death.[54]

Scholarly studies carried out during the post-war years – including Elliott Jaques's reflections on the midlife crisis – similarly tended to regard the male life course as the human norm: Daniel Levinson's study of the 'seasons of a man's life' first appeared in 1979, seventeen years before his comparable study of women's lives.[55] Yet, as narratives of age identity reveal, the aspirations and experiences of ageing men should not be taken as representative – or be allowed to reduce the value – of women's experiences across the life course. Women's time, as Julia Kristeva pointed out in the early 1980s, possessed its own social, as well as biological, periodicity and meaning.[56] The life cycles of men and women across the twentieth century were certainly sculpted by shared socio-political contexts, but they were structured differently by the gendering of work and love – 'the twin engines of age anxiety', as Gullette put it.[57] In a cross-cultural study of perceptions of the adult life course, based on field work carried out during the 1980s, Charlotte Ikels and her colleagues suggested that Chinese men and women in Hong Kong staged their life courses in similar ways (in terms of youth, middle age and old age), but that the freedom and responsibilities associated by women and men with particular stages varied:

> Women are somewhat more likely than men to link the life course to family and child-rearing while men are more likely to talk about work ability, in terms of strength, drive, competitiveness, and achievements, than women. Both sexes see a reduction in pressures in the 40s and 50s. Women focus on the free time gained, while men talk about seeing the results of their work efforts and finally being in a position where one's words and opinions are respected.[58]

If love and work – or more accurately work and family – provided the principal yardsticks by which men and women measured their lives for much of the twentieth century, literary sources reveal how middle age was narrated differently according to gender. Lynne Segal has shown how fictional accounts of ageing heterosexual men were marked primarily by concerns about declining sexual potency and the 'increasingly unrealizable' life of desire, both of which appeared as key motifs in late twentieth-century representations of the male midlife crisis.[59] In some women's writings, by contrast, ageing was expressed in more positive tones: for post-war feminist writers such as Germaine Greer, Betty Friedan and Gloria Steinem, the passing of youthful sexual passion allowed women to be 'free at last'.[60] Yet, as Segal shows, this dichotomy between male and female perceptions of shifting sexuality across the life course was overly simplistic. Like men, women ageing through midlife regretted the loss of their freedom to express love and desire or to 'compete with the appeal of younger women'.[61] Equally, in terms of the complexities and variability of the life course, there are too few sources – and certainly too few scholarly studies – to determine whether and how perceptions of age, work, love and family differed or not among same-sex couples; how those who remained single or did not work measured the stages and transitions of their lives; or how constructions and reconstructions of personal identity across the life course were influenced by family relations, as well as by social change.[62]

Mid-twentieth-century theorists conceptualized and labelled the stages and transitions of the life course in different ways. According to the influential feminist sociologist Alice Rossi, interwar and post-war interests in socialization during childhood, adulthood and old age led to longitudinal and cross-sectional studies hoping to explain the processes of change and stability across the life span.[63] The work of Marjorie Fiske Lowenthal and colleagues on coping strategies across 'four stages of life' serves to illustrate Rossi's point. According to Lowenthal, all life events could be stressful. But longitudinal cohort studies of middle-class participants indicated that while early life changes – relating to work, college, marriage and parenthood – were regarded as voluntary and socially valued, later life events – including the post-parental 'empty nest' and retirement – were considered enforced and negative.[64] Studies by sociologists and economists, by contrast, were concerned not with perceptions and experiences of individual life stages and transitions, but with the extent to which the timing of events across the life cycle – whether determined or not by personal choice – impacted on levels of unemployment, financial security and family stability.

Although the precise model varied, developmental psychologists operated within a different framework again, preferring to situate 'any specific phase of life in the broad context of the larger life span'.[65] The work of German-born developmental psychologist Charlotte Bühler provides one example. Bühler's early reflections on understanding the 'curve of life' through biographies were followed in the 1960s by more detailed analyses of self-development and self-determination within the context of 'a person's history, constituted by dates and events' that only made sense when 'assembled and seen together'. From Bühler's psychodynamic perspective, the Western life course – with its potential for both stability and crisis – was shaped consciously or otherwise by the pursuit of certain goals, such as the satisfaction of need, effective adaptation, creative expansion and a sense of accomplishment that preserved psychological equilibrium.[66]

Scholarly debates about the life course – and how to study it – were not merely academic, certainly in relation to midlife. During the middle decades of the century, the middle-aged were becoming a more visible and more powerful proportion of Western populations. John Benson's study of Britain indicates that both the absolute number and the percentage of the population between the ages of 40 and 59 increased steadily across the early and middle decades of the twentieth century.[67] Recognizing the ambiguity of the term, post-war commentators pointed to the rapidly rising proportion of the American population that could be regarded as middle-aged. 'While our total population increased 98 per cent in the last half-century,' wrote American politician Thomas Desmond in 1956, 'our middle agers increased by 200 per cent.'[68] More importantly perhaps in the context of commitments to social reconstruction and economic recovery during the Cold War, the middle-aged could be at the peak of their earning power and play significant roles in the business and political life of the nation. According to Clark Tibbitts, a prominent American researcher on ageing and adjustment, the middle-aged were living longer in better health and were able to harness their experience and wisdom to work more efficiently than younger employees.[69] There were, however, barriers to the capacity of middle-aged men and women to contribute to social stability and economic growth. A feature article in *Time* magazine in 1966, which used Lauren Bacall as the exemplar of graceful and productive ageing through midlife, claimed that the abilities of the middle-aged were being devalued by a 'stultifying Youth Cult' that was thought to be 'intimately related to the American denial of death'.[70] These articles and others like them expressed one of the paradoxes of midlife at mid-century: while middle age emerged as a luxury or privilege associated with urban or suburban affluence, it also carried assumptions that any worthwhile measure of life had, by midlife, already been lived.

WILLIAM OSLER'S INSISTENCE on the 'comparative uselessness of men above forty years of age' and on the need for men over the age of sixty to retire from commercial, political and professional life was not spoken entirely in jest. Presenting to his colleagues in 1905 on the occasion of his departure at the age of 55 from the faculty of Johns Hopkins University, Osler argued that the life course could be divided into various 'fixed periods' according to intellectual and practical productivity. The 'effective, moving, vitalizing work of the world', he claimed, 'is done between the ages of twenty-five and forty – these fifteen golden years of plenty, the anabolic and constructive period, in which there is always a balance in the mental bank and credit is still good'.[71] After forty, men's powers declined until at the age of sixty their work became not only redundant, but potentially dangerous, littered with social and political mistakes.[72] Osler's barbed reflections on ageing owed much to Anthony Trollope's satirical novel *The Fixed Period* (1882), in which members of an island community were to be admitted to a 'college' at the age of 67 before being offered a peaceful 'departure by chloroform' precisely one year later.[73] But given his professional prominence, as he moved from America to take up the Regius Chair of Medicine at Oxford, Osler's opinions became influential in defining middle age.

Deliberately provocative, Osler's partitioning of the life course into fixed periods drew on contemporary representations of the life cycle in terms of rising youthful vigour, a plateauing or gradual decline of ability during the middle years, and more rapid descent towards decrepitude in later life. While the rigidity of his framing of midlife and his dismissal of the accomplishments of older men were not always accepted, Osler's outline of the stages of the ageing process inspired Hall's thoughts on senescence and helped to reinforce and perpetuate accounts of men's middle age in terms of a relatively fixed period of stagnation – at best – between the ages of forty and sixty.[74] British social anthropologist Edmund Leach, for example, regarded people over the age of 45 as relatively useless, largely because rapid cultural change rendered their knowledge and skills redundant. 'In our runaway world,' he wrote in 1968, 'no one much over the age of forty-five is really fit to teach anybody anything. And that includes me. I am fifty-seven. It is hard to accept but that's just the point.'[75] The early to mid-forties signified a watershed in other cultures. Throughout the Edo period in Japan, it had been customary for men in some rural villages to retire at the age of 43, possibly because 42 was regarded as the 'great climacteric' of a man's life, marking the end of his active career.[76]

Weighing the stages of life according to mental and physical capacity was not restricted to men in the early twentieth century. In a scathing critique of marriage as a trade that primarily benefited men, published in 1909, the English writer, actor and suffragist Cicely Hamilton exposed how women were valued or dismissed according to their age.

> A friend of my own (who will forgive me for repeating her con-fidence) told me the other day of a happening in her life that, to my mind, exactly illustrates the awakening of class-consciousness among women. It was the careless speech of a man, addressed to her while she was still a very young girl, to the effect that all women over fifty should be shot. The words were lightly spoken, of course, and were probably intended half as a compliment to her manifest youth; certainly they were not intended as an insult. But their effect was to rouse in her a sense of insult and something akin to a passion of resentment that she and her like should only be supposed to exist so long as they were pleasing, only so long as they possessed the power of awakening sexual desire. She took them as an insult to herself because they were an insult to women in general; and, lightly spoken as they were they made upon her an impression which helped to mould her life.[77]

Negative assessments of the worth of women over fifty surfaced elsewhere. In *The Seven Ages of Woman*, published in 1915 as an instruc-tion manual for 'young wives and mothers', the London gynaecologist Mary Scharlieb adopted a similar image of life's rise and fall through youth, middle age and old age, periods marked in turn by evolution, stability and involution.[78] The pinnacle of physical development in women, Scharlieb argued, was attained around twenty years of age; little material difference then occurred until fifty, an age that coin-cided with menopause and was followed by changes in physical ability and personal appearance.[79] While Scharlieb's work aligned studies of women's life cycles with those of men and recognized the 'social value of older women', she was nevertheless influenced by strongly gendered expectations that women were responsible for upholding family stability across the life course even in the face of their own personal transitions.

Osler, Hamilton and Scharlieb had highlighted a key feature of subsequent models of the modern life course, namely that the stages of life constituted distinguishable periods that were bracketed by crises. Middle age constituted the exemplar of this formulation of a standard life course punctuated by episodes of pivotal transition. Entrance into middle age at around the age of forty was thought to be characterized by deepening awareness of the loss of youth and emerging conflicts between intimacy and isolation, as Erik Erikson put it in 1950.[80] The termination of middle age at around sixty or sixty-five was marked by a further conflict between integrity and despair, or by what the French author Jean Frumusan had referred to graphically in his 1922 study of rejuvenation as entry into 'the cold melancholy valleys' of old age.[81] Although its boundaries were flexible and its problems and potentialities often ignored by psychologists and physicians more interested in adolescence and later life, by mid-century middle age was recognized as a distinct stage in the Western life cycle, with its own demographic and economic characteristics; its own iconography and meaning; its own mentality or state of mind; its own language and literature; its own clichés and stereotypes; its own peculiar prospects of personal and family dissolution; and its need for a dedicated brand of medical care and marital support.[82]

Yet, by the post-war years, the consensus that emerged around the parameters and characteristics of middle age was already being challenged by the ambiguities, contradictions and reconfigurations of midlife that appeared in medical, popular and political discourses. As the work of Clark Tibbitts and others highlights, negative visions of middle age in terms of more frequent illness, occupational redundancy, social ineptitude and a sense of time lost or slipping away were being tempered by a growing belief that midlife could also constitute 'the prime of life', a period marked – at least among the middle classes – by professional success, economic independence and family stability.[83] The demonization of middle and old age as periods of gradual disengagement from society – a process mirrored by social distancing from the elderly – was countered by emphasis on the benefits of experience and wisdom across, and beyond, the middle years.[84] From the 1930s through to the 1970s, the psychoanalytical and psychosocial studies of Carl Jung, Erik Erikson and Elliott Jaques, for example, stressed how psychological maturity and the integration of personality during the middle years could generate greater capacity for caring and coping, renewed creativity and an enriched sense of self.[85] It was this clash between experiencing declining health and well-being at midlife, on the one hand, and recognizing that middle age could – or should – be the prime of life, on the other, that made forty the 'nightmare birthday', one that could precipitate the midlife crisis identified by Elliott Jaques in 1965.[86]

The depiction of midlife as a crossroads, or even more positively as an opportunity for a second chance in life, figured in post-war studies on the development of personality, particularly those influenced by the interpersonal theories and therapeutic approaches of the American psychoanalyst Harry Stack Sullivan and the German psychiatrist Frieda Fromm-Reichmann. In the work of Jane Pearce and Saul Newton, who founded the controversial Sullivan Institute for Research in Psychoanalysis in 1957, middle age constituted a critical life stage in which a clear choice had to be made between growth and deterioration. 'The decision to grow or die', they wrote in 1963,

> is the crisis of middle age. Resignation often masquerades as maturity after forty, but resignation is not growth; it is the person's decision to progressively write off his life as a waste of breath. Therefore, many people die during middle age, although they may wander through the world like zombies waiting to be buried decently for thirty years or more.[87]

References to midlife in terms of potential loss and profit appeared in the columns of journalists and agony aunts responding to concerns expressed by their readers about the perils of ageing. 'Age does not only mean the loss of physical elasticity', wrote Evelyn Home (a pseudonym for Peggy Makins) to one reader in 1938. 'It means greater understanding, greater tolerance and, above all, the possibility of creating something worthwhile now that you know which things are worthless.'[88] Articles such as this illustrate the intensity of efforts to counteract widespread fears of personal decay, an endeavour that was not without political resonance in an age troubled by fears – and the reality – of economic decline and recession.[89] They also reveal the gendered dimensions of age anxiety. Men struggled with competition, work-related insecurities and a sense of receding masculinity, evidenced by hair loss and reduced libido.[90] These male anxieties were expressions of contemporary preoccupations with measuring, managing and maximizing economic productivity, thereby binding men to the ticking of the factory or office clock.[91] Women's crises were thought to be linked to their reproductive, maternal and marital roles, yoking their aspirations and fulfilment to the biological and family clock. At least until women joined the workforce in increasing numbers during the 1960s, anxieties about their physical appearance and the execution of domestic duties overshadowed any interest in women's contributions to the economy outside the home. It was partly this double standard, which was both ageist and sexist, that led post-war feminist authors to decry superficial evaluations of women's social worth and challenge masculine models of the midlife crisis.

As midlife changed – its lower and upper limits teased apart by the shifting rhythms and expectations of family life and work – so too did studies and theories of adult development. In particular, differences between men and women, and between the middle and lower classes, in terms of the timings and meanings of transitions across the life cycle suggested to post-war researchers that there was no normative midlife crisis – no singular or inevitable 'threshold shock' on entering middle age, as Frieda Fromm-Reichmann referred to it in 1959.[92] Rather, there were multiple trajectories marked by numerous entrances and departures, regular tipping points or epiphanies, and a series of alternating equilibria and disequilibria in identity, personality and relationships across time. Even as middle age emerged as a distinctive stage in the life course, large-scale longitudinal surveys, interviews, literary analyses, evolutionary studies of senescence and clinical accounts of the menopause were already serving to divide adulthood into segments, no longer measured only by the almanac, but by variably constructed periods of demands and responsibilities.

Moments of crisis and transition between and across life stages were generated and accentuated by broader socio-economic conditions. According to Erikson, writing in 1959, American democracy was placing peculiar pressures on post-war populations as they strove to tally political promises of self-fulfilment with the realities of adjusting to the 'changing necessities of booms and busts, of peace and war, of migration and determined sedentary life.'[93] Such factors were thought to contribute to the peculiar challenges of middle age, which threatened to become 'the nonsense time, the in-between time, the worst time of your life', according to American authors Robert Lee and Marjorie Casebier in their 1973 study of 'weathering the marriage crisis during middlescence.'[94] It was during middle age, they argued, that boredom, economic pressures, domestic conflict and frustrated expectations created a growing sense of separation between partners, as well as disenchantment with the world. The period of self-appraisal that followed, beginning in 'dead earnest around the age of forty-three',[95] stimulated an appetite for advice literature that offered prescriptions for healthy ageing or, as sociologists Alva Myrdal and Viola Klein put it in 1956, for 'starting afresh at Forty'.[96]

IN AN INTERVIEW published in the *Pittsburgh Press* on 10 April 1917, just four days after America had entered the First World War, Matilda I. Cruice Parsons, the widow of an army officer, implored American women to 'train for the duties that war time may bring'.[97] Drawing on a wide range of evidence, including the work of Granville Stanley Hall and her own experiences training pupils in schools and colleges, Parsons had for some years been advocating a form of 'New Education' that emphasized the role of physical exercise in developing the brain and balancing the emotions.[98] In 1917 she argued that preparing for war was analogous to preparing for 'wifehood and motherhood' and demanded that attention be paid to women's physical training for military, as well as domestic, responsibilities. Her comments were directed particularly at 'the adipose woman of forty' who had neglected to care for herself: 'It is a paradox of life,' Parsons claimed,

> that we do not begin to live until we begin to die. Death begins at thirty, that is, deterioration of the muscle cells sets in. Most old age is premature, and attention to diet and exercise would enable men and women to live a great deal longer than they do to-day. The best part of a woman's life begins at forty.[99]

Applied initially to women, whose health and fitness Parsons believed to be vital to the war effort, during the interwar and post-war years the expression 'life begins at forty' was adopted as a catchphrase by self-help authors on both sides of the Atlantic. During those decades, Parsons's idiom was not merely used to encourage individuals to develop their own physical and creative potential. It was also mobilized as a tool for boosting economic recovery by fostering – or exploiting – middle-class, middle-aged aspirations for prolonged youth and personal fulfilment.

Mid-century attempts to ensure that life did not end at forty embraced two principal strategies. On the one hand, they focused on restoring merely the appearance of youth and vitality or, as Forbes Lindsay had put it in *Harper's Weekly* in 1909, 'obliterating the footprints of Time'.[100] During the early decades of the twentieth century, cosmetics and pharmaceutical companies marketed soaps, creams, shampoos and hormone preparations designed to restore healthy skin and hair; or they promoted fitness regimes, supplements, training courses, spa treatments and appliances for arresting middle-aged spread and enhancing attractiveness.[101] For women in particular, the sales strategies of Elizabeth Arden in America or Boots in Britain testify to the level of popular demand for skincare products – or 'skin food' – for those over forty.[102] Commodities for perfecting appearances and improving energy were

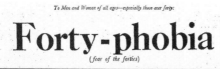

'Forty-phobia (fear of the forties)', *The Times*, 28 April 1938.

not limited to the surface of the body, but included tonics designed to steady frayed nerves and combat 'forty-phobia'.[103] According to the makers of Phyllosan, forty marked 'the end of youth and the beginning of a period of change and re-adjustment, frequently characterised by anxiety and mental stress'. Regular consumption of Phyllosan tablets would enable readers to 'feel younger as they grow older'. Fears of turning forty were commonplace across the second half of the twentieth century. In a Mass-Observation survey on midlife transitions in 2009, for example, a 72-year-old retired clerk recalled that she 'had gone peculiar at 40, but I got over it by remaining 39 for 10 years'.[104]

Men's physical shape and fitness were not ignored in advertisements for anti-ageing products, particularly given the emerging link between body size, heart disease and the ability to work; indeed, the advertisement for Phyllosan appears to be directed primarily at the middle-aged man.[105] But the majority of marketing strategies and advice literature targeted young and middle-aged women, whose primary value was tied to their capacity to attract and retain a husband. Attention was focused particularly on a woman's face, which provided a 'canvas upon which she paints a revised, corrected portrait of herself', as Susan Sontag put it in 1972.[106] Such emphasis played on popular beliefs – and the reality – that when husbands started affairs or remarried after divorce, it was usually with a woman far younger than their wives, who remained largely ineligible for future relationships on account of their age.[107] Of course, the means to preserve at least the image of youth was not available to all. Rather, it was limited to the prosperous middle classes, who had both the desire and the resources – in terms of time and money – to retain their youthful appearance.

The quest for youth could take a second, less superficial route, one that not merely concealed surface cracks and greying temples, but offered to restore physical, intellectual and economic potency across the life course. In 1932 Walter B. Pitkin, professor of journalism at Columbia University and author of numerous self-help guides between the 1920s and the 1940s, used the phrase 'life begins at forty' for the title of a popular advice book that offered readers an antidote to the seemingly inevitable downward spiral of energy and aptitude after midlife.[108] Pitkin enticed his readers with a vision of the excitement and riches on offer in a modern machine age that had reduced the 'hours of toil' and increased opportunities for leisure. His prescription for health and happiness – like Parsons's admonition to middle-aged women – harnessed anxieties about economic recession and the threat of military conflict, as well as contemporary beliefs in the freedom and upward mobility associated with the American dream. For men, contentment came from continued learning, shorter working hours and increased leisure in later life; for women, satisfaction was to be found in embracing new opportunities for work and creativity. 'Life's afternoon is brighter,' Pitkin insisted, 'warmer, fuller of song; and long before the shadows stretch, every fruit grows ripe.'[109]

After the publication of Pitkin's book, 'life begins at forty' became a popular slogan in Britain as well as America, providing the basis for the 1935 comedy *Life Begins at Forty* and a number of songs.[110] In her autobiography published in 1951, the American singer and actress Sophie Tucker admitted that one of her most popular songs was Jack Yellen's 1937 hit 'Life Begins at Forty'. 'It's a hot song,' she wrote, 'and, I insist, it's not dirty. It expresses what everybody who shivers at the word "middle-aged" feels; that is the longing to make life over, to live it more fully and freely. To have more love and a lot more laughs.'[111] The phrase was also satirized in popular culture. In the 1942 film *Life Begins at Eight-thirty* – based on Emlyn Williams's play *The Light of Heart* – the central character struggles with a familiar pattern of midlife challenges: a failing career, growing debt, addiction to alcohol and the fragmentation of family life. Although intended as comic entertainment, *Life Begins at Eight-thirty* portrayed the hopes and disappointments of a generation of middle-agers in a privileged Western world.

As forty came to be regarded in the West not merely in terms of chronology, but as a symbol of personal and often painful transition, the phrase 'life begins at forty' attracted the – largely disparaging – attention of scholars.[112] In their 1956 study on women's dual roles at home and work, Alva Myrdal and Viola Klein were sceptical about advertisements that tried to 'persuade women that they can look 20 at 65', and dismissed the 'element of pep-talk' embedded in claims made by Pitkin and others that it was possible to remain glamorous after forty.[113] Nevertheless, they acknowledged that Pitkin's work revealed the scale of public interest in maintaining active, healthier lives, as well as more appealing bodies, through and beyond middle age. According to Myrdal and Klein, the proliferation of self-help books constituted evidence of 'a widespread desire to extend the period of continued development and growth of personality and bear witness to a still somewhat nervous and self-conscious refusal to "take up one's final position"'.[114]

Contemporary faith in self-improvement through the forms of materialistic consumption promoted by Pitkin had already been parodied in Sinclair Lewis's novel of 1922, *Babbitt*, in which the principal character's selfish pursuit of prosperity and civic status – and his eagerness to hide his heaviness, with its hint of 'fatness' – threatens to destroy his family before he recognizes the emptiness and futility of his grandiosity and 'cre[eps] back' to his wife.[115] But, as Myrdal and Klein recognized, Pitkin's message that modern populations could now progress from 'making a living' to 'living' still proved attractive to aspiring middle-class middle-agers keen to enjoy – and display – their well-earned capacity for consumption and leisure.[116] Pitkin accepted that metabolism and vitality decreased with age and that midlife transitions might be the result of 'some obscure shift in the endocrine balance.'[117] He insisted, however, that biological limitations need not prevent people from living more contentedly as they aged. Health and fulfilment in later life were becoming more attainable and more desirable in a period when standards of living and economic growth were emerging as matters of national, as well as personal, importance.[118] An increased capacity to afford goods and make the most of their leisure time, Pitkin argued, allowed the middle-aged to attain the 'emotional poise which underlies enduring happiness.'[119] 'Happiness', he suggested, 'comes most easily after forty.'[120] Contemporary novelists agreed. In 1939 the eponymous protagonist of Jan Struther's *Mrs Miniver* embraced the joys of turning forty.

> Stepping lightly and quickly down the square, Mrs. Miniver suddenly understood why she was enjoying the forties so much better than she had enjoyed the thirties: it was the difference between August and October, between the heaviness of late summer and the sparkle of early autumn, between the ending of an old phase and the beginning of a fresh one.[121]

The optimism expressed by Pitkin and others challenged prevalent anxieties about the accelerating passage of years and decades. Pitkin countered concerns about approaching old age and death by stressing the value of time: 'Time is neither a medium nor is it exchangeable,' he wrote. 'It is the inmost stuff of life itself.'[122] But his invocation to spend time, as well as money, wisely across the life course in order to prolong health and happiness was not a disinterested form of advice to beleaguered middle-aged men, whose problems outweighed those of older women, according to Pitkin. In addition to being a form of self-help and self-promotion, *Life Begins at Forty* was a prescription for social stability and recovery from the Great Depression. Austerity and automation, Pitkin claimed, had limited the number of jobs for young people and adversely affected their capacity to purchase either 'goods and services for simple subsistence' or those which helped 'toward self-improvement both vocational and cultural'.[123] Pitkin's manifesto for personal fulfilment after the age of forty was underscored by the belief that economic growth, and indeed America's future, now depended primarily on harnessing the spending power, managerial capacities and wisdom of the middle-aged. Success would expand employment prospects for the young, encourage independence and self-sufficiency, enable more people to work part-time, promote longer lives in better health and provide greater opportunities for leisurely self-realization.[124] As with other self-help literature published before and after the Second World War, Pitkin's emphasis on individual accountability for active ageing was aligned with political ambitions to promote model citizens and a stable society without necessarily addressing the socio-economic determinants of health across the life course.[125]

In his own guide to healthy living, first published in 1965 and aimed at men and women approaching what he regarded as the new midlife threshold of fifty, Walter Pitkin's son reflected on the impact of his father's work. By focusing popular and professional attention on '*the subjective, or inner life* of the middle-aged and aging person', he argued, *Life Begins at Forty* had encouraged readers to believe that life could be creative, happy and challenging after the onset of middle age. In the process, Pitkin Jr argued, his father had launched 'a whole industry' of inspirational literature for the middle-aged.[126] As his son recognized, and as historians have noted, Pitkin was by no means the only writer of lifestyle manuals for the middle-aged during the middle decades of the twentieth century, although he was arguably the most prominent and most influential.[127] Numerous books on diet, relaxation and yoga were marketed directly at those over forty – or in the depths of middle age – to help them counter the effects of the stress, tension, poor diet, limited exercise, excessive work and inadequate rest that were thought to lead to nervous breakdowns, chronic ill-health and premature death.[128]

The belief that a 'full and happy life is a balanced one' – particularly for the overworked, middle-aged, male executive – figured particularly strongly in self-help texts for those at midlife.[129] In their 1938 discussion of the merits of relaxation in a frenzied world where few could 'attain equilibrium', the British physician E. J. Boome and speech therapist M. A. Richardson emphasized the role of relaxation in achieving equanimity: 'The balance and stability which can be obtained by the practice of relaxation,' they suggested, 'enables a man to face and deal fearlessly with responsibility and trouble instead of trying to evade them.'[130] Guides to yoga stressed the value of moderation in diet and work, alongside breathing exercises and postures, for those over forty seeking to retain their youthful vigour as well as their figures.[131] And Gayelord Hauser's bestselling *Look Younger, Live Longer* focused on the manner in which readers could ensure good health in later life not only by adopting balanced diets, but by balancing their personality, mind, activities, emotions, recreation, friends, budgets and marriages.[132] 'You have learned that the secret of good health is a balanced diet, that the secret of good looks is a balanced blood stream,' he insisted in a passage that revealed the multivalence of balance as a key health concept. 'What is the secret of a good life? Balanced living.'[133]

The importance of balance in combatting midlife malaise was also emphasized by clinicians and social scientists on both sides of the Atlantic during the middle decades of the twentieth century. Nadina R. Kavinoky was a Swiss-born gynaecologist and the first female president of the American National Council on Family Relations, an organization that had been founded in 1938 to promote marriage and family life. In 1944 Kavinoky claimed that individual and family mental stability depended on an appropriate balance of work, recreation and rest. Recreation in particular, Kavinoky argued, facilitated the rehabilitation of 'men wounded in body and spirit' and enhanced the capacity of couples and their children to cope with the physical and emotional demands of modern living.[134] In Britain, too, advice for the middle-aged highlighted the importance of relaxation – or even idleness – as a means of counteracting the impact of stressful lifestyles on health.[135] Yet not all writers prioritized leisure over work. Tom Lutz has pointed out that during the 1920s work was portrayed by American physicians as a solution to boredom and lassitude, a means of invigorating mind and body, controlling or 'working through' emotions, and realizing the self. Both women and men needed some form of work in order to foster feelings of self-worth. While for men satisfaction was thought to come from the office or factory, for women their 'real work was not the monotony of cleaning but the more significant, ennobling job of raising a family'.[136]

Advice literature for women beyond the age of forty was shaded by the prejudices of middle-aged men, as well as by social commitments to bolstering marriage and the nuclear family. The importance of restoring or maintaining family stability before and after the Second World War influenced debates about paid employment for women, as well as shaping discussions about their capacity for self-fulfilment.[137] According to the older Pitkin, wives and mothers whose children had left home and whose husbands were 'sunk deeply in the miry ruts of their own business offices' needed to identify educational and career opportunities that utilized their skills and experience in order to prevent boredom, unhappiness, and periods of personal crisis. By contrast, educated college women needed to temper their commitment to work with more opportunities for play.[138] In a rather cursory and patronizing chapter on the travails of 'idle women of middle age', Pitkin argued that balancing work and leisure in these ways would enable women in their forties and fifties to achieve a greater sense of utility and satisfaction in later years.[139]

There were alternatives to Pitkin's heavily patriarchal tone, at least in some parts of the world. In offering advice to middle-aged women in the 1950s and '60s, the Canadian gynaecologist Marion Hilliard partially mirrored Pitkin's conservative expectations of women as they aged through – and beyond – marriage and the nuclear family. In particular, she reiterated traditional beliefs in women's principal role in maintaining marital happiness and domestic stability and in the biological determinants of women's physical and emotional well-being.[140] At the same time, however, Hilliard challenged contemporary opinion that women should invest energy in attempting merely to retain their youthful looks, or in 'grappling fiercely with such an inevitable force as time itself', as she put it in 1963.[141] She insisted that married women should be able to work beyond the home. Wives, like their husbands, needed the satisfaction of occupation not only to combat the tiredness so often associated with the demands of motherhood and the pressures of modern life, but to restore self-esteem. 'Women need to work to gain confidence in themselves', Hilliard wrote in 1956. 'Women need to work in order to know achievement. Women need to work to escape loneliness. Women need to work to avoid feeling like demihumans, half woman and half sloth.'[142]

Hilliard's belief in the synergistic benefits of work and recreation for women – and indeed men – in their forties and fifties was not always accepted. Medical writers warned that middle age could bring an increased risk of heart disease, cancer and stress-related depression, the effects of which were often exacerbated by the loss of social support following separation and divorce. Martin Roth, professor of psychological medicine at the University of Durham, acknowledged the sense of optimism that had been initiated by Walter Pitkin's *Life Begins at Forty*, as its 'sales rocketed to millions' and it crystallized 'the attractive image of youthful middle-age which beguiles us from the pages of American magazines'.[143] But he also highlighted the prevalence of health hazards that challenged Pitkin's enthusiastic belief that happiness could improve beyond midlife. The ability of middle-aged men and women to capitalize on opportunities that had been made possible by earlier marriages, smaller families and prolonged life expectancy – at least among the affluent middle classes – was tempered by recurrent fears of divorce, decline and death.

IN THE EPILOGUE to his sweeping history of American civilization, *The Epic of America*, published in 1931, James Truslow Adams set out the principal features of modern American aspirations for health and prosperity. The language of the American dream had first been deployed in the late nineteenth century to describe shared commitments to democracy, freedom, education and equality. Sarah Churchwell has pointed out that, although the notion sometimes spilled over into passionate nationalism – captured by the term 'America first' – it was more often used in the early twentieth century to critique the selfish accumulation of wealth and to challenge 'economic inequality and laissez-faire capitalism'.[144] Adams reinforced this militant version of the dream. The American dream, he insisted, was 'not a dream of motor cars and high wages merely, but a dream of social order in which each man and each woman shall be able to attain to the fullest stature of which they are innately capable, and be recognized by others for what they are, regardless of the fortuitous circumstances of birth or position'.[145] Although dreams of opportunity and achievement had been realized more fully in America than elsewhere, Adams acknowledged that growing obsessions with 'business, money-making and material improvement' had lured modern populations into forgetting how to live 'in the struggle to "make a living'".[146] As Adams was aware, remedies for the imminent collapse of American aspirations for self-fulfilment – such as Pitkin's insistence on encouraging the middle classes to use time and money wisely to boost the economy – simply pushed power and responsibility further into the hands of business leaders, who were anxious to develop and exploit new markets. Adams's preferred solution was not to promote consumerism, but to reinvigorate the 'art of living', as he referred to it in 1929. Individuals should be empowered to acquire and exercise 'courage, thought and will' without feeling the pressure to conform or to worry about what 'Mrs. Jones' or any other neighbours might be thinking or doing.[147]

Adams was optimistic that, in the 1930s, America had not yet been sufficiently overrun by 'Babbitts' – or by 'high Babbitry', as Pitkin put it – to make the dream impossible.[148] But Adams's idealism did not last. According to many middle-aged novelists on both sides of the Atlantic, by the immediate post-war years the American dream had already turned sour, curdled by a combination of personal greed, political paralysis and economic austerity. As one reviewer of John Braine's *Life at the Top* commented in 1962, the 'good life' that the archetypal angry young man Joe Lampton had eventually created for himself was now 'hanging by a thread'.[149] Sloan Wilson's *The Man in the Gray Flannel Suit*, written in 1955, and its sequel published in 1984, similarly reveal the aspirations, experiences and disappointments of midlife.[150] Having returned home from the war in 1946, the principal character, Tom Rath, is confronted by what appears to him to be an ailing and alien world. Caught between his own feelings of anger and anomie, on the one hand, and the need to support his wife and three children, on the other, Rath begins to resent the suffocating conformity of work and marriage – particularly given the stark contrast between the intensity of wartime experiences and his dull, joyless life in the suburbs. Like many male protagonists – and male novelists perhaps – Rath's mental health and his sense of identity are salvaged by his wife, who at least in the first novel provides the inspiration to close the gap that had appeared between them during and after the war and to restore relative tranquillity to a marriage disrupted by separation and infidelity.

In line with scholarly and popular literature on middle age, Wilson chose to reveal the fault lines in 1950s domestic and social relations through the eyes of a narcissistic middle-aged man, whose personal and domestic experiences exemplified what appeared to be the universal contours of midlife. In the trailer for the 1956 film adaptation of the novel, Gregory Peck explained the appeal of *The Man in the Gray Flannel Suit*: 'America took this great best-seller to its heart because it could be the story of any American, your husband or wife, your mother or father, your boss, even yourself.'[151] Of course, Peck's reference to the apparent universality of mid-century midlife angst was disingenuous; most novelists and self-help authors remained obsessed only by the rebellion of white middle-class middle-aged men. In his series of Rabbit novels, John Updike offered graphic portrayals of male fantasies across the life course, fantasies that smouldered during early adulthood and erupted into violence and destruction at midlife, before petering out – at least in Rabbit Angstrom's case – into resignation at approaching death. Norman Mailer's *An American Dream* (1965) constituted an even more torrid warning about how self-serving male impulses to rebel against social conventions could lead to nightmarish sexual brutality and murder.[152]

In contrast to fictional portrayals of male agency, novels in which the protagonist was female tended to depict women reacting to, rather than driving, the changes in marital relations that came to define their midlife experiences. In Simone de Beauvoir's *The Woman Destroyed* (1967), Monique's descent into bitterness is triggered by her husband's adultery with a younger woman. As Beauvoir pointed out, Monique's passivity in the face of aggressive male greed was not unique. 'It's a matter of statistics,' Monique's daughter tells her. 'When you put your money on married love you take the risk of being left flat at forty, empty-handed. You drew a losing ticket; you're not the only one.'[153] Beauvoir's blistering critique of male selfishness clearly reveals how ageing women were blamed for men's crises and the breakdown of family relations at midlife. 'I had an inspiration this morning,' Monique writes in her diary one evening:

> the whole thing is my fault. My worst mistake has been not grasping that *time goes by*. It was going by and there I was, set in the attitude of the ideal wife of an ideal husband. Instead of bringing our sexual relationship to life again I brooded happily over memories of our former nights together. I imagined I had kept my thirty-year-old face and body instead of taking care of myself, doing gymnastics and going to a beauty parlour. I let my intelligence wither away; I no longer cultivated my mind – later, I said, when the children have gone.[154]

Monique's belief that time changed women's bodies, minds and expectations more than men's highlights how the double standard of ageing operated in the post-war decades. It also suggests that midlife crises were never entirely individual, but always relational. According to some studies in the 1960s, married couples who were discontented at midlife were 'unhappy not so much because they were all married as because they were all Forty'.[155] Similarly, midlife theorists such as Elliott Jaques continued to insist that the midlife crisis was primarily the product of personal disillusionment, rather than marital or relational discord. But midlife and its attendant problems were inevitably structured and constrained by relationships with partners, children, parents and peers, or even more specifically by what Richard Titmuss referred to in 1958 as the 'stresses and strains of married life'.[156] In the context of concerns about the perils of unrestrained individualism and rising levels of separation and divorce on both sides of the Atlantic through the 1950s and '60s, the midlife crisis was often construed – and perhaps experienced – quite overtly as a marriage crisis.

3
SCENES FROM A MARRIAGE

'But a world in which people may reorient their whole lives at forty or fifty
is a world in which marriage for life becomes much more difficult.'
MARGARET MEAD, 1949[1]

At a time when marriage was regarded as a social institution, rising trends in separation and divorce constituted a social crisis. If stable marriages were key to the post-war reconstruction of family life and the restoration of social and political order, as many contemporary British and American commentators believed, the severance of marital bonds and the fragmentation of families signalled 'an extremely grave social problem' that required urgent public attention.[2] References to the importance of marriage and families to society were already commonplace in the interwar years. In 1928 Marie Stopes had insisted that nobody 'could doubt that the stability of the nation depends on the health and *happiness* of its homes'.[3] At the heart of Stopes's romantic vision was a belief that the home – rather than merely the house – was built on faithful married love, on mutuality, on the creation of a unified pair of lovers, rather than simply on the cohabitation of 'a couple of isolated individuals'. 'This duity,' as she referred to it in *Enduring Passion*, her guidebook for married couples at midlife, 'this unit composed of two like but dissimilar lives interlocked so as to make one unit existence, is an extremely important item in the social system of any State desiring permanence, continuity and stability.'[4]

Although Stopes and others feared that there was a tendency in Western societies towards the disintegration of marital relations, levels of divorce before the Second World War were generally low, at least in countries where statistics are available. But as divorce rates began to rise immediately after the war and across the post-war decades, Stopes's admonitions about the importance – for couples and children – of sustaining marriages across the life course became increasingly cogent, prompting sociological, legal and political interest in analysing and addressing the causes and consequences of marital breakdown. In spite of the increasing likelihood of divorce, marriage remained popular, as the establishment of the Marriage Bureau in 1939 indicates.[5] However, the number of marriages varied across the middle decades of the century: peaks occurred at the start of and after the Second World War – in 1940 and 1947; numbers then fell to a low in 1958, before rising again to further peaks in 1968 and 1972.[6]

More significant in terms of patterns of marriage and divorce were the ways in which the nature and expectations of marriage – rather than the absolute numbers – were changing. After the war, greater prosperity, the availability of labour-saving home appliances and the changing status of women helped to popularize the notion of 'companionate' or 'conjugal' marriage, in which men and women were expected to be bound to each other by enduring romantic love rather than by pragmatism, to share domestic duties more equitably and to spend leisure time together within the haven of the nuclear family.[7] According to the American anthropologist Margaret Mead writing in 1953, modern marriages were supposed to be based on 'greater frankness, greater articulateness, greater sharing than any we have known before in this country'; couples were expected to focus on 'having children in comradeship'.[8] Mead's assessment of a significant shift in values was repeated across the post-war decades. A report of the Marital Studies Advisory Panel of the Tavistock Institute suggested that prior to the 1950s married couples had been expected to be 'efficient executants of their roles as bread-winner and house-wife'; by contrast, couples marrying during the 1960s and '70s 'should be people who like one another'.[9]

The realities of married life seldom matched up to the principle of companionate marriage. In his study of British marriage over four centuries, John Gillis pointed out that 'the conjugal has always been more an illusive dream than an attainable reality', not a 'source of liberation', as some believed, 'but a new form of tyranny', as hopes for greater equality were disappointed.[10] According to the British pioneering researcher in social administration Richard Titmuss, writing in 1958, the post-war period constituted 'an indefinable stage in the process of "democratizing" marriage', a stage in which couples' experiences did not yet tally with expectations of intimacy, leading them to become disenchanted with their marital relationships.[11] Aspirations and frustrations within marriage were not evenly distributed. There was significant diversity in attitudes and experiences between partners, between and across socio-economic classes, and across time. Studies of family life after the war have revealed a multiplicity of practices in relation to marriage, child-rearing and domestic responsibilities. In many working-class communities marriage remained a labour contract 'far removed from cosy companionship'.[12] Although post-war feminists highlighted the demands and disappointments of bourgeois domesticity, experiences of marriage, home and family also varied widely across the middle classes. In addition to considerable differences in the extent to which men were involved in family life across the second half of the twentieth century, the capacity of couples to cope with the stresses of married life were shaped by kinship networks and working practices.[13] Writing in 1964, American sociologists Peter Berger and Hansfried Kellner suggested that the stability of a marriage was dictated not only by the two partners, but by a 'chorus' of children, friends, relatives and acquaintances.[14]

In the light of anxieties about the impact of broken homes on social cohesion, patterns of marriage and divorce – like many other intimate areas of emotional life in Britain and America – became public, rather than merely private, issues. This was especially the case when the custody of children was involved, as the final report of the Denning Committee on Procedure in Matrimonial Causes stressed in 1947.[15] The extent of British interest in marriage, separation and divorce is evident in the number of public lectures on the subject, as well as in television programmes produced by the British Broadcasting Corporation (BBC) during the 1960s. Estimating that one in seven marriages ended in divorce, a *Panorama* programme in 1963 explored proposals to extend the grounds for divorce to include separation for seven years. The Matrimonial Causes Bill introduced that year by Leo Abse, Labour MP for Pontypool, was intended to enable divorced partners to more easily remarry, thereby ensuring that any children from the new relationship were legitimate. The purpose of the Bill was to promote a move towards no-fault divorce, in which spouses could effectively define the breakdown themselves. Abse's efforts to reform the law failed. Through the mid-1960s adultery continued to constitute the archetypal 'matrimonial offence' and the most commonly cited reason for divorce – although it was often seen as a consequence, rather than the cause, of marital breakdown.[16]

In 1964 a series of three television programmes entitled *Marriage Today* interviewed couples and individuals of all ages in order to reflect on marriage as a social institution, to consider attitudes to sex, pregnancy, parenthood and infidelity, and to investigate how experiences and opinions of marriage ranged from 'the romantic to the self-consciously modern'.[17] The final programme in the series not only revealed middle-class expectations and experiences of marriage, but included insights from psychologists, lawyers and anthropologists about why marriages were apparently less robust than in the past. Margaret Mead's contributions made it particularly clear that contemporary patterns of marriage and divorce were dependent on the emergence of the modern life cycle, including the tendency for an extended middle age to induce crises. According to Mead, a number of factors made it more difficult to sustain marriages in post-war Western societies. The tendency to marry earlier and live longer, more frequent opportunities to meet people beyond the home as a result of greater social and occupational mobility, the potential to change direction at midlife, and shifting educational expectations and employment prospects for women were together promoting a new brand of individualism that threatened the cohesion and stability, or indeed the desirability, of the nuclear family.[18]

Mead had made similar points in her 1949 study of the 'two sexes', *Male and Female*, which was based on extensive fieldwork in America and seven South Sea cultures. 'But a world in which people may reorient their whole lives at forty or fifty', she argued, 'is a world in which marriage for life becomes much more difficult.'[19] One solution to this challenge, according to Mead, was to provide people with the option of sequential marriages for different purposes at different stages of life: a first marriage for youthful passion, for example, a second for parenthood, and a third for companionship in later life.[20] Mead's interest in multiple marriages was not entirely dispassionate. She had herself been married three times: first, in 1923, to an American theology student Luther Cressman (her 'student marriage'); second, in 1928, to a psychology student from New Zealand, Reo Fortune; and finally to the British anthropologist Gregory Bateson, to whom she was married for fourteen years and with whom she had a daughter. But Mead was by no means alone in recognizing the potential for serial relationships to resolve some of the challenges of maintaining love and intimacy across the life course. 'Ideally for those of us who find women attractive and are attracted to them', wrote one man – born in 1934 – in response to Mass-Observation's later directive on having an affair, it would perhaps be better if it was the accepted way that you changed wives and husbands about every ten years. It would have to have meant that it was the husbands who moved out and the wives who kept the properties and in most cases the children, even the innocent injured husbands would have to leave. Of course if you were ideally happy with your wife you would remain wedded until one of you died. I think that that being the normal accepted behaviour of wedded couples would suit 80% of married couples, I think most couples try to make the most of none too happy marriages because it causes less distress to everyone involved than if they split up.[21]

As pressure to reform the divorce laws peaked during the 1960s, the BBC turned its attention to debates about how best to prevent, or more constructively regulate, the breakdown of marriages.[22] A three-part *Man Alive* television series on marriages under stress, presented by Desmond Wilcox and broadcast in January 1967, focused in turn on the impact of marital tensions and divorce on children, the reasons why some marriages reached breaking point, and the ways in which men and women coped with separation and divorce.[23] The programmes revealed complex patterns of crisis, triggered by – and manifest in – a range of behaviours that left marriages under strain. Husbands were violent and neglectful towards their wives, or committed adultery with younger women, resulting in the 'clichéd, corny eternal triangle', as Wilcox referred to it.[24] Wives were unfaithful while their husbands were away on business. Husbands left the marital home to return to parents. Single women were duped by men who lied about being married or claimed that they had an 'unhappy home life' in order to initiate an affair.[25] Coping strategies varied. Some couples managed to reconcile and learned to live with the lack of trust generated by their husband's or wife's infidelity. Others separated and divorced, after which they sought to reduce social isolation by meeting new partners at 'Ex-clubs' or 'Second Time Around Groups' that were geared 'specifically to the needs of the recently widowed and divorced of all age groups'.[26] But, whatever the outcome of marital discord, intimate televised accounts of betrayal and separation indicate that the emotional trauma and social tragedy of divorce rarely receded from contemporary narratives of love, marriage and family at midlife.

IN 1949 AMERICAN sociologist Reuben Hill claimed that political awareness of the level of disruption evident in post-war families was finally
leading to calls for the development of a 'national policy for family life'.[27]
Hill chose wartime separation as a case study to investigate the capacity
of families to cope with the stress of interrupted relationships, especially
after the honeymoon-like glow of reunion had faded.[28] Contemporary
preoccupations with the consequences of separation were also evident
in British documentaries and studies on health and marriage at midlife.[29] In the 1967 *Man Alive* series, participants revealed how separation
between work and home – or that generated by military service in
some countries – created opportunities for adultery by either one or
both partners. As families moved to the suburbs, the daily commute
fatigued men and women who worked outside the home and created
a sense of distance – both temporal and spatial – between spouses. In
1937 the English physician Macpherson Lawrie had already highlighted
the ways in which modern transport served to physically separate husbands and wives and increase temptation, leading to the disruption of
'domestic sentiment' in ways that were detrimental to married love.[30]
For other couples, separation was manifest in the slow violence of emotional – rather than physical – detachment or in mounting intolerance
and resentment within the marriage. 'How many separate informally,'
asked a Mass-Observation report on the state of matrimony in 1947,
'and how many who do not separate live together in mutual sufferance
under the same roof?'[31]

The physical, emotional and economic distance that appeared
between partners resulted in what Robert Lee and Marjorie Casebier
referred to in 1973 as 'the spouse gap'.[32] Psychological estrangement
was thought to deepen across the middle years of life. But emotional
detachment was often complicated by proximity, leaving some partners
living together as 'intimate enemies', as the psychotherapist George
Bach and journalist Peter Wyden put it in 1969 in their account of how
to harness aggression creatively and reconcile marital conflicts through
more effective communication.[33] Such studies challenged men's claims
that their wives did not understand them. On the contrary, the con-
verse might well have been true. Marital discord at midlife – and the
tendency for men to seek more sympathetic partners – emerged not
because wives no longer understood their husbands, but because
they understood them too well.[34] Maintaining intimacy in the face
of midlife complacency was difficult. According to Margaret Mead,

couples 'living in a complex modern world' that placed peculiar strains on marriage were often unable to grow together at the same rate, a fact that one day, she argued, might be regarded as a 'legitimate reason for divorce'.[35]

In 1950 marital separation constituted a distinct category in the American census for the first time.[36] It also became a conspicuous theme in cinematic treatments of midlife malaise in the post-war years. In the 1960s American films such as the Academy Award-winning *The Apartment* (1960) and *The April Fools* (1969) explored adultery not merely as a release from loveless marriages, but also as a tool for securing influence with colleagues and employers. One of the most prominent examples of preoccupations with emotional and physical distance within relationships is Roberto Rossellini's *Journey to Italy* (1953), starring George Sanders and Ingrid Bergman as a middle-aged couple, Alexander and Katherine Joyce, travelling to Naples to arrange the sale of a house inherited by Alex from his uncle. The emotional distance between the couple soon becomes apparent: 'I realize for the first time,' Katherine says when they reach the hotel in Naples, 'that we are like strangers.' Alex agrees: 'That's right. After eight years of marriage it seems like we don't know anything about each other.' Throughout the film, the couple's isolation from each other is reinforced by geographical distance: while Alex socializes – and flirts – with friends in Capri, Katherine visits museums and archaeological sites around Naples either alone or with a guide. Rossellini makes clear that separation – largely the result of Alex's commitment to work – has been a prominent feature of their relationship throughout the marriage, only brought into greater relief during the journey to Italy. The spouse gap that emerges between Alex and Katherine is bridged eventually by a contrived physical proximity. Having agreed to divorce, the couple decide to return home. But their exit from Naples is obstructed by a carnival, allowing them time to reflect together on the consequences of separating. Realizing that life is short, Katherine and Alex reconcile in the closing scene of the film.[37]

The Seven Year Itch (1955), directed by Billy Wilder and based on a play by George Axelrod that had premiered on Broadway in 1952, adopts a comic, but no less critical, tone to analyse the dynamics of marital separation and infidelity during middle age.[38] After the 38-year-old Richard Sherman has seen his wife and son leave for the summer vacation, he befriends and begins to seduce a younger woman, played by

Marilyn Monroe, who lives in the apartment upstairs. The film reveals many of the bland assumptions, as well as nuances, of post-war discussions about marriage and divorce. As an editor for a publishing house, Sherman is reading *Of Man and the Unconscious*, a manuscript submitted by Dr Ludwig Brubaker, which explores the roots and consequences of repressed sexual urges in middle-aged men. One of the author's key arguments is that 'the urge curve in the middle-aged husband rises sharply during the seventh year of marriage.' This 'unfortunate urge', the author suggests, 'which strikes 84.6 per cent of the married male population, rises to an alarming 91.8 per cent during the summer months', that is, during the peak period of physical separation between husbands and wives.[39] Wilder provides the texture for his depiction of Sherman's midlife crisis by parodying David Lean's more earnest film *Brief Encounter* (1945), which was based on Noël Coward's play *Still Life* (1936). Wilder's homage to Lean surfaces most compellingly in the soundtrack. The unconsummated affair between Celia Johnson and Trevor Howard in *Brief Encounter* is accompanied by excerpts from Rachmaninov's Piano Concerto No. 2 in C minor, a composition that was used in a number of films and television series across the twentieth century. In *The Seven Year Itch*, Sherman creates the atmosphere for seduction by playing the same concerto by 'good old Rachmaninov' on the gramophone.[40] As in *Journey to Italy*, resolution of the marital crisis is achieved by collapsing the distance between Sherman and his family. Ashamed of his adulterous thoughts, Sherman leaves Manhattan to join his wife and son in the country. The final frames of *The Seven Year Itch* suggest that for post-war populations, minimizing physical separation between spouses – whether in the home or the marriage guidance counsellor's office – enabled emotional reconciliation between husbands and wives, obviating the need for divorce.

According to Canadian psychiatrist Eric Berne, marital 'games' of the type displayed in cinematic treatments of middle age provided the 'scaffolding for married life and family living'.[41] In *Games People Play*, a study of the psychology of human relationships published in 1964, Berne highlighted the variety of manipulative behaviours that often functioned as barriers to intimacy and triggers for infidelity. Disputes between husband and wife generated typical scenarios: 'harried housewives' shouldered responsibility for domestic duties alone; spouses offered or withdrew sexual privileges; and both partners attempted to demonstrate how hard they had worked at the marriage in order to justify petitioning for divorce.[42] Although conceptual and populist, Berne's framework for exposing fault lines in relationships can be seen in contemporary films. The most evocative example of the gradual dissolution of a marriage in this way can be seen in Ingmar Bergman's *Scenes from a Marriage* released in 1973. The film traces the collapse of a previously happy ten-year marriage between Marianne and Johan. Superficial contentment with their professional careers and family life – brought into relief by the unhappiness of other characters who are coping with loveless or querulous marriages – conceals deepening cracks between Johan's and Marianne's beliefs and aspirations. The tipping point in the marriage is Johan's admission that he is having an affair with a younger woman, triggering re-evaluation of their personal lives and relationships. Divorce in this instance fails to resolve either individual or shared conflicts, leading eventually to a renewal of intimacy. Bergman's interpretation of marital despair at midlife – made more painful by the camera's scrutiny of Marianne's barely perceptible responses to her husband's revelations of adultery – captures the complexity of the emotional pathways towards, through and beyond betrayal, separation and divorce in the post-war period.

'MARRIAGE IN OUR society', wrote Peter Berger and Hansfried Kellner in 1964, 'is a *dramatic* act in which two strangers come together to re-define themselves.'[43] Achieving and maintaining a partnership between two individuals was not simple, particularly given the public rituals of married life – from the wedding to the honeymoon and portentous anniversaries – and the heavy expectations that marriage would bring prescribed forms of happiness and sexual satisfaction. According to Berger and Kellner, the anticipated, socially legitimated benefits of the drama of marriage, evident in all strata of society, included 'romantic love, sexual fulfilment, self-discovery and self-realization.'[44] Pressure on couples to realize these dimensions of marriage were relatively new in the post-war period. According to the Marital Studies Advisory Panel at the Tavistock, the gradual loss of a collective framework for values and norms had left individuals responsible for defining themselves, ensuring personal growth and maturity, and preserving 'integrity of the self' in the face of external challenges. Within this context, companionate or symmetrical marriage became pivotal to personal and social stability, a prime location for enabling the development of personality – but also, of course, an emergent source of conflict and tension between partners.[45]

Changes in the expectations of marriage were not immaterial to the emergence of the midlife crisis. In their study of the 'collision of interests between love, family and personal freedom', Ulrich Beck and Elisabeth Beck-Gernsheim argued that in the twentieth century 'deep cracks' appeared 'across the picture of the family'. New opportunities and pressures to 'break free and discover one's true self', they argued, meant that the midlife crisis often manifested itself as a marriage crisis, one made possible by the coincidence of three factors: 'individualization in general, female individualization in particular and increased life expectancy'. From this perspective, the challenge of middle age was not initiated primarily by a growing awareness of personal death, but by the escalating struggle for two individuals 'to survive within a shared life'.[46] Post-war commentators on marriage and the family were of a similar opinion. In their 1960 study of stress in American suburbia, Richard E. Gordon, Katherine K. Gordon and Max Gunther referred to the manner in which the marriage knot was beginning to fray, creating first temporary and then permanent schisms between husbands and wives.[47] Ten years later, American journalist Alvin Toffler pushed the image of rupture further: newly streamlined – or nuclear – families were being fractured by growing acceptance of the transient or obsolescent nature of relationships, as well as materials. Living longer and moving more frequently for work increased the odds against maintaining a successful marriage across several decades and encouraged reassessment of realistic marriage trajectories.[48] By disrupting the sense of stability and identity previously made possible by traditional gender roles and normative notions of the nuclear family, the forces of individualization were encouraging men and women to escape from what were now seen as the constraints of companionate marriage.[49]

The image of fraying and fractured families was increasingly apt as rates of marital breakdown and divorce rose across the second half of the twentieth century. Before the Second World War, no more than 7,000 couples were divorced in England and Wales annually, at a rate that was substantially lower than in other European countries or America at that time.[50] Of course, a low divorce rate did not mean that marriages were happy. On the contrary, according to some commentators, 'discord in marriage' was 'extremely frequent'.[51] 'The prevalence of divorces illustrates a bent,' wrote Macpherson Lawrie in 1937, and it represents an infinitesimal proportion of unsatisfactory marriages. Where one case reaches the divorce court thousands upon thousands of marriages, among the rich and poor, portray an irritability, a lack of companionship and a 'tension' more in keeping with a tilt yard than with congeniality.[52]

Rather than signifying largely stable marriages, the low divorce rate in Britain during the interwar period reflected the fact that divorce was both costly and difficult to obtain, particularly for women, even after the 1937 Matrimonial Causes Act had expanded the grounds for divorce beyond adultery to include cruelty and desertion.[53] 'Legal and financial sanctions' against divorce, stressed a Mass-Observation report in 1947, had now 'reinforced the moral ones'.[54]

After the Second World War, the number of divorces – and the proportion of marriages that ended in divorce – rose in Britain, from 15,634 in 1945 to 30,870 only five years later. A sharp rise in divorce petitions during the immediate post-war years was explained by government enquiries and the media as a 'symptomatic feature of the disturbance brought about by war in the field of family relations'.[55] Extramarital affairs on the part of both men and women during periods of separation, as well as the challenges of readjusting to domestic life and civilian work after the war, generated what *The Times* referred to in 1946 as a 'flood of cases' of divorce relating to service personnel, some of whom were thought to have married hastily just before or during the war.[56] Studies of the repatriation of British prisoners of war demonstrated the difficulties generated by men returning to family life. Soldiers found that once familiar domestic and social conventions and habits no longer held the same meaning. Unable either to experience pleasure or to invest fully in work and home again, some men abandoned their wives and children. For soldiers' wives, who had become emotionally and financially independent during their husbands' absence, reunion – however keenly anticipated it might have been – created a disequilibrium that often proved fatal to their marriage.[57] It was precisely this troubled dynamic between partners after the war that provided the focus for Sloan Wilson's fictional analysis of Tom and Betsy Rath's struggles to maintain marital stability, family cohesion and occupational satisfaction in *The Man in the Gray Flannel Suit*, first published in 1955.[58]

Pressure on divorce courts during the late 1940s and early '50s led to calls for greater resources being made available to expedite proceedings.

It also increased political demands for urgent solutions to the lack of adequate housing following the war, a situation that left many newly married couples with the stress of beginning their lives together while residing with parents or relatives. Although the immediate post-war bulge in divorce petitions soon receded, by the 1960s the number of divorces began to rise again, reaching 37,785 by 1965 and rising even more steeply after the passage of the 1969 Divorce Reform Act, which stimulated a spate of publications offering advice about how to navigate the process.[59] Coming into force in 1971, the Act replaced the increasingly problematic notion of 'matrimonial offence' with the principle of 'irretrievable breakdown' of the marriage, allowing couples to divorce after a period of separation, as well as in cases of adultery, cruelty and desertion.[60] It was not only the rate and social impact of divorce that became of public and political interest. The health and well-being of families were threatened by unhappy – as well as broken – marriages. In the *Man Alive* series aired in 1967, Desmond Wilcox claimed that while one in ten marriages ended in divorce, nine out of ten marriages came close to it, potentially exposing partners and children to the traumas of family discord.[61]

Britain was not alone in experiencing dramatic changes in rates of divorce across the middle decades of the twentieth century. A similar pattern emerged in North America, where a perceived crisis in marriage and family was regarded, already by the late 1930s, as equally serious as the crisis in the 'economic system and political order'.[62] In response, the National Conference on Family Relations was established in 1938 in

YEAR	NUMBER OF DIVORCES
1945	15,634
1950	30,870
1955	26,816
1960	23,868
1965	37,785
1970	58,239
1975	120,522
1980	148,301
1985	160,300

Number of divorcing couples in England and Wales, 1945–85.

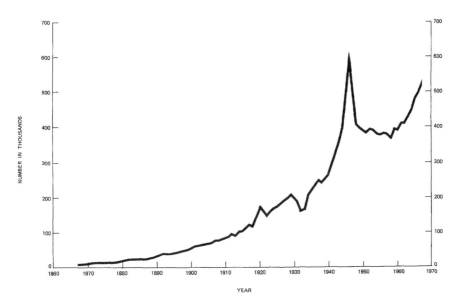

Number of divorces in the United States, 1867–1967.

order to 'advance the cultural values that are now principally secured through family relations, for the advantage of the individual and the strength of the Nation'.[63] A report on marriage and divorce statistics in the United States, published in 1973, highlighted a gradual rise in divorce across the first half of the twentieth century, a sharp peak immediately after the Second World War and then another steady increase through the 1960s.[64] Rates of separation and divorce varied across socio-economic groups. Using long-term data sets, Steven Ruggles has suggested that, in addition to changing cultural values and norms, patterns of marital breakdown were linked to employment opportunities and economic conditions: 'All we can say for sure', he argues, 'is that the more working women and fewer working men in a district, the higher the likelihood of being divorced or separated.'[65]

In 1965 the marriage counsellor David Mace highlighted national differences in approaches to divorce.[66] Comparative studies certainly reveal distinctive patterns of divorce, as well as different legislative provisions, across space and time. In spite of traditional commitments to family, divorce rates in Japan had been higher at the end of the nineteenth century than in most other countries, an unfavourable comparison that generated concern in the Japanese media. As Harald Fuess's detailed study of divorce in Japan has shown, during the early decades of the twentieth century rates began to decline to levels below those in the West, perhaps as a result of changes in legislation and the registration of marriages and divorces. From the 1960s, however, Japanese divorce rates rose rapidly in line with trends seen in Europe and America. This trend was linked not primarily to judicial reform – as was partly the case in Britain – but to a revolution in attitudes and behaviour. The social stigma attached to divorce receded, married women became more economically independent as access to wage labour increased, and family and community control over marriage arrangements declined as individual choice of partner and 'love marriages' became more widely accepted.[67]

Other countries, such as Canada and the German Democratic Republic, also experienced rising rates of divorce – and sometimes lower rates of marriage – across the post-war decades as changing social and economic conditions after the Second World War made it increasingly possible for women to end marriages blighted by infidelity, physical violence and alcohol abuse.[68] But divorce rates varied according to class, race and religion and remained low in some countries. In Catholic countries, opposition to divorce hardened rather than relaxed across the twentieth century. In Russia, where monogamy was enforced by State regulations and patriarchal norms until 1968, divorce was uncommon.[69] Of course, even in these contexts, many couples were still able to separate – or to live separate lives in the same house – without formally divorcing. As the Polish-born anthropologist Bronislaw Malinoski argued in a series of debates with the French surgeon and anthropologist Robert Briffault, broadcast by the BBC in 1931 but published in 1956, formal divorce was not necessary to mark the end of a marriage: 'Marriage ceases', he stressed in his first lecture on 'the present crisis' in marriage, '*when* it ceases to exist.'[70]

In Britain, a number of government commissions were established to consider how to strengthen the institution of marriage and to safeguard the well-being of children when marriages did break down. The steady increase in rates of divorce across the post-war decades, particularly among the middle-aged, was attributed to a number of factors other than the war. In 1946 the Denning Committee argued that the exhausting 'mechanics of everyday life' were reducing women's marital satisfaction and happiness in particular. From the 1950s the availability of legal aid (introduced in 1949) and improved employment opportunities enabled women to gain greater financial independence and end unhappy marriages more easily by petitioning for divorce.[71] Benita Eisler's study reveals how in the 1950s some middle-aged women, unhappy in their married lives, carefully planned for divorce by saving sufficient money from full-time or part-time employment to allow them to live independently.[72] Ten years later, the widely-discussed Royal Commission on Marriage and Divorce suggested that friction between husbands and wives and any resultant family instability could be traced to demographic and socio-economic factors such as 'the housing shortage, the earlier age of marriage, the higher standard of living, the transformation in the social position of women, and the change in attitudes towards non-marital sexual relations'.[73]

Rising divorce rates in Britain were also linked to the manner in which relationships were seemingly being weakened by the 'atomistic tendencies of modern life', as the British psychiatrist Alexander Wilson put it in 1949.[74] According to the 1956 Royal Commission, trends in divorce could be attributed to the inclination 'to regard the assertion of one's own individuality as a right, and to pursue one's personal satisfaction, reckless of the consequences for others'.[75] These claims – and the evidence on which they were based – were not universally accepted, but the rapid increase in divorce rates continued to be regarded by some as an 'index of domestic decay', as a product of greater divorce-mindedness among post-war couples, who were supposedly becoming more hesitant to commit fully to marriage and less inclined to resolve marital difficulties when they arose.[76] The cultural potency of the image of the reluctant couple was not lost on journalists and cartoonists commenting on the ambivalent and precarious nature of contemporary international, as well as personal, relations. In 1967 Michael Cummings cleverly juxtaposed contemporary concerns about amending the divorce laws with political debates about the benefits – and potential drawbacks – of the United Kingdom joining the European Economic Community.

Fault lines characteristically appeared at two distinct moments in the life cycle of a marriage. In the first instance, there was some support for the notion of a seven-year itch. The belief that couples could experience particular difficulties after seven years of marriage was not new. In 1913 the British writer Philip Gibbs had explored how, by 'the eighth year', the excitement and thrill of marriage had often given way to loneliness, boredom, work pressures and economic stress. Such factors resulted in couples being slowly torn apart by what he referred to as a 'new creed of selfishness' that encouraged people – especially

" If the worst came to the worst, Lord Gardiner, would I be able to get a divorce ?"

Michael Cummings, 'If the worst came to the worst, Lord Gardiner, would I be able to get a divorce?', *Sunday Express*, 7 May 1967.

women, he believed – to seek escape through infidelity and divorce.[77] American statistics compiled after the Second World War endorsed Gibbs's earlier appraisal of the chronology – if not the precise dynamics – of marital breakdown and divorce. According to a brief note in the American journal *Marriage and Family Living*, the median duration of marriages ending in 1955 was 6.4 years.[78] Further statistical analysis in 1973 revealed that the time span of American marriages before divorce had changed little over the previous century: from a median of 7.4 years in 1867 to 7.1 years in 1967.[79]

Comparable figures emerged from studies elsewhere. In Japan, the mean duration of marriage before divorce was 5.3 years in 1950, rising to 10 by the mid-1980s.[80] In Britain, the Registrar General's annual returns and independent surveys suggested not only that divorce was higher during the second quinquennium of married life, but that the proportion of marriages dissolving before ten years was increasing across the post-war years.[81] Ronald Fletcher's analysis of British families and marriage, in which he challenged contemporaries who were proclaiming the 'death of the family', indicated that the highest percentage of divorces and annulments (30.6 per cent) in 1957 occurred between five and nine years of marriage. The second highest percentage (21.3 per cent) of divorces occurred between ten and fourteen years, after which the proportion of marriages that ended in divorce dropped.[82] The British psychiatrist Jack Dominian similarly calculated that in 1963 divorces reached 'a peak six to seven years after the start of the marriage', probably as the result of a failure to establish a robust physical and emotional relationship. Of course, as Dominian warned, figures relating to the duration of marriages were not a reliable guide to the timing or prevalence of marital discord, which could surface well before the point of separation and divorce.[83]

The seven-year itch was not, however, the only marital crisis point. If couples successfully negotiated the initial stages of conjugal life, they subsequently became subject to different stresses. Marriages were put under strain by the changing personality traits and needs of their partners, the reappearance of unresolved emotional difficulties with parents, the departure of grown-up children from the home, and obstacles to maintaining or refashioning social lives – that is, to the myriad challenges of middle age. The impact of such situational factors on the happiness of married couples across the life course became a key focus for interwar and post-war sociologists.[84] Failure to adjust successfully to transitions through midlife, it was assumed, increased the risk of unhappiness, infidelity, separation and divorce. In 1955 a study of domestic unhappiness in American married couples (as rated by their siblings) concluded that midlife constituted a pivotal moment for many marriages: 'the study suggests the late forties and early fifties as a crisis period for married women and the fifties as a critical decade for marital happiness in the life cycle of men.'[85] A feature article in the *Daily Mail* in 1965 similarly stressed that middle age constituted a conspicuous 'danger time for marriages', a time at which 'marriages, happy for years, suddenly go on the rocks'.[86] And in 1967, Kenneth Soddy and Mary Kidson pointed out that the fifth decade could be a 'restless decade, during which the stability of marriage may be threatened'.[87]

Potential solutions to the difficulties of maintaining happy marriages across the life course were not hard to find in self-help guides for the middle-aged or in the popular media on both sides of the Atlantic. Marriage guidance counsellors, doctors and agony aunts in tabloid newspapers and magazines regularly offered advice on how to revitalize relationships, share interests and hobbies, address anxieties about sex, improve physical appearance and cope with inevitable midlife changes. But approaches to preserving what Marie Stopes had referred to in 1928 as the 'rare contentment' of a happy marriage were complex and culturally specific.[88] Patterns, experiences and outcomes of marriage varied widely according to class and gender. In his 1955 study of English character, influenced by the work of Margaret Mead, Geoffrey Gorer used questionnaires to examine – among other issues – the hopes, fears and experiences of marriage and divorce across the country. Gorer's findings suggested that English men most admired their wives' skills as housewives and mothers, that is, their ability to keep house, cook and look after the children. Women by contrast referred more often to their husband's personal qualities – understanding, thoughtfulness and sense of humour. While happy marriages required 'give-and-take', understanding, love, equanimity and mutual trust, the principal causes of unhappiness within marriage were a lack of trust, having no house of one's own, a partner's self-ishness or temper, sexual incompatibility, poverty and neglect – few of which constituted grounds for divorce. Infidelity supposedly con-stituted a far less important cause of marital unhappiness, although opinions about its significance varied between partners. Men were far more likely than women to believe that adultery should 'automatically terminate the marriage'.[89]

Men and women cited different reasons for the breakdown of a marriage. According to Gorer, husbands tended to reproach their wives for careless spending and nagging. Wives accused their husbands of cruelty, drunkenness, laziness and neglect. Neither men nor women, however, necessarily blamed their partner's conduct directly for mari-tal tensions, even in cases of adultery. Instead they often referred to deeper, longstanding flaws within the marriage or admitted to the impact of their own behaviour on the stability of the marriage. For men, self-reflection involved considering why their wives had turned away from them and whether or not they were themselves 'free from guilt', as one 46-year-old man put it. Women tended to focus on their physical appearance, exhorting their peers to 'look in the mirror', make themselves 'as attractive as possible' and let their husband's affair 'die a natural death' so that he would return to the matrimonial home.[90] 'I suggest she stands in front of a mirror and examines her reflection in detail,' wrote one 38-year-old working-class woman from Sunderland, 'then she should examine her conscience carefully, and finally review her attitude towards her husband. Inevitably she will find the fault lies within herself and as soon as she remedies it, her husband's affair will cease.'[91] Such forthright appraisals on the part of wives reveal the extent to which the physical manifestations of ageing in women were thought to reduce sexual attraction and trigger marital disaffection during middle age. A woman's changing appearance was regarded as an explanation – and justification – for male midlife adultery.

MIDLIFE REBELLION COULD occur in unmarried – as well as married – people in their forties and fifties.[92] But across the post-war decades, crises in middle age were primarily understood in the context of marriage – or rather, in terms of marital unhappiness, infidelity, separation and eventual divorce. Although attempts to reform the divorce laws were aimed primarily at bolstering the institution of marriage for social and political purposes, they were also intended to reduce the personal distress associated with unhappy marriages, a factor that was instrumental in encouraging support for reform from the Church of England.[93] The arguments for closing the gap and preserving harmony between husband and wife were compelling for many contemporaries. In a 1925 essay, Carl Jung had emphasized that feelings of unity and identity within marriage constituted a 'genuine and incontestable experience of the Divine'.[94] Less spiritual in their assessment of the capacity of marriage to enrich lives, post-war commentators nevertheless similarly regarded a flourishing marriage as a source of happiness. 'There is no greater happiness than a successful marriage,' wrote the Austrian urologist and pioneer in sexual medicine Oswald Schwarz in 1947, 'whereas an unhappy marriage is a foretaste of damnation. The one provides the greatest freedom towards the perfection of our personality, the latter is a prison in which two innocent unfortunates serve a sentence for life.'[95] Some years later, the American social psychologists Marjorie Fiske Lowenthal and Lawrence Weiss pursued the argument even further when they suggested that, in the absence of external stress, most individuals were able to live satisfying lives 'only through one or more mutually intimate dyadic relationships'. Lowenthal and Weiss identified two groups most at risk of losing marital intimacy and becoming ill. Middle-aged women entering the post-parental stage of the life cycle struggled to cope with dependent parents while also supporting their husbands through retirement. Overloaded by the pressures of work and home, middle-aged men became vulnerable to heart disease, mental illness and suicide.[96]

According to Schwarz, marital breakdown resulted from people either not being suited to each other or not being suited to marriage.

As a result, he advocated a policy that had already been embraced by eugenicists – but largely rejected by legislatures – earlier in the century. For Schwarz, the solution to unhappy marriages lay not in relaxing or toughening the divorce laws, but in making marriage itself more difficult – by raising the age at which marriage was permissible or by ensuring that 'physically and psychologically unfit people should not be allowed to marry'. While Schwarz's despotic approach to regulating marriage and reproduction was outdated and politically contentious, he had identified an important incongruity in post-war approaches to marriage and divorce, namely the conflict between popular expectations and experiences of married life – or between marital aspirations and attainment – that lead to greater separation between spouses. Whatever people might suppose, marriages were not 'made in Heaven', he insisted, but 'contracted in a Registrar's office'. Schwarz argued that it was largely this secular shift in practice – if not in perception or desire – that had generated 'the crisis of marriage which we are assured is now upon us'.[97] Against the backdrop of major social and cultural transitions, discrepancies between hope and reality often proved fatal to marriages at midlife. Men and women frequently held very different views of marriage and family – propagated by middle-class myths about the American dream, according to Germaine Greer – leading to tensions and conflict within the home.[98]

The idealized Victorian family – with heterosexual marriage at its heart – had been built, at least among the middle classes, on some degree of separation: between home and the office; between earning a salary and caring for children; between work and leisure; between public and private; between men and women; and indeed between generations. But the traditional logic of socially prescribed distance between partners fitted poorly with the changing structures of family life that were slowly beginning to blur boundaries between the educational, occupational and domestic opportunities and responsibilities of men and women during the middle decades of the twentieth century. As women worked increasingly outside the home in order to boost family finances, roles and relationships became entangled, separation between career and family more opaque, and feminist demands for greater parity within the home and workplace more insistent.[99] In 1958 Richard Titmuss pointed out that the 'sharply defined roles and codes of behaviour set by the Victorian patriarchal system' were slowly being replaced by 'the idea of companionship in marriage'.[100] Some years later, in their analysis of 2,644 interviews with Londoners, Michael Young and Peter Willmott referred to this new form of partnership as a 'symmetrical relationship' or 'symmetrical family', one that carried expectations of mutual love and respect, shared duties, equal educational and occupational opportunities, and joint pleasures.[101]

Experiences of companionate marriage, at least in Britain, differed markedly across socio-economic classes. Working-class marriages and domestic life rarely matched the image of marital symmetry promoted by middle-class self-help authors and marriage counsellors.[102] But, regardless of class, roles remained gendered. According to Oswald Schwarz, while women struggled with the multiple pressures of being at once 'an attractive woman, a wife to her husband, mother to her children, and successful in her work', men refused to relinquish 'some of the time-honoured privileges of a husband', which they still took for granted.[103] On-going commitment – on the part of men at least – to the separation of roles between the sexes may have provided families with a reassuring sense of continuity and stability, but it allowed husbands to pursue self-fulfilment and the realization of their own dreams at the expense of their wives and children. The continued separation of duties between men and women also provided a barrier against the encroachment of feminist critiques and liberal values on patriarchal social and family structures. The image of 'synthetic family bliss' may well have been dented by the permissiveness of the 1960s, wrote Beata Bishop in *Punch* in 1968, but women remained as 'unfree as ever', still as helpless as 'a Victorian wife'.[104]

Physical and psychological distance between spouses at midlife was regarded as both cause and symptom of marital difficulties. In a culture in which emotional intimacy and companionship constituted the hallmark of a successful marriage, and in which 'cold war paranoia', as Elizabeth Wilson put it, encouraged a peaceful return to established gender roles, any noticeable detachment between spouses was thought to signify failure.[105] Post-war researchers recognized that establishing and maintaining an appropriate balance between 'togetherness and distance' in a relationship was not simple, but they often warned that if such tensions were not adequately addressed early in the marriage, then breakdown and divorce were more likely during middle age.[106] According to Marion Hilliard, writing on love and life in 1958, if the 'gap that began in the tenth year has never been mended, another crisis will occur at the twenty-fifth anniversary', when the couple 'is now middle-aged and the children grown and gone'.[107] At that point, both men and women began to re-evaluate their marriages as they realized that they might still live for another thirty or forty years.[108] Responsibility for bridging the midlife marital gap – or for ensuring that the couple did not 'settle for separate lives under the same roof' – was not shared equally, in Hilliard's view. The onus for maintaining marriages still lay more heavily on wives, who were expected to understand and satisfy the multiple needs of their husbands.[109]

In spite of allegiance to the principle of companionate marriage, assumptions that women were primarily responsible for marital and domestic happiness – and subservient to their husband's emotional and sexual demands – persisted in marital advice literature and studies of middle age through the 1960s. The work of Kenneth Hutchin constitutes a prime example of contemporary – and largely male – concerns that women were not fulfilling their traditional marital obligations, leaving families and homes vulnerable to fragmentation. During the 1960s and '70s Hutchin published a series of popular books offering advice on how to preserve health and relationships across the life course – most notably *How Not to Kill Your Husband* in 1962 and, three years later, *How Not to Kill Your Wife*. The messages embedded in Hutchin's work were clear: 'the husband's health must take priority,' he advised women in 1962, because the well-being of the rest of the family depended on him. The marital consequences of women failing to fulfil their duties as custodians of their husbands' health and happiness could be devastating for couples. During middle age, when men felt that they had remained 'younger sexually' than their wives, it was supposedly a wife's frigidity and intolerance that stereotypically drove her husband into the arms of a more understanding younger woman. In cases of male adultery, where men were simply 'satisfying a physical need', wives were not blameless, but complicit in the breakdown of the relationship. In order to preserve the marriage, Hutchin insisted, a woman should be prepared to 'simulate enjoyment' and act as a buffer against the 'shocks and worries' of her husband's overloaded life.[110]

Feminist writers interpreted the responsibilities of middle-aged women in different ways. Women's dissatisfaction with marriage and family at midlife – particularly in the suburbs – stemmed not from ignorance or laziness, but from the isolation, boredom and hidden conflicts experienced by housewives after the Second World War. 'Nagging, overweight and premature ageing', wrote Germaine Greer in 1970, were not products of women's inadequacies, but the result of misery caused by the drudgery of surviving from day to day.[111] In spite of Greer's insistence on the social, rather than psychological, drivers of midlife malaise in women, post-war housewives who were tired, listless and irritable continued to be accused of having let themselves go. And wives and mothers who ate and drank too much or became addicted to antidepressants, tranquillizers and stimulants in order to survive were dismissed as neurotic or psychologically ill-equipped to adapt to the demands of married life.

Notwithstanding feminist resistance to attempts to restrict women's roles to childcare, housework and supporting their husbands, Hutchin's brand of chauvinism was pervasive and not confined to advice literature written by men. In 1952 Mary Macaulay had high-lighted the pivotal role that marriage and family played in the social life of the nation. But even within 'democratic marriages', the burden of ensuring a husband's loyalty and fidelity rested on the shoulders of his wife: 'The husband who knows he will be warmly welcomed in the home and warmly welcomed in the bed', she wrote in a chapter on middle age, 'has no need to look elsewhere for reassurance that he is loved and appreciated.'[112] According to Macaulay, whose opinions on marital problems at midlife were influenced by her professional life as a doctor and her work with Merseyside Marriage Guidance Clinic in Liverpool, happy marriages were apparently seldom troubled by the husband – or indeed the wife – being offered love and appreciation elsewhere. Unhappy marriages, by contrast, could lead quite easily to compulsive infidelity at midlife.

Marriages were disrupted by both internal and external factors. In their survey of two hundred urban working-classes families, car-ried out between 1943 and 1946, the British physician Eliot Slater and social worker Moya Woodside argued that happiness in marriage was compromised by the presence of neuroses in one or both partners, as well as by a husband's absence from the home for work.[113] Drawing largely on psychoanalytical theory, other writers pointed out that psy-chological problems – such as narcissism, age-anxiety and the fear of death – surfaced more visibly at midlife to trigger a crisis within the marriage.[114] Writing in 1959, the congregational minister Leslie Tizard and psychotherapist Harry Guntrip argued that 'some deterioration of personality' was likely during an individual's forties and fifties, leading to the reappearance of earlier anxieties and uncertainties and the disruption of previously stable relationships.[115] The resurgence of suppressed emotional instability during middle age became a popular refrain in mid- to late twentieth-century accounts of marriage problems. 'Middle age, then, intensifies all the difficulties we thought would go away some day – either in our own behaviour or that of our spouse,' wrote Robert Lee and Marjorie Casebier in 1971.

> But there they are, waiting for us at mid-life, bigger than ever. Sometimes the crisis problem is a more intense repetition or variation of a problem we've always lived with. But now the spouse can no longer stand it and no longer expects it to go away. A sense of frustration and of time fleeting finally stirs a person to act. The search for help may lead to relief from the old tension – to real growth and change – or it may come too late.[116]

The gap between spouses during middle age was not only generated by emotional immaturity. It was also amplified by emergent stresses on individuals and families at midlife. Financial pressures, political instability, unemployment, entry of women into the workplace, occupational frustrations, coping with the developmental crises of adolescent children, caring for ageing parents, fear of the empty nest and awareness of physical decline all served to magnify differences between spouses, leading them to grow further apart or retreat into a protective insularity. In her study of English cultures published in 1965, the British psychotherapist Josephine Klein claimed that in traditional working-class communities rifts between husbands and wives deepened during times of financial stress. 'The man will work more overtime,' she argued, 'and so be in the house less than before. The woman will rely more on her kin, and hence be less involved with her spouse than before. The poorer the family is, the more restricted their lives will become, and the less man and wife will have to share emotionally and socially.' By contrast, when stress lifted or when standards of living rose above subsistence level, allowing families to spend more time together, 'affectionate relations' could be restored.[117] In many cases, the distance between partners generated by stress had already become too wide for reconciliation, leaving at best the uneasy indifference captured by one 27-year-old respondent to Mass-Observation in 1947: 'He don't talk much. He just says hello and goodnight.'[118] At worst, however, couples lived in what Barbara Fried referred to in

1967 as 'corrosive togetherness'.[119] 'If intimacy simply goes down the drain through lack of attention,' wrote Lee and Casebier, 'the marriage may one day break up on the rocks of loneliness and neglect.'[120] Lack of intimacy, the failure to communicate and a tendency to drift into the damaging marital games described by Berne could lead almost imperceptibly to animosity and betrayal.

THE AUSTRIAN-BORN AMERICAN psychoanalyst Edmund Bergler could well have been the prototype for George Axelrod's fictional character Dr Ludwig Brubaker in *The Seven Year Itch*. From the 1930s through to the '50s, Bergler drew on extensive clinical experience to write a number of advice books on marriage, middle age and divorce. In *The Revolt of the Middle-aged Man*, published in 1958, he set out the compulsive and destructive behaviour of men struggling with the stresses of life and the imminence of personal death – that is, with a condition that was so common that he referred to it as the 'measles' of middle age.[121] According to Bergler, one striking feature of midlife rebellion was the 'essential sameness' of the problems experienced by men: 'So nearly identical are the complaints, rationalizations, defenses, and eventual surrender that characterize progression of this typical, and typically abortive, uprising that these men seem to merge into one composite, hardly differentiated figure.'[122] Similarities between men's beliefs and behaviour at midlife were the product of the parallel personal and family pressures generated by a standardized life course and common experiences at work and within the home. They were also shaped by cultural emphasis on the significance of love in dictating individual choice: the paradox of love, Germaine Greer pointed out, was that it appeared to justify 'both marriage and illicit encounters'.[123] Bored and frustrated by the suffocating demands of domestic and corporate life, midlife rebels justified capitulation to the lure of a new partner in stereotypical terms:

> I want happiness, love, approval, admiration, sex, youth. All this is denied me in this stale marriage to an elderly, sickly, complaining, nagging wife. Let's get rid of her, start life all over again with another woman. Sure, I'll provide for my first wife and my children; sure, I'm sorry that the first marriage didn't work out. But self-defence comes first; I just have to save myself.[124]

Bergler's caricature of middle-aged men's narcissistic search for what he referred to as 'happiness in a hurry' resonated with the concerns of post-war populations anxious about the impact of marital unhappiness on social stability – and particularly about the causes and consequences of adultery, which was the most commonly cited ground for divorce. Enticed by a cast of younger women – crudely characterized by Bergler as Miss Mild Resignation, Miss Illusion, Miss Magic Gesture, Miss Revenge, Miss Professional Troublemaker, Miss Rescue Fantasy, Miss Gold Digger and Miss Promiscuous – the typical man of forty sought attention elsewhere in order to resolve internal psychological dilemmas. The attempts of middle-aged men to escape unhappy marriages through adultery, Bergler argued, were unlikely to succeed, partly because any woman who succumbed to the rebel's advances would necessarily have emotional problems of her own, but also because simply trading partners failed to resolve inner conflicts. Yet while male midlife revolt was unavoidable, its symptoms were not necessarily incurable. Instead of seeking stimulation outside the marriage, Bergler believed that men should learn – with the help of a counsellor – to avert psychological chaos by channelling disruptive drives into more creative outlets.[125] 'Divorce won't help,' Bergler had already insisted in 1948.[126] 'Before running to the nearest divorce lawyer', he argued, troubled middle-aged men and their wives should 'run to the nearest psychiatrist' in order to first resolve their own emotional conflicts.[127]

Post-war preoccupations with the damaging effects of adultery – often softened by the use of terms such as misconduct – were reinforced by surveys of the sexual behaviour of American and British men and women, who increasingly appeared to regard adultery as 'a matter of little moment' according to the British judge Lord Denning in 1954.[128] The most widely reported and perhaps most contentious studies were those carried out by the American sexologist Alfred Kinsey, whose initial investigations into the sexual behaviour of 12,000 men in 1948 were followed five years later by a comparable study of nearly 8,000 women. According to Kinsey and his colleagues at Indiana University, whose work triggered Geoffrey Gorer's survey of English character, over one-third of married men admitted that they had 'some experience in extramarital intercourse', most often with other single or married women 'of their own class', but also with prostitutes. Male adultery was usually sporadic and rarely continued with the same partner for any length of time.[129] Although women were apparently far less interested in having a variety of sexual partners, Kinsey's survey suggested that approximately one-quarter of married women had had affairs by the age of forty – with a peak incidence of adultery in the mid-thirties and early forties. Sanctions against unfaithful wives were generally more stringent, however, than those against their husbands, whose extramarital affairs were largely tolerated so long as the stability of the home was not threatened. According to Kinsey, American men rated a partner's extramarital activities as cause for divorce twice as often as their wives did.[130] A similar double standard was evident in Japan, where, until 1947, only men were entitled to petition for divorce on the grounds of their partner's adultery.[131]

Kinsey's findings attracted considerable media attention.[132] Midlife adultery became a touchstone in post-war discussions of the regulation of marriage and divorce, leading to a blossoming trade in hiring private investigators to obtain evidence from hotel staff and registers to prove extramarital affairs.[133] But there was a diversity of practices and attitudes to infidelity across the twentieth century. Adultery appears to have been justifiable among early twentieth-century British working-class couples, for whom separation and divorce were not affordable options.[134] During the interwar years, commitments to the depth and significance of married love allowed some couples to survive infidelity, although then – as at other times – infidelity in men was regarded as a reasonable response to wives becoming dowdy.[135] Claire Langhamer's analysis of a Mass-Observation survey of sexual behaviour in post-war Britain indicates that the sexual permissiveness of the 1960s was offset by an apparent 'hardening of attitudes to extra-marital sex' in the context of increased commitments to companionate marriage.[136] In response, adultery was simply reframed – at least by middle-aged men – as a legitimate route to self-fulfilment.

Infidelity became a pivotal focus for post-war commentators on the crises of middle age and their impact on marriage and families. This was particularly evident in the work of marriage guidance counsellors in Britain. In *The Challenge of Middle Age*, published in 1962, J. H. Wallis drew on his experiences as a counsellor to explore the ways in which many of the emotional uncertainties of adolescence recurred at midlife, generating comparable patterns of unpredictable behaviour and cataclysmic personal upheaval. Preoccupations with youthful looks and energy, commercial pressure to make the most of middle age and failure to adjust to new occupational and domestic stresses created the space for disillusionment as physical health declined and aspirations remained unfulfilled. In such circumstances, it was not unusual for people to blame their partners for their crises or to direct their anger outwards at employers, social circumstances or political systems.[137] Psychological insecurities and anxieties of this nature led to arguments and recriminations that blighted many marriages at midlife.

According to Wallis, the most visible and startling manifestation of midlife despair was 'the sudden compulsive infidelity that not infrequently comes the way of the counsellor'. It was infidelity, he argued, that constituted the paradigmatic – and eventually clichéd – feature of what he termed 'the middle-age crisis'. The 'emotional typhoon' that occurred in both men and women at midlife could afflict apparently secure relationships. 'One is given the picture of a happy, normal, stable marriage,' he wrote, 'with the usual ups and downs, but on the whole rewarding and fulfilling – until *this* happened.' The impact of betrayal on what many people referred to as 'the innocent party' could be profound. 'It is not easy', wrote Wallis in 1962, 'to describe the sense of desolation, of panic, that these events usually cause, of utter bewilderment and loss.'[138] Wallis's appraisal of the devastation caused by sudden infatuation and infidelity was echoed in the retrospective reflections of respondents to a Mass-Observation directive on having an affair. 'Generally,' wrote one retired married man, 'affairs cause immense harm, often leading to divorce, trust between couples is destroyed, children are baffled, angry and upset.'[139]

Adultery also figured in literary, cinematic and personal accounts of marriage and divorce at midlife. In *The Woman Destroyed*, published in 1967, Simone de Beauvoir referred to 'the abyss of sadness' that engulfs a middle-aged woman when she discovers her husband's affair.[140] Sadness was often amalgamated with anger. In 1962 the American poet Sylvia Plath reacted to Ted Hughes's adultery by tearing 'some of his papers in half'.[141] Plath went further than many contemporaries in caricaturing the crises of middle age in men, describing Hughes's midlife shift in personality as 'part of a syndrome' triggered by – or manifest in – his relationship with another woman.[142] Sometimes, sadness and anger gave way to resignation. In the words of Gail Sheehy's female protagonist in *Lovesounds*, published in 1970, couples simply came 'uncoupled'.[143] Adultery, divorce and remarriage at midlife were highrisk strategies. Wallis, for example, insisted that infidelity rarely resulted in happiness even for the 'guilty' party, but was liable to jeopardize reputations and damage children. Like Bergler, Wallis believed that marriages could be maintained or repaired by preventing the mundane demands of family life from suffocating creativity. Marriage guidance would enable middle-aged men and women to dispel fears of ageing and death, obviating the need to seek comfort and affirmation elsewhere.[144]

IN 1947 THE final report of the Denning Committee recommended greater state investment in marriage guidance services in order to help couples deal more effectively with 'the post-marital causes of unhappiness'.[145] Denning was not alone in pressing for greater support for unsettled or failing marriages. Although the Archbishop of Canterbury recognized that many voluntary societies, marriage guidance clinics, Citizens' Advice Bureaux and church bodies offered couples assistance in 'saving endangered homes', he argued that without public money the work of these organizations 'was diffused, the numbers engaged in it too few, and their effort limited'. What every town needed, he suggested, was a centre 'where married people could discuss their troubles and obtain expert advice confidentially – spiritual, medical, psychological, legal'.[146] Other writers on marriage agreed that greater support was necessary for couples to address the underlying causes of divorce, ensure a loving home environment for their children, reduce the likelihood of juvenile delinquency and ensure companionship in later life.[147]

In the immediate post-war period, options for married couples were limited in Britain – as indeed they were in other countries. The Marriage Guidance Council, Family Welfare Association and Catholic Marriage Advisory Council offered advice and therapy, but their services were not distributed evenly across the country; in fact, many of them were available only in London, leaving couples elsewhere struggling to cope with marital difficulties on their own.[148] Since maintaining successful marriages was regarded as a prerequisite for – and a symbol of – effective post-war social reconstruction, Denning's recommendations for greater financial support were eventually endorsed, enabling the expansion of advice services through the 1950s and '60s. The Marriage Guidance Council was founded by the Methodist minister David Mace, the Presbyterian minister Herbert Gray and their colleagues shortly before the Second World War in response to what Mace later referred to, in deliberately sensationalist terms, as a 'marriage crisis'.[149] Insisting that successful marriage was the 'foundation of happy family life' and 'vital to the well-being of society', the Council aimed to help young couples understand the responsibilities and rewards of marriage, promote the value of monogamy and support those who were encountering marital difficulties.[150] The initial plan to ease troubled marriages had been formulated in 1938 and, supported by individual subscriptions and donations from the Eugenics Society, the Council was formally established in May that year.[151] Over the next few years, the Council began to coordinate services around the country, becoming the National Marriage Guidance Council in 1947. By the mid-1960s – at which point Lord Denning was president of the Council – there were 107 local councils across England and Wales, although not all of them were members of the national organization.[152]

Mace's conviction that divorce 'was nearly always the end of a long and sad story' that could have been avoided was not the only mid-century articulation of the need for effective marriage guidance.[153] In 1938 the National Conference on Family Relations was founded in America in order to promote family values – including upholding marriage – for the benefit of individuals, couples and their communities.[154] In addition to providing counselling services, the National Conference published an academic journal – initially entitled *Living*, but changed to *Marriage and Family Living* in 1941, and then in 1964 to the *Journal of Marriage and Family*. The journal was influential beyond America, publishing research into family life, predictive factors in marital success and preventative and therapeutic approaches to couples in conflict. Indeed, according to Mace, it was American authors such as Carl Rogers, one of the leading proponents of client-centred psychology, who provided the clearest articulation of the nature and value of counselling.[155] Similar services were instigated in other countries, such as New Zealand and the German Democratic Republic, where state-run marriage guidance services, Free German Youth and workplace collectives offered advice and support to couples whose marriages were threatened by unrealistically high expectations, inadequate housing and separation between spouses as a result of military service.[156]

Mace's approach to providing guidance across the marital life course was not new. During the 1920s and '30s Marie Stopes had offered advice not only to couples at the start of their relationships, but to those in middle age whose marriages had become tinged by 'a common sadness' as they failed to maintain intimacy and passion. Stopes regarded crises within marriage as products of maladjustment and ignorance triggered by the 'artificiality of civilisation', a pessimistic refrain commonly voiced in the interwar years.[157] Her prescription for promoting lifelong passion and fidelity emphasized effective communication as a means of countering melodramatic media accounts of inevitable decline in middle and older age. While interwar advice literature, such as the work of Walter Pitkin, focused primarily on individual strategies for self-fulfilment, Stopes and others approached marriage difficulties from a relational perspective, foregrounding the necessity for couples to work together through demanding periods in their relationship and cultivate shared pleasures as they aged.

For many post-war marriage guidance counsellors – whatever their professional background – it was also the dynamics of the marital dyad that provided the principal focus for analysis and intervention. Some writers explicitly acknowledged Stopes's relational approach. In 1952 Mary Macaulay thanked Stopes in the preface to *The Art of Marriage*, in which Macaulay argued that middle-aged couples needed to study and respond to 'each other's interests' if they were to avoid apathy and infidelity.[158] Similar arguments for recognizing the needs of others permeated psychological understandings of marital difficulties. In 1938 William Brown, Director of the Institute of Experimental Psychology at the University of Oxford and renowned for his work with shell-shocked soldiers during the First World War, suggested that successful adjustment to marriage – and indeed to middle age – required individuals to surrender 'the very pronounced degree of narcissism which we all have in our earlier years' and see life from the perspective of their partners, particularly once a couple had children.[159] Only then could two people live closely together as husband and wife. Appeals against narcissism also inflected the work of the National Marriage Guidance Council: 'Spiritual, emotional and physical harmony in marriage', the Council claimed, could only be achieved 'by unselfish love and self-discipline.'[160]

Marriage guidance in Britain and America was delivered by probation officers, social workers, nurses, occupational therapists and doctors, who were provided with specialist training for the practical and emotional challenges of working with couples experiencing difficulties. Counselling was sometimes dismissed as a 'technique in search of a theory' and became the butt of cartoonists' jokes.[161] But political concerns about rates of divorce ensured that the methods and outcomes of marriage guidance attracted considerable public, media and professional interest. The approaches adopted by marriage counsellors were clearly set out in the description and analysis of the work of the National Marriage Guidance Council written by J. H. Wallis and his colleague H. S. Booker in 1958, entitled *Marriage Counselling*. The first part of the volume reflected on the principles and practices of marriage guidance. The significance of the couple – evident also in Wallis's later reference to the 'Us' of marriage – was clear throughout.[162] Even when counsellors were approached initially by only one partner, they were to remember that 'in marriage counselling there are no problems independently of the marriage, independently of husband and wife.' After one or more individual consultations, counsellors were expected to invite the other partner to join them.[163]

Drawing on the narratives of 25,000 couples seeking advice between 1952 and 1954, Booker's contribution to *Marriage Counselling* explored the factors that precipitated requests for help from the Council, contextualizing the data in relation to family income, the number and age of any children, the educational, occupational and religious status of the spouses, and the ratio of wives to husbands who first sought guidance.

"As a first step let us try to get back to the love-hate relationship."

John Whitfield Taylor, 'One step at a time', *Punch*, 26 February 1964.

In 1952 more women (57.5 per cent) than men (37.5 per cent) initially approached clinics; partners attended together in only 5 per cent of cases.[164] The causes of crises in marriage varied. The most commonly cited reasons for discord were ill-health, living conditions, parental interference, sexual difficulties, personal defects such as selfishness, emotional immaturity, drinking and gambling, periods of separation caused by war or work, and husbands 'running after women'.[165] Known or suspected infidelity – most often on the part of the husband – constituted a factor in 16 per cent of cases in 1952 and 17.5 per cent in 1953. Infidelity was linked to the family life cycle, especially to the demands of midlife. Adultery was particularly prominent in marriages of approximately twenty years' duration – that is, in couples who were in their early forties.[166]

Booker's analysis traced the outcome of counselling, identifying cases where marriage difficulties had seemingly been overcome completely (19 per cent), improved to some extent (16.5 per cent), or showed no change (31.5 per cent).[167] Enriched by abbreviated case studies, *Marriage Counselling* revealed the relational dimensions of midlife marital crises. Descriptions of 37 cases of infidelity on the part of the husband and 15 on that of the wife – often after many years of marriage – highlight the manner in which couples apportioned blame for the breakdown of a marriage. In one case, a marriage of 31 years and four children had ended when the husband left his wife to live with 'a third party', citing his wife's lack of affection and her tendency to talk 'like a parrot, never ending'. Another couple had been 'happy for fifteen years' before the husband – who was described as overbearing and cruel – had begun 'an affair with the widow of a friend'. Wives also deserted dull and insecure husbands, seeking excitement or greater financial stability with new partners.[168]

The focus of counsellors on couples rather than individuals stemmed directly from contemporary commitments to reinvigorating family life. The need to stabilize families and restore social order constituted a reason to strengthen the interpersonal and emotional, rather than merely economic, foundations of marital relationships through the provision of marriage welfare services.[169] By contrast, psychodynamic approaches to marital and midlife crises tended to ignore existing family relationships, focusing instead on promoting self-expression and self-fulfilment. Yet not all psychotherapists neglected the relationship between partners or the dynamics of the family in seeking to resolve marital tensions. One key feature of the social casework carried out by staff at the Family Discussion Bureau (later the Institute of Marital Studies) – which had been founded at the Tavistock Clinic in 1948 – was its emphasis on individual personality development. But, in line with the focus of the Tavistock Institute of Human Relations on understanding the social, political and psychological determinants of behaviour, caseworkers at the Bureau recognized how marital discord could be traced to the incommensurate expectations of love between two partners. 'Since in our society marriage is primarily a love relationship,' wrote Kathleen Bannister and her colleagues at the Family Discussion Bureau in 1955,

> most difficulties which lead to marital breakdown can be seen as disturbances of emotional equilibrium – ultimately the balance of love and hate, of positive and negative impulses – between the two partners. Its success as a going concern, a growing organism, depends in the last resort on the partners' capacities for an emotional give-and-take of a maturing kind; the capacity to give and receive love, to belong to each other and yet to tolerate their separateness and fundamental individual and sexual differences, and to deal with the feelings of frustration and even of hostility which will inevitably arise between them.[170]

Funded by grants from the Home Office, London County Council and Gulbenkian Foundation, caseworkers at the Family Discussion Bureau developed a team approach that focused not on 'the individual but the marriage, and behind it the family'.[171] Indeed, the term 'family discussion' had been chosen explicitly instead of 'marriage welfare' in order to recognize the importance of the family to relationship difficulties at midlife and signal a supposedly more neutral stance to the preventative and therapeutic work carried out as a joint venture by clients and caseworkers.[172] Although clients were seen individually, particularly in the initial consultation or if one partner was reluctant to attend, emphasis on the couple as a single analytical unit necessitated involving both parties in attempts to address marital problems. Anonymized narratives of marital tensions presented by members of the Bureau revealed the web of norms and assumptions that structured couples therapy as well as the marital problems that it was designed to resolve. Extensive case reports of the Bureau's work aimed to link marital problems with family background, courtship and marriage, the birth of children and individual aspirations and perceptions of marriage. As staff at the Bureau pointed out in 1955, open discussion of marriage difficulties was intended to enable the couple to convert 'the vicious circles of intolerance and resentment' into a 'beneficent spiral of readjustment and growth' that continued after counselling had ceased.[173] Successful therapy helped to reduce marital tensions, facilitated the well-being of the family unit and improved social relationships beyond the marriage.

The value of joint, rather than individual, psychotherapy was most forcefully articulated by the British psychiatrist Henry Dicks, who in 1967 set out the principles and practices of therapy employed by caseworkers in his independent Marital Unit at the Tavistock Clinic. Although he criticized David Mace for his 'reliance on clichés', Dicks's analysis was similarly shaped by contemporary truisms about the importance of investigating 'disturbed marriages' in order to stem the 'trail of unhappiness' generated by 'broken homes' after the Second World War. Dicks's approach, however, was more clearly structured by an understanding of the complex interrelations between cultural norms, social expectations, emotional growth and what he termed 'marital pathology'.[174] Drawing on findings from a pilot study initiated in 1949, Dicks developed a strategy for diagnostic interview and joint therapy that moved well beyond the dyadic approach advocated by marriage guidance counsellors.[175] For Dicks, effectively working through and remedying relational tensions required establishing a novel system of joint interview and joint therapy involving both partners and two therapists.[176] Over time, this 'four-person relationship', Dicks suggested, would allow couples, whether married or not, to uncover and resolve conflicts generated by disappointed role expectations, the power of past identifications and the projection of one partner's repressed needs or characteristics onto the other.[177] It was perhaps his emphasis on maintaining or restoring the strength and security of the couple – with its reliance on 'keeping faith' – that led Dicks to regard adultery as 'the most serious threat to the great majority of marriages', as the 'symbolic final treason'.[178]

Factors other than those linked to personality and emotional immaturity impacted on marital harmony. Marriages became strained under the influence of in-laws, economic and housing difficulties, the double burden of home and work, and clashes of culture. In addition,

Dicks argued, marriages contracted under certain forms of stress –
such as 'a child on the way, the rebound from another affair, or as
a desperate remedy for social loneliness' – were often doomed from
the start.[179] In some instances, external factors – such as occupation
– served as potential solutions to marital tensions. Although both partners working beyond the home created challenges for couples and
families, middle-aged women on both sides of the Atlantic sought paid
work not only to restore self-esteem, but to escape domestic boredom, responsibility for childcare, financial constraints and unhappy
marriages.[180] However, unlike the authors of marriage guidance and
self-help literature aimed at the middle-aged, Dicks insisted that social
circumstances still needed to be understood primarily along psychoanalytical lines, that is, 'in terms of the meaning they have for the two
intrapersonal worlds'.[181]

The Family Discussion Bureau's casework methods and the
Tavistock Clinic's approach to couples counselling attracted considerable interest from the popular media and professional press. Although
some reviewers criticized what they regarded merely as a form of 'lay
psychotherapy', as well as a tendency to focus still on treating individuals
rather than marital and family relationships, the value of incorporating
'well-written, succinct case-material' into the Bureau's publications was
especially welcomed.[182] Dicks's extensive body of research prompted
more detailed comments from his peers. On its publication in 1967,
Marital Tensions was reviewed in medical, public health and psychology journals, and in popular and specialist publications such as *The
Observer*, *New Society* and *Marriage Counseling Quarterly*. Critics
highlighted weaknesses in Dicks's theoretical framework, which relied
– like the work of Elliott Jaques – partly on psychoanalytical models
established by Melanie Klein, and reprimanded him for neglecting the
work of the National Marriage Guidance Council. Dicks's identification
of human relations, rather than socio-economic factors, as the primary
cause of marriage problems was also challenged on the grounds that
most of the couples studied were from the middle classes. Nevertheless,
the 'four-person' approach advocated by Dicks was regarded as genu-
inely innovative, and the sensitive manner in which he had revealed the
'psychological sub-soil on which many a shaky marriage is built' was
appreciated.[183] An extended review in the *Times Literary Supplement*
suggests that Dicks's work also struck a chord with contemporaries
wanting to promote marriage as 'more than the sum of 1 and 1', or

struggling to contain the damage caused to partners and children by the shifting axis of love at midlife.[184]

Given his commitment to reading both individual and dyadic development in psychoanalytical terms, as well as the fact that he worked alongside Elliott Jaques at the Tavistock Institute during the 1950s, it is not surprising that Dicks was one of the first writers on marital distress to cite Jaques's formulation of the midlife crisis.[185] According to Dicks, it was the rediscovery of personal identity during middle age – that is, once the period of collaborative 'nest-building' was over – that threatened the stability of the 'social atom' that had been created by marriage. Nearly half of the couples seen at the Tavistock Clinic were in their thirties and a similar proportion of divorces occurred during that decade. The effects of the crisis that afflicted people at midlife continued to reverberate through subsequent years of marriage. Levels of conflict between partners remained high between the ages of forty and forty-nine, after twenty years or so of marriage.[186] During the post-war years, marriage guidance counsellors, psychoanalysts, state agencies and proponents of divorce law reform on both sides of the Atlantic believed that midlife crises, marital breakdowns and fractured families were largely inseparable.

IN *ROCKET TO THE MOON*, a three-act play first performed at the Belasco Theatre in New York in 1938, the American dramatist Clifford Odets highlights the ways in which mid-century models of marriage and home were creating expectations of mutual happiness that were often crushed by the pressing realities of work and domesticity. For Odets, 'taking a rocket to the moon' was a metaphor for rebelling against the conformity and monotony of adult life. Almost forty years old, Ben Stark's dental business is failing; his marriage is laced with undertones of intolerance and regret; a young dental assistant – precisely half his age – seems to present an opportunity for sexual solace and contentment; and the mocking insolence of his father-in-law, who offers to fund Stark's practice, generates only further insecurities and self-doubt. Although the plot appears to revolve primarily around Ben Stark's dilemmas, Odets pays careful attention to the imposed passivity and emotional despair of Stark's wife, Belle, as the distance between the couple increases and a distorted triangle of frustrated expectations, boredom and disillusionment begins to form. Indeed, Odets skilfully creates far greater sympathy for Belle as a neglected and dispossessed wife than he does for Ben, who surfaces from the dialogue merely as a sad, narcissistic middle-aged man in crisis. While her husband has lazily taken everything for granted, including his wife, Belle alone has the strength and presence to assert the importance of the companionate marriage that characterized the aspirations of middle-class, middle-aged couples at mid-century: 'A woman wants to live *with* a man – not next to him,' she insists.[187]

When *Rocket to the Moon* was reprised at the Apollo Theatre in London in 1982, the English critic and broadcaster Sheridan Morley described it in *Punch* as the 'long-lost Clifford Odets drama of American marital menopause'.[188] Although Morley's conflation of the relational with the biological dimensions of midlife could be read as flippant, his reference to the association between marital tensions and a particular stage in the life course was shrewd. The term 'marital menopause' neatly captured prominent post-war concerns about the internal and external drivers of midlife crises in both women and men. Morley's reference to menopause was in some ways chauvinistic, displaying and replaying attempts to consign women, wives and mothers to domestic duties and their sexual and reproductive destinies. But, at the same time, it diverted interest away from glamorized descriptions of the behaviour of the rogue male towards recognizing critical turning points in the life course of women and the effects of crises on marital harmony as well as individual health. As attention shifted to women at midlife, crises were no longer construed entirely in negative terms. Experiences and accounts of the menopause in women provided momentum for women to seek happiness and self-fulfilment beyond the home. Constrained by the everyday ties of the nuclear family, but liberated by growing economic independence, women left their husbands not necessarily for *someone* else, but always for *something* else, as Ellen Goodman put it in the *Daily Mail* in 1975. For women divorce could be 'more of a declaration of confidence than of defeat'.[189]

Although film producers and novelists increasingly foregrounded the capacity of women to leave philandering husbands and the drudgery of domesticity, there was a backlash against women's attempts to seek freedom from their roles at home and within the family. Reactionary responses to feminist critiques of masculine hegemony focused on the biological determinants of health and happiness. The socially constructed timetable of women's lives was reframed in terms of the ticking of a natural biological clock, reducing women's social value to the period in which they were able to reproduce. 'Empty nest syndrome', understood in terms of the loneliness and disillusionment experienced by parents when their children left home, was traced not only to women's fading social roles as mothers and wives as they aged, but to the physiological and emotional lability widely associated with menopause. And in attempts to reinvigorate sympathy for the physical, emotional and occupational travails of men at midlife, doctors and self-help authors insisted that middle-aged men also suffered from hormonal imbalances during their forties and fifties, leading to – and perhaps justifying – the impulsive behaviour associated with the midlife crisis.

4

BIOLOGICAL CLOCKS

'The crisis of the menopause rudely cuts the life of woman in two.'
SIMONE DE BEAUVOIR, 1949[1]

In a series of experiments initially conducted in the early 1920s as part of his doctoral research, the American biologist Curt Richter intimated that many animal behaviours – such as physical activity, nest-building and feeding – followed recognizable rhythmic cycles governed by endogenous clocks.[2] Through the middle decades of the twentieth century, Richter's laboratory research focused on exploring and explaining the circadian, monthly and longer-term rhythms that regulated behaviour. Although his experimental work used the Norway rat as the principal model for investigating innate rhythms, Richter extrapolated his findings to humans. In a seminal paper published in 1960, he argued that disordered clocks could lead to, or exacerbate, recognizable physical and psychiatric conditions, most notably certain forms of recurrent arthritis, Parkinsonism and manic depression.[3] Indeed, for Richter many of the clocks harboured by humans were discernible only in pathological states. Under normal circumstances, the rhythmic nature of mental and bodily processes had 'become submerged in one way or another during the process of evolution'. In modern times, Richter suggested, only 'slight, if any, diurnal variations' and the 'emotional changes associated with menstruation' remained visible in humans.[4]

Richter's pioneering studies of the role of intrinsic 'timing devices' in self-regulatory or homeostatic behaviour helped to establish the nascent field of chronobiology and to popularize the term 'biological clock' during the 1960s, a decade in which sociological, psychological and literary references – and objections – to the clockwork corporate and commercial regulation of working patterns, leisure time and family life cycles were becoming commonplace. Richter was not alone in drawing scientific and medical attention to the significance of biological cycles in this period. At the same time, behavioural physiologists such as Jürgen Aschoff, Erwin Bünning and Arne Sollberger were employing animal models to explore the properties of physiological clocks and the drivers of circadian rhythms and applying their findings to human pathology.[5] Unlike Richter, whose work focused almost exclusively on the biology of keeping time across the days, months and years, Aschoff in particular was interested in investigating social cues in the environment (referred to as '*Zeitgebers*' or 'time givers') that might affect the ability of employees – including night shift workers and pilots – to adjust safely to different regimes of work and rest.[6] Only if circadian rhythms were aligned to external circumstances, Aschoff argued in 1965, would organisms be able to master 'changing conditions in a temporally programmed world'.[7]

Interest in biological clocks was evident not only in individual studies of animal behaviour, but in a number of international conferences convened in the post-war decades. In 1956 Richter contributed a paper on 'hormones and rhythms in man and animals' to the Laurentian Hormone Conference coordinated by Gregory Pincus, an American biologist renowned for his work on the development of the oral contraceptive pill.[8] Four years later, a Cold Spring Harbor Symposium on biological clocks brought together papers from a wide range of scholars analysing the general properties, metabolic aspects and physiological and ecological dimensions of circadian rhythms, as well as preliminary studies of longer tidal, lunar and annual periodicities in birds and marine organisms.[9] Scientific obsessions with the mechanisms and limits of physiological regulation deepened across the 1960s and '70s, most notably in debates about homeostasis and stress-related diseases, which were seen as manifestations of a failure to adapt over time to environmental stimuli. As a result, the term 'biological clock' became more extensively, and more loosely, applied to rhythms beyond the circadian; to monthly, seasonal and annual variations in mood, function and survival; to the evolutionary and epigenetic drivers of ageing being investigated across the 1940s, '50s and '60s by scientists such as Conrad Waddington, Peter Medawar and George Williams; and to the temporal limits of procreative potential across the life course.[10] As Aschoff pointed out in his address to the Cold Spring Harbor Symposium, 'organisms possess several different clocks with perhaps extremely different periods.'[11] It was the synchronicity or misalignment of these multiple biological clocks that came to define – or predict – the achievements, crisis points and duration of life.

Biological periodicity was not the only determinant of fluctuations in human behaviour across the life span. Social and cultural rhythms also dictated aspirations for – and experiences of – entry into the workplace, marriage, parenthood and retirement. Just as there were different life clocks, all with discrete movements and periods, so too were there distinctive moments of personal transition between the hours, days, months, years and stages of life that shaped the health of individuals and families across the life course. Coincidences or dissonances between biological, cultural, chronological, career and family calendars could elicit crises, especially at midlife when individual and collective rhythms across generations conspired to create episodes of undue conflict and estrangement. Richter and his wife, the psychiatrist Phyllis Greenacre, suffered their own crises during middle age, as the strain of overwork, Greenacre's struggles to defy prevailing conventions and combine career with motherhood, and Richter's affair with a younger woman resulted in separation and divorce in their mid-thirties.[12] The midlife traumas of Greenacre and Richter reveal a key feature of contemporary formulations of clock time: while men's clocks were shaped primarily by the socially prescribed time span of occupational productivity and extended sexual prowess, women's value across the life cycle was tied to what were regarded as the natural temporal limits of their reproductive and maternal capacity. In this way, the ticking of the biological clock emerged as a metaphor for the diminishing chances of middle-aged women to fulfil their generative role before the advent of what the psychoanalyst Helene Deutsch referred to in 1947 as the 'partial death' of menopause.[13]

The notion that life was governed by a biological clock was given especial prominence in 1978 by the American journalist Richard Cohen, who outlined the seemingly inevitable dismay of the 'career woman', whose chances of motherhood were fading as she entered her thirties. It was the image – or sound – of the ticking clock that symbolized the fears of post-war Western societies that women were neglecting their procreative and domestic duties.[14] As birth rates fell – apart from a sharp peak in the early 1960s – and divorce rates rose, women who had no children and mothers who worked were often regarded as an affront to conventional valuations of motherhood and wifehood, a threat to the health and well-being of husbands and children, and a danger to the security and wealth of nations. Patriarchal presumptions that the social capital of women was programmed by biology, rather than constructed by culture, were met with defiance. Post-war feminists vigorously contested attempts to reduce women's hopes and prospects to marriage and motherhood, arguing that such constraints damaged the emotional and physical health, as well as the social status, of women of all ages.[15] Not only women's lives were constrained by feudal conventions. Carefully guarded distinctions between work and domesticity in the capitalist conditions of advanced Western societies similarly limited men to a single, politically manipulated dimension. Sociological studies by Herbert Marcuse and William H. Whyte, as well as the fictional works of Sloan Wilson and David Ely, exposed the intensity of men's despair at the straitjacket of work pressures and family life after the war. Even feminist critiques of traditional gender roles acknowledged – if only half-heartedly – that men's lives were constricted too.[16] While the notion of companionate marriage encouraged men to spend more time at home, growing aspirations to achieve the freedom and prosperity promised by the American dream consigned them to the routines and rhythms of the workplace and distanced them physically and emotionally from their wives and children. Resistance was seen to be futile for both men and women. The change of life, waning virility, middle-aged spread and post-parental emptiness all indicated that, regardless of efforts to stem or reverse the flow of time, the biological – as well as social – clock was always ticking.

ACCORDING TO ELLIOTT Jaques, the midlife crisis was often 'obscured in women by the proximity of the onset of changes connected with the menopause'.[17] Jaques's dismissive gesture to the problems of women at midlife was remarkable for its ignorance of contemporary biology and psychology. In physiological terms, women's experiences made it clear that menopause occurred most often around the age of fifty, well beyond Jaques's timing of the typical midlife crisis.[18] At the same time, Jaques ignored – or was unaware of – an expanding psychoanalytical literature on the psychology of women across the life course. The most extensive studies in this area were carried out by Helene Deutsch, whose work during the middle decades of the twentieth century shifted focus away from Freudian accounts of sexuality that continued to interpret key physiological transitions in women primarily in terms of castration.[19]

Instead, Deutsch argued that the onset and cessation of menstruation, as well as other physiological and psychological changes throughout the life course, generated conflicts between narcissistic and maternal impulses. Emphasizing that its biological significance was unknown – partly because there was no analogous transition 'either in the human male on the one hand or in the animal kingdom on the other' – Deutsch claimed that menopause constituted a psychological struggle against the 'physiological regression' that was most likely to occur between a woman's mid-forties and mid-fifties. But she also believed that women could experience emotional resistance to age-related changes at a much earlier stage in the life course – that is, during their thirties, well before the organic changes of the menopause had begun to impact on their lives and more clearly in line with accounts of the midlife crisis in men.[20]

In *The Second Sex*, published in French in 1949, Simone de Beauvoir – citing Deutsch at one point – highlighted how women in their early forties began to feel the 'fatal touch of death itself', triggering hypomanic attempts to conceal the physical features of ageing, as well as precipitating a 'morbid state of melancholy' that might require treatment.[21] Yet, in spite of attempts to align women's experiences at midlife with men's emotional crises at a similar stage in the life course, it is clear that post-war accounts of middle-aged women were dominated by the biology of the menopause. The tone of post-war discussions of the reproductive destiny of women had already been set in the late nineteenth and early twentieth centuries.[22] In 1915 the British gynaecologist Mary Scharlieb emphasized the physical involution that occurred after the onset of menopause at around fifty. Decline was evident in 'the accumulation of unnecessary fat', a reduction in bone density and changing cardiac function and digestion, as well as the cessation of menstruation.[23] Although she regarded menopause as a normal process, Scharlieb recognized that the transition could prove difficult. She warned that women might be afflicted with minor pains, emotional instability and a variety of more serious diseases of the reproductive organs. Given the persistence of the traditional Victorian model of domestic economy, which figured men as the principal breadwinners, responsibility for adapting to menopausal symptoms and maintaining the stability of the home lay with women, not with those around them. 'If the whole household is not to be disorganised,' Scharlieb wrote, 'and if the woman is to retain her self-respect, she must resolutely call up her powers of self-control and learn how to suffer not only in silence but in cheerfulness.'[24]

Interwar accounts of menopause continued to linger on images of crisis, decline and catastrophe. One of the most prominent studies of the 'climacteric' or 'critical age' was first published in 1919 by the Spanish pathologist Gregorio Marañón and translated ten years later into English. For Marañón, the menopause constituted a 'complex endocrine crisis', analogous to the 'pubescent crisis' and manifest not only in ovarian changes but in alterations in thyroid, suprarenal, hypophyseal and nervous functions.[25] The result, in Marañón's view, was not merely the cessation of menstruation, but a series of physical and emotional changes that led women to re-evaluate their lives and recognize the need for 'improving one's time' – a subjective position that he referred to as the 'emotion of hurry'.[26] Marañón's text read like a treatise on hormones, which is perhaps not surprising given the prominence of endocrinology and the development of synthetic oestrogens to treat menopausal symptoms in the interwar years.[27] But he was not insensitive to the cultural dimensions of the menopause. Both the timing and manifestations of the climacteric varied according to social conditions. Class and race, as well as the local environment, could determine how and when menopause expressed itself. Women of the lower social classes 'cruelly lashed by life', Marañón argued, tended to experience menopause earlier than their more affluent peers, who could concentrate on 'the cult of the person, simply because their economic circumstances permitted it'.[28]

Marañón's evidence that the physiological, psychological and chronological markers of menopause were culturally determined was considered by some reviewers to be flimsy.[29] But emphasis on the cultural dimensions of menopause proved to be a rich vein of research for subsequent anthropological, sociological and biomedical studies of women at midlife. Experiences and interpretations of menopause were by no means universal in either social meaning or physical expression. Whether the change of life was regarded as a relief or a crisis and how it manifested in specific symptoms depended on social and cultural contexts operating in tandem with biological factors. In some cultures, as American anthropologist Marcha Flint pointed out in her studies of Indian women in the 1970s, the menopause and its aftermath were regarded as reward rather than punishment, as opportunity rather than burden, as an elevation rather than reduction in social status, resulting in fewer or less-pronounced physical and psychological symptoms during the change.[30] Developmental psychologists cautioned researchers and clinicians against accepting that every midlife problem was attributable to menopause or even that menopause constituted a crisis – or a pause – at all.[31] And Margaret Lock's studies of American and Japanese women demonstrated how menopause carried quite different meanings depending on social attitudes to ageing and women's roles across the family life cycle.[32] Throughout the second half of the twentieth century, beliefs that menopause constituted an almost inevitable and painful rupture in the lives of middle-aged women were limited to Western biomedical valuations of women's bodies and identities.

Margaret Gullette has suggested that decline narratives of ageing were beginning to lose potency during the early and middle decades of the twentieth century.[33] Certainly, the belief that cataracts of emotion would necessarily erupt around the time of the menopause began to be contested in that period, most notably by Marie Stopes, who regarded Marañón's work as 'more subtle, sensitive, and full of understanding' than other studies – even though, unlike Stopes, he clearly equated the climacteric with crisis.[34] In *Enduring Passion*, Stopes criticized self-help authors for intimidating women who were approaching the menopause, insisting instead that the physiological and psychological changes that could occur at that stage of life were usually minimal and transitory. In particular, she dismissed the 'stupid idea' that couples 'must necessarily cease from sex' after menopause, a notion that she pointed out had been propagated by Mary Scharlieb, among others, but one that Stopes regarded as a 'fantastic misrepresentation of physiological fact'.[35] Stopes not only argued that many women began to enjoy sex 'spontaneously and happily' perhaps for the first time after the change of life, but cautioned men 'not to be disheartened' at this time and 'break up the married unity by going elsewhere' – especially to prostitutes. After menopause, she claimed, couples could enjoy a 'second honeymoon', a period of mutual discovery unencumbered by the responsibilities of family and work.[36]

In *Change of Life in Men and Women*, published in 1936, Stopes painted an even more positive and less demeaning portrait of menopausal women. Although she recognized that menopause was accompanied by physical and mental changes as the 'harmony of the hormones' was disrupted, she was adamant that the notion of a climacteric crisis had been 'artificially created' by male doctors and pharmaceutical companies keen to profit from women's anxieties about the change. 'The "difficulties" of the menopause in women', Stopes wrote,

Advertisement for
Parke, Davis & Co.,
1930s.

"*I was afraid of the Menopause, too!*"

To a woman of middle age, the very word "Menopause" often conjures up a frightening picture.

A picture of an abrupt termination of all the things a woman holds dear. Infinitely precious things like charm…health…appeal…peace of mind. Largely due to whispered old wives' tales which have drifted her way since adolescence, she may regard "change of life" as a nightmarish entrance to old age.

If you are one of those who dread the Menopause, you are likely to get some good news from some understanding friend who has gone through change of life herself within the past few years.

The chances are she'll say something like this: "I was afraid of it, too. But it isn't nearly the ordeal you think it is. Nowadays, doctors can give you so much help that you'll probably have very little trouble."

Yes, doctors can do more about the Menopause today—thanks to a wealth of medical research. Your doctor will tell you that modern treatment can go far towards relieving the physical and mental upsets accompanying Menopause—a measure of relief undreamed of 10 short years ago.

Moreover, at no time in a woman's life is sound diagnosis more important. For many women, knowing that they are passing through the Menopause, tend to blame it for all their ills. Yet, they may have some additional and entirely unrelated trouble. Something which, left to itself, may become serious before it is detected.

Under your doctor's wise guidance, you can face this period of glandular readjustment calmly and without apprehension. You are apt to be pleasantly surprised at how little it will alter your usual daily routine. And when it passes, the chances are that your life can be just as happy and serene as ever.

PARKE, DAVIS & COMPANY
Detroit, Michigan

The World's Largest Makers of
Pharmaceutical and Biological Products

See your Doctor

'are chiefly the physical expression of mental states induced by fears of all the falsehoods and hoodoos put into circulation by rumour.'[37]

Stopes's emancipatory rhetoric and her refusal to equate physical signs of ageing with declining social value were echoed in other inter-war and wartime studies. In 1930 the British physician George Riddoch suggested that many of the manifestations of menopause – at least in middle-class women – were merely the inescapable consequences of middle age. Wrinkles, greying hair, greater conservatism and fears of 'diminished physical attractiveness', he argued, were not confined to those experiencing the change of life, but common to many women passing through midlife.[38] Three years later, an expansive clinical survey of 1,000 women, carried out by the Council of Medical Women's Federation, concluded that 90 per cent of interviewees 'carried on their daily duties without a single interruption due to menopausal symptoms', regardless of whether they were married or single.[39] As Julie-Marie Strange has pointed out, this survey was not without political purpose. Its attempt to challenge the belief that menopause was a pathological process was linked to efforts to recognize women's capacity to contribute to the workforce, as well as to arguments for equal pay and improved working conditions.[40] The findings of the Council's survey found some support, but its impact on popular attitudes to women working, even during wartime labour shortages, may have been limited. Citing the Council's findings in a debate about the call-up of older women during the Second World War, the British Labour politician Ernest Bevin insisted that women in their forties were perfectly capable of working during their menopausal years without compromising their health. Indeed, he suggested that work might improve the emotional well-being of middle-aged women and reduce the growing distance that often appeared between husbands and wives – and between adolescent children and their mothers – during this period of their lives. However, Bevin acknowledged that public opinion differed: objections to women working during middle age continued to be expressed by men and children, who had come to regard their wives and mothers as fixtures in the home.[41]

In spite of feminist accounts of menopausal women in terms of increased – rather than reduced – capacity to work, the language of crisis and involution continued to inflect post-war debates about women at midlife, helping to perpetuate feelings of shame and anxiety during the menopause. The denigration of menopausal women was per-haps not always deliberate. The British obstetrician Joan Malleson was a key figure in the radical movement to legalize abortion, having referred a young rape victim to the gynaecologist Aleck Bourne, triggering a landmark legal case that led indirectly to the passage of the Abortion Act in 1967.[42] Yet her clinical publications in the 1950s, like those of many doctors on both sides of the Atlantic, tended to pathologize the menopause, explaining it primarily in terms of ovarian failure that was amenable to treatment with oestrogen.[43] According to Malleson, meno-pause constituted a physiological disturbance of the hormones 'outside the range of normal endocrine balance'. Hormonal instability created what Malleson referred to as a 'negative-state balance', a term that echoed earlier formulations of menopausal women in terms of deficit and decline. Reflecting chauvinistic stereotypes of the roles of mothers and housewives, she emphasized the impact of menopause on women's ability to function effectively either domestically or in the workplace. Irritability at this time of life, she argued, could be a 'devastating force in the home and in industry, and among teachers, nurses, and others'.[44] Malleson believed that succumbing to the restlessness and misery of menopause could lead to a deterioration in family relationships. In a paper published just after her death, she blamed women directly for domestic tensions. 'Home can be disrupted', Malleson wrote in 1956, 'by the nagging of a wife, children made unhappy, whilst the woman herself is wretched with temper and remorse.'[45]

Malleson's popular advice literature for middle-aged women – and ostensibly for their partners – was arguably less judgemental. In *Change of Life: Facts and Fallacies of Middle Age*, published in 1949, Malleson focused not only on the physiological and emotional disturbances of menopause, but on the more general challenges raised by midlife. She admonished women who became lazy and gained weight during middle age and believed that it was a wife's responsibility to remain sexually active – sometimes in the face of diminishing desire – in order to maintain her husband's virility.[46] But she also insisted that 'liberation from menstrual and menopausal burdens' could lead to 'great change and development', to a 'new life of the mind and the spirit' – words that were intended to console and energize those women who felt empty and purposeless after children had left home or lonely after the death of their parents.[47] The solution in these instances, she argued, was not necessarily pharmacological, but psychosocial. Drawing on her work with women experiencing marital difficulties, Malleson suggested that older women should pursue creative and social outlets that would help them to maintain a sense of individuality and self-esteem. She accepted that this could be difficult for the 'average housewife' unaccustomed to social situations, but she insisted that new activities were essential for women's satisfaction and security beyond menopause.[48]

The tone of Malleson's recommendations for self-help were not unlike contemporary emphases on the benefits of leisure through the middle years. Nor were they dissimilar to beliefs in the ability of sublimation to resolve midlife marital tensions; or to literature reassuring women that they could 'feel good' through the menopause and look 'happily ahead' to later life.[49] Malleson's approach to the challenges of middle age also resonated with clinical attempts to address what were still often regarded as the most difficult years of a woman's – and her family's – life. At a 1954 conference of the Medical Women's International Association, the earlier work of which Malleson had cited in her academic publications, a number of contributors highlighted the accumulation of worries that both reflected and contributed to deteriorating conjugal and family relationships around the time of the menopause. The realization that 'the years of fertility, of sexual attractiveness, and of expectations, will soon be ended', one speaker suggested, could precipitate physical symptoms and depression in women just as they were thought to in middle-aged men.[50]

Although intended to free women from overly biological interpretations of menopause, such accounts often reinforced gendered stereotypes of ageing, in particular those that identified women as the cause of their husbands' midlife distress. In *The Art of Marriage*, which sold 15,000 copies between 1952 and 1956, the physician Mary Macaulay accepted that both women and men could be difficult to live with in their forties and fifties. But it was wives who were responsible for ensuring that their husbands did not 'leave them for someone younger and more responsive'.[51] Women became scapegoats for their husbands' dissatisfaction, and husbands felt themselves justified in expressing animosity towards their wives.[52] Kenneth Hutchin's self-help books continued the assault on middle-aged women. In some respects, Hutchin was sensitive to women's midlife transitions, advising men and children to be supportive even though they were experiencing work stress and adolescent crises of their own. But he nevertheless pointed out that wives and mothers remained accountable for domestic harmony: 'The woman who makes the most of her symptoms', he wrote in 1963, 'can turn the climacteric into a time of misery for the whole family ... Whether it is in family life or in married life, women in the climacteric should try not to take things too seriously.'[53] In a world in which family stability was seen as crucial for effective social reconstruction, the happiness of men and children took precedence over the health of wives and mothers.

Ambivalent evaluations of women's worth during and after menopause, and the belief that women remained primarily responsible for mitigating midlife pressures within the nuclear family, were contested. Throughout the post-war decades, Bernice Neugarten regularly dismissed assumptions that menopause necessarily implied crisis. Neugarten and her co-workers used the Blatt Menopause Index – a measure of self-reported symptoms and clinical ratings that had been introduced in the 1950s – to establish the health and well-being of middle-aged women. Her work demonstrated that there was considerable variability in menopausal symptoms and that menopause, like many other life changes, was a normal – but not necessarily traumatic – turning point in a woman's life course: 'a psychology of the life cycle', she argued, 'is not a psychology of crisis behavior so much as it is a psychology of timing'.[54] On occasion, the change of life could be portrayed in even more positive terms. Judith Houck has argued that, although menopause was often regarded as a 'family disease' for which women were responsible if separation and divorce were to be avoided, American advice literature also emphasized the 'liberating aspects of life' beyond the change.[55] While the mid-century medicalization of menopause reinforced women's reproductive and domestic responsibilities, there was another side to post-war debates about menopause, one that was inspired, Houck suggests, by comparing it to the painful, but necessary, 'transition from a war-time economy to a peace-time economy'.[56] The menopause was certainly interpreted by some authors as a refreshing opportunity to relinquish the frustrations experienced by women during their thirties and forties and to discover the emotional balance and peace of later life. According to Marion Hilliard, for example, menopause could be a woman's 'greatest blessing', marking the end of periodic volatility, the resurgence of libido and growing recognition that it was no longer worth investing finite stores of energy in 'keeping up with the Joneses'. 'The first, and, best sensation when the menopause is finished', Hilliard reassured her readers in 1958,

> is that the woman has reached a plateau of constancy. She can depend on her moods, which won't fluctuate unduly. She can depend on her body and energy to be faithful. With this goes a sense of rebirth and exhilaration beyond description. Now that the fear of pregnancy is past, many women find themselves enjoying sexual relations with their husbands for the first time in their lives . . . The change – if that's what you're determined to call it – begins at forty-five but, believe me, life begins at fifty.[57]

In spite of attempts to highlight its more positive attributes, Western societies continued to regard menopause in terms of physical deterioration, the loss of sexual identity and death. For women struggling to cope with the change of life, Marcha Flint insisted, 'fear begins at forty and it's downhill after that, with death waiting at the end.'[58]

The endeavours of post-war feminist writers to emphasize the ways in which middle-aged women were demeaned by cultural stereotypes failed to unsettle dominant masculine medical narratives of menopause as a gateway to barren old age. Writing in 1949, Simone de Beauvoir emphasized the symbolic – rather than merely physiological

– significance of the change of life, particularly in women who had 'staked everything on their femininity'.[59] The promise of a new, more creative life after menopause, she argued, was largely an illusion, middle-aged women's restlessness merely 'a defence reaction' against despair. It was only by giving up 'the struggle against the fatality of time' that a woman's dangerous age would pass – although challenges to maintain her 'place on earth' persisted. In spite of feminist resistance to reductive biological readings of women's bodies and minds, it was still the case, according to Beauvoir, that the 'crisis of the menopause rudely cuts the life of woman in two'.[60] Like the despair at the downward curve of life that came to define men in middle age, menopause encouraged women to take stock: 'In this perspective,' wrote Beauvoir, 'she reviews the past; the moment has come to draw a line across the page, to make up her accounts; she balances her books. And she is appalled at the narrow limitations life has imposed upon her.'[61] But even here, it was biology that governed the sense of disillusionment that women shared with men at midlife.

Menopause cut the world, as well as the lives of women, in two. Although middle-aged men faced impotence and waning virility, their experiences constituted only a shadow of the hormonal, psychological and social ruptures experienced by women during their forties and fifties. The significance of this distinction surfaced in Jean Baudrillard's idio-syncratic reflections on a politically polarized world. 'Democracy is the menopause of Western society,' he wrote in 1987, 'the Grand Climacteric of the body social. Fascism is its middle-aged lust.'[62] Crudely simplistic in its imagery, Baudrillard's words nevertheless captured the potency of the social and sexual forces that separated women from men – or 'Us' from 'Them', as Marilyn French put it in her classic novel *The Women's Room* in 1978.[63] Indeed, French highlighted even more starkly the symbolic and substantive distance between women and men at midlife. Towards the end of the novel, Val's embittered reaction to her daughter being raped – 'all men are rapists', she asserts to one of her friends – is trivialized by Howard after Val's death: 'She was great, you know, really great. Once. My theory is that she went nuts in menopause. Women do, you know? She was getting old, she was no longer attractive to men, and her basic hostility to them took over.'[64]

There were few ways for women to escape derogatory assessments of their minds and bodies at midlife. The personal, social and political challenges faced by women as they aged could not be resolved by resort-ing to skincare products or tonics, either to suspend the ticking of the clock or to guarantee a husband's continued fidelity. On the contrary, as post-war feminists insisted, the production and marketing of cosmetics, as well as the promotion of labour-saving domestic appliances, further belittled and dehumanized women as they aged, exposing them more blatantly to the appraisal and approval of men. The fears of middle-aged women as they approached and passed through menopause were accentuated by the images of docile, accommodating housewives that appeared in post-war magazines, novels, films, advertisements and television series.[65] Reinforced by beliefs that maternal deprivation could permanently scar the next generation, post-war media representations and commercial marketing strategies confined women more tightly to caring for husbands, children and the home, and exacerbated – rather than alleviated – menopausal and post-menopausal feelings of loss, redundancy and emptiness.

EMPHASIS ON PHYSIOLOGICAL changes in men at midlife served not to confine husbands to domestic or occupational responsibilities, but to allow them freedom to look beyond the marital bed, factory floor and office desk for satisfaction. The notion of a male climacteric had been raised by European medical practitioners in the early and mid-nineteenth century. Although not the first writer on the subject, in 1865 the English physician C. M. Durrant pointed out that, while the constitutional changes associated with menopause in women were well known, it was less commonly accepted that analogous changes could occur in men. Between the ages of forty and fifty-five, he argued, the 'decline of life' in men was evident in constitutional disturbances not dissimilar to those witnessed in women, including fatigue, pain, anxiety, circulatory problems and insanity. Although emphasizing the biological determinants of these symptoms, Durrant claimed that climacteric changes in men – unlike those in women – could be triggered or exaggerated by financial loss, an 'ill-assorted marriage' or the pace of modern business life.[66] During the late nineteenth and early twentieth centuries, the existence and principal features of the male climacteric were contested. Marañón had no doubts that men experienced a 'critical age', although its evolution and limits were diffuse. Given the far more gradual decline in testicular, as opposed to ovarian, function with age, he suggested, the male climacteric lacked 'the menopausal phenomenon as a point of reference'.[67] Symptoms in men included diminished erectile power, a variety of physical conditions including weight gain, hypertension and diabetes, and – as in women – a tendency to impatience and emotional instability expressed both at home and at work. While the manifestations of age were thought to render women unappealing during and beyond midlife, physical decline did not necessarily make middle-aged men unattractive, Marañón insisted. As emotional maturity and intellectual control increased with age, so too did a man's capacity to achieve financial success, leading to greater sexual appeal and an increased tendency for 'young women' to marry 'men already mature'.[68]

Marie Stopes also believed that middle-aged men underwent physiological and psychological changes equivalent in many ways to those experienced by women. Indeed, in her 1936 volume on the change of life, Stopes discussed the determinants and features of the male climacteric before considering the change in women.[69] As both Marañón and Stopes acknowledged, however, many of their contemporaries were more cautious about accepting the existence of a distinct change of life in men. In *Psychology of Sex*, first published in 1933, the British sexologist Havelock Ellis insisted that, at least in physiological terms, the male climacteric constituted only a 'vague and comparatively unimportant period' in a man's life.[70] Ellis did not discount the potential for men at midlife to experience physical changes triggered by fluctuations in hormones, but he focused on the psychological manifestations of crisis. In contrast to many authors who suggested that the climacteric generally occurred in men during their late forties and fifties, Ellis believed that crises were more common around the 'age of 38', leading to a pattern of behaviour similar to that described by Elliott Jaques some years later:

> The man suddenly realizes that the period of expanding power has reached its limits, even that there is a comparative failure of power, this also manifesting itself in the sexual sphere, and by a sudden revulsion of feeling he may begin to feel that he is no longer a young man but an old man. Such a recognition with advance of age may involve not only the liability to an eruption of sexual activity but also the development of a certain egotism and callousness which facilitates its manifestations.[71]

Sometimes drawing explicitly on Ellis's work, mid-century writers on age-related changes in health and well-being continued to debate whether the male climacteric – if it existed – was primarily a physio-logical or psychological phenomenon and whether its symptoms should be alleviated by pharmacological or psychotherapeutic means.[72] On occasion, researchers considered the role of cultural factors in gener-ating men's midlife problems. In 1954 Otto Billig and Robert Adams rejected the notion that the male climacteric had a physiological basis. Instead, they argued that it was a psychiatric syndrome triggered by Western cultural emphasis on achieving success in a competitive world. Viewing men's passage through midlife from a psychoanalytical per-spective, Billig and Adams suggested that emotional disturbances in middle-aged men were primarily Oedipal, but made visible only in specific circumstances. The competition of a younger colleague at work, or a son's adolescence and emerging adulthood, could reactivate a man's unresolved anxieties about losing parental love and social approval if he proved to be a failure.[73] Such interpretations were incorporated into academic and literary studies of the midlife crisis. In 1967 Barbara Fried used an Oedipal framework to explain the emergence of aggres-sive impulses in middle-aged men as they sought sexual and emotional renewal outside the marriage.[74] And in Joseph Heller's 1974 anatomy of an American midlife crisis, *Something Happened*, Bob Slocum's lech-erous – and eventually murderous – impulses are driven partly by his fear that he is being eclipsed by his children.

Given the chronology of the modern life course, men's midlife angst coincided not only with their children's adolescence but perhaps with their partners' menopause and their parents' deteriorating health, lead-ing to a 'conflict of generations' that could further destabilize individuals, marriages and families.[75] As Edmund Bergler had pointed out in 1958, the crises of middle-aged men were complex matters of timing as much as they were simple manifestations of declining potency. One of the tragedies of family life, he argued, was the 'peculiar synchronization of woman's change of life and man's middle-age revolt'.[76] Partners who had been similar in age when they married began to follow different trajectories at midlife, leading men to lose interest in – and sympathy for – their wives as they approached and passed through the menopause. Bergler challenged physiological interpretations of the behaviour of middle-aged men, insisting that it was inappropriate to draw analogies between men and women at midlife. 'Medically speaking,' he argued in 1958, 'not a shred of proof has been offered that there is a biological basis for man's middle-age revolt.'[77] Claiming that nothing 'comparable to the ovary's functional death' occurred in men, Bergler – like Ellis – explained men's crises in psychosexual terms.

> Men consider that their sexual powers are on the downgrade, become morbidly preoccupied with approaching age, and resign themselves to prostate troubles, urinary disturbances, heart troubles, and even cancer of various organs that they believe to be imminent. The radius of their fears increases; the other organs are engulfed. The end result is a typical hypochondriacal picture. Middle-age hypochondria has found its typical patron.[78]

According to Bergler, subsequent events in the midlife journey of anxious, disaffected men followed a stereotypical script: the entrance onto the stage of a younger woman enabled them to express their frustrations with work, wife and family. In the middle-aged rebel's mind, his wife – who by now 'is old, while he himself is still young' – no longer understands him, legitimating his decision to seek comfort elsewhere.[79] It was this conviction – or delusion – that Billy Wilder had already drawn attention to in *The Seven Year Itch*. Richard Sherman's rationalization of his attraction to Marilyn Monroe drew on chauvinistic beliefs that women aged more rapidly than men: 'It's just a simple biological fact,' insisted Sherman in relation to his wife's appearance. 'Women age quicker than men. Yeah, I probably won't look any different when I'm sixty. I have that kind of face. Everybody'll think she's my mother.'[80] Rather than equating men's crises with the biological changes of menopause, Bergler was adamant that men's sense of exhaustion, their rebellion against the demands of their wives, worries about sexual potency and attempts to prove their masculinity with younger women were manifestations of a 'second emotional adolescence'.[81] Sexual infidelity at midlife was not a direct product of waning testicular function; rather, it was the result of narcissistic fears that virility and capability were receding with each week, month and year that passed.

In spite of psychosocial interpretations of midlife turbulence, the male climacteric was arguably medicalized more stridently during the 1950s and '60s than the female menopause. According to Elizabeth Siegel Watkins, this process in America was driven not primarily by clinical studies, but by a blossoming popular literature on what became known in this period as the 'male menopause'.[82] Journalists and self-help authors – as well as pharmaceutical companies – framed midlife in terms of declining levels of testosterone, prompting the development and marketing of synthetic hormones to rejuvenate ailing middle-aged men who were hoping to start afresh after forty.[83] Hopes of renewal were not available to all men. As commentators through the 1960s and '70s pointed out, men from lower social classes were unlikely to be able to indulge in – or afford to resolve – a midlife crisis. 'While the blue-collar worker may be experiencing similar changes,' wrote one journalist in the *New York Times* in 1971, 'medical experts agree that he is less likely to have the time or the opportunity to dwell on them than his more afflu-ent, middle-class counterpart.'[84] Biologically determined and amenable to pharmacological treatments, the male menopause was often viewed as a transitory stage in the life course, a crisis from which many men emerged into a vigorous old age. However, as the writers of self-help and marriage guidance literature were aware, by that time irreparable damage to health, work, relationships and families may already have occurred as middle-aged men strove to silence the ticking of their own biological, psychological and social clocks by searching beyond the home and office for personal, sexual and occupational fulfilment.

Men's preoccupations with preserving and displaying their virility reflected a contemporary crisis of masculinity, a crisis that had first manifested itself in early twentieth-century debates about the causes of shell shock and neurasthenia in soldiers in the First World War.[85] Concerns about the meanings of masculinity and the limits of male resilience persisted across the interwar years, but they surfaced more forcefully again during and after the Second World War, when a number of organic and psychological conditions were linked not only to combat stress, but to the challenges that soldiers faced as they returned to civil-ian life. In their pioneering study of 'men under stress', Roy R. Grinker and John P. Spiegel recognized in particular the pressures associated with adjusting to the realities of home life – realities that failed to match up to the 'peaceful and happy life' that servicemen had imagined while overseas.[86] The emotional and sexual difficulties experienced by wives during periods of separation and repatriation were less openly acknow-ledged. In line with studies of military stress, post-war novelists such as Sloan Wilson, David Ely and Joseph Heller highlighted how men – rather than their wives – were struggling to cope with the tedium and monotony of domestic routine, companionate marriage and corporate life after the war. Along with the shell-shocked soldier, the fatigued worker and the stressed executive, it was the figure of the disgruntled, frustrated and impotent husband – perhaps more than the bored suburban housewife – that came to embody the stresses and strains associated with chasing the American dream.

The inability of middle-aged men to perform sexually – at least within marriage – symbolized anxieties about whether, in a rapidly changing world, traditional Western models of masculine hegemony could withstand the political threats of communism or feminist attacks on the double standards of sexuality and ageing. The two were not unrelated. As Jessamyn Neuhaus has shown, while American politicians were concerned about being perceived as 'soft on communism' during the Cold War, marital advice books published during the 1950s and '60s discouraged men from succumbing to 'soft living' if they were to avoid losing sexual potency and social status.[87] According to the American historian Arthur Schlesinger, Jr, writing in 1958, American men were no longer sure of their role in society, no longer confident about their sexual identity. A crisis in masculinity was evident in – perhaps partly driven by – the merging of male and female roles within the household and the blurring of tasks within the workplace. Schlesinger dismissed arguments that men's anxiety was simply a product of 'the onward rush of American women'. Rather, he believed that it had become more difficult for men – and women – to fashion stable identities in a world dominated by large corporations and mass-produced entertainment. 'For men to become men again', he argued, 'their first task is to recover a sense of individual spontaneity', to reject the conformity imposed by the organizations for whom they worked.[88]

If male impotence constituted a mark of personal inadequacy and a metaphor for political weakness, adultery evolved as a necessary and justifiable – if aggressive – strategy for reaffirming muscular Western authority. In this sense, Marilyn French was quite right to highlight men's capacity for violence towards women. Post-war male writers sometimes – reluctantly – endorsed French's diagnosis. Allen Wheelis's novel *The Seeker*, published in 1960 and cited in Barbara Fried's study of the male midlife crisis, may have been less overtly brutal than Norman Mailer's *An American Dream*, John Updike's series of Rabbit novels or Joseph Heller's accounts of midlife malaise in *Something Happened* and *Good as Gold*. But Wheelis's portrayal of male lust equally acknowledged – without quite condemning – men's narcissistic exploitation of women. Early in the novel, Wheelis's protagonist, a 38-year-old psychoanalyst struggling to find meaning in his life, betrays his subconscious dreams of masculine domination – dreams that to some extent he acted out through the remainder of the book.

> A second change, beginning only in recent months, had been an upsurge of lecherous preoccupations. Desire for my wife had decreased, and desire for every other woman increased. There was nothing carefree about this. I had been beset with an intense and indiscriminate lust, a hunger for variety and possession and penetration that would gather up and devour all the women of the world.[89]

Beliefs that male infidelity at midlife was determined largely by a biological imperative – namely to satisfy and sustain generative potential across the life course – absolved men from the guilt of betraying partners and children. They also implied that it was a wife's responsibility to maintain the marriage, either by ensuring her husband's continued sexual satisfaction or by forgiving an extramarital affair. However, as the American journalist and writer Nancy Mayer pointed out in her later study of the male midlife crisis, biological accounts of men's midlife itch appealed not only to men, but to wives seeking a rational explanation for their husband's impulsive pursuit of younger women. According to Mayer, it was easier for a wife to think that her husband was 'sick', rather than 'sick of her'.[90] Although privilege and autonomy were not equally shared in relation to sex either within or outside the marriage, both men and women colluded in normalizing and legitimizing adulterous reassertions of masculinity. Seemingly overworked and misunderstood, the midlife man was given licence to enjoy the comfort provided by a younger woman with whom he could recapture his youth and confirm his manhood – even though it might end in divorce and remarriage.

During the nineteenth century, second marriages had usually been the result of the death of a spouse and had most often taken place between an older man and a younger woman – far more rarely between an older woman and a younger man. Fictional accounts of January–May marriages – as they were known – revealed not only the likely male exploitation of younger women, but the more complicated sexual politics from which both men and women of different ages could benefit.[91] While women offered older men sex, companionship, domestic service and more children, young wives gained greater security since their husbands had already demonstrated their capacity to raise and

care for a family.[92] Some early twentieth-century commentators, however, emphasized the dangers of a significant age difference between
husband and wife, especially in relation to concerns about the inappropriate behaviour of senescent men and the eugenic implications of late
fatherhood. Employing a different seasonal metaphor from that used
by his predecessors, in 1922 Granville Stanley Hall referred to the 'tragic
consequences to health, occupation, and even life, that follow when
December weds May': older men were prone to become jealous of their
younger wives, to age more rapidly and to father children less likely
to survive into adulthood.[93] The seasonal metaphor for relationships
between older men and younger women became a motif in popular
culture, appearing in Kurt Weill's 'September Song' (1938), William
Dieterle's film *September Affair* (1950) and much later the British
television sitcom *May to December* (1989–94).

As life expectancy increased across the twentieth century in many
Western countries, divorce began to replace death as the most common
grounds for a second chance to achieve marital happiness, particularly
after the Second World War. If the creation of a life unencumbered by
marital boredom and fears of physical decline was the aim for middle-
aged men, adultery was largely the means. An extramarital affair with
a younger woman was seen by most writers as the archetypal symptom
of the male menopause: 'A man of a certain age becomes depressed:
It's menopause,' wrote Martha Weinman Lear in the *New York Times*
in 1973. 'He loses his sex drive: It's menopause. He regains it with a
woman half his age. Indeed, it's menopause.'[94] Lear drew on the work
of a number of psychiatrists, as well as on the personal accounts of men
experiencing physiological and psychological symptoms of the climacteric between the ages of approximately forty-five and sixty. She also
interviewed Margaret Mead, who highlighted the importance of men's
occupational achievements keeping pace with their chronological and
biological age if they were to avoid midlife malaise. When men began
to feel that external success was no longer attainable or commensurate
with their position, Mead argued, they looked elsewhere for 'exogenous
solutions – as in getting a young wife'.[95]

The emergence of the male menopause as a distinct syndrome,
rather than merely a manifestation of middle age, after the Second
World War reflected fresh understandings of how hormonal, psychological and socio-cultural factors converged to create crises at midlife.
Acceptance of the complex determinants of the syndrome offered

potential social, as well as pharmacological, remedies. According to Lear, feminism had encouraged deeper analysis of the social roles and expectations of both women and men. If women's roles were 'defined less explicitly in terms of childrearing and physical attractiveness', she argued, the menopause would be less traumatic. Similarly, if masculinity 'were less a matter of power and performance', men's experiences of declining energy beyond midlife would not be so painful.[96] Lear's concluding remarks, however, revealed men's continued reluctance to accept responsibility for their behaviour during middle age. Male physicians responded to suggestions that they were particularly prone to menopausal crises by insisting that 'the primary cause of the Medical Man's Menopause was neither his hormones nor his neuroses nor his environment but, in fact, his wife.'[97] The blame for a man's desertion of his family apparently lay not with him – or indeed with his mistress – but more often with the failure of his first wife to remain attractive or to respect his right to sexual satisfaction and domestic contentment.

ACCORDING TO THOMAS Desmond, writing in 1956, the disadvantages of middle age had too often been exaggerated, leading men and women to 'waste their middle years' and ruin their chances of health and happiness in later life. Drawing inspiration from Pitkin's insistence that life could begin – rather than end – at forty, Desmond and other post-war writers drew attention to 'the assets of middle life', criticizing the tendency for researchers to emphasize the results of 'tests which spotlight decay and decline'.[98] Middle age carried multiple benefits. Longer life and better health introduced new opportunities for work and leisure. A steadier income and fewer responsibilities enabled couples to spend more time together, just as they had done when they were first married but without financial constraints or the stresses of parenthood. On the surface, the cult of youth continued to disable middle-agers, particularly in tight labour markets. But midlife brought status, maturity, insight and resilience, allowing men and women to reassess their lives and capitalize on a 'second chance' for fulfilment – not merely by pursuing external recognition and reward, but by satisfying internal drives. 'We see this spirit of reassessment of life's goals,' wrote Desmond,

> in the middle-aged mother who decides she would like to go back to college to earn her teaching license, the middle-aged reporter who

gives up a glamorous, well-paying job as Capitol correspondent for a lower-paying post teaching journalism. It is more than external change. The business man who quit his steel concern to enter the ministry and the woman in her fifties who works every day as a volunteer in a hospital are redirecting themselves internally.[99]

Desmond's positivity, which spoke primarily to the concerns and aspirations of the affluent middle classes, did not eradicate fears of middle age. Experiences at midlife were shaped not only by anxieties about the approaching change of life, but by awareness of the increased risk of physical and mental illness during adulthood. In the light of evidence that morbidity and mortality associated with obesity, heart disease and cancer increased steadily after the age of forty, midlife pessimism was not unrealistic, as the English psychiatrist Kenneth Soddy and his technical assistant Mary Kidson pointed out in 1967. Soddy and Kidson were reluctant to accept that individual behavioural changes in men during their forties could be traced unequivocally to a male climacteric or any other physiological transition. They preferred instead to explain the sexual restlessness of middle-aged men in terms of shifting social and cultural attitudes to sex, marriage and fatherhood. But they acknowledged that physical appearance and capacity clearly changed through middle age: vision, hearing, taste and smell deteriorated; basal metabolic rate decreased; height declined, while weight increased, particularly in women; and the chronic illnesses that led to death in later life arose first in middle age.[100] The visible perils of middle age outlined by Soddy and others were captured by post-war novelists. In *The Seeker*, Allen Wheelis's arrogant, egotistical hero – or anti-hero – reflects on the outward signs of ageing and their significance:

> Sometimes, combing my hair, I would suddenly stop and examine the man before me. The hair, such as there was, was getting gray. The gums were receding, and the teeth appeared larger. The skin was pale, the muscles flabby. The eyes were calm and thoughtful, but with a trace of pain. This man was a victim, and the trouble was he had no adversary. More than half of his life had been lived, but the face in the mirror was that of a stranger.[101]

Visual evidence of physical change suggested that middle age was itself a period of danger, a pathological state that required preventative and therapeutic attention. Understanding midlife in terms of risk was driven partly by concerns about the economic burden of an expanding and ageing population and the need to forestall undue public expense that might be incurred in caring for those in later life. As care of the elderly came to be regarded as a 'major social problem' requiring adequate research and resources, attending effectively to health hazards earlier in the life course was seen as increasingly important.[102] British and American post-war public health programmes – and international initiatives – prioritized the well-being of those at and beyond midlife.[103] State-sanctioned educational campaigns, medical journals and self-help literature recommended balanced diets, increased levels of exercise and recreation, the reduction of alcohol intake and continued social interactions if personal health and family relations were to be maintained into older age.[104] Such advice carried economic and political benefits. Preserving the health of those over the 'critical age' of forty would diminish the demand for costly on-going medical care, decrease mortality rates and help to prevent the loneliness and social dislocation associated with bereavement.[105] Healthier lifestyles also promised to mitigate the effects of the accelerating stresses and strains of modern living, particularly those associated with the workplace, thereby reducing the incidence of sickness absence and its costs to employers and employees. In addition, improving fitness across the life course was thought to ensure continued physical attraction between partners, leaving men supposedly less likely to be unfaithful and more committed to marriage and family.

One of the key physical markers of middle-age – and one that created problems for the vulnerable midlife psyche – was excess weight. In 1956 a popular English guide to 'medical, marriage and motherhood problems' advised readers that maintaining a healthy body weight constituted the single most important factor in ensuring a long and healthy life. Providing a table of the ideal weights of men and women of different heights, the editor of the volume suggested that adjusting eating habits according to fluctuations in weight was better than 'messing about with diet sheets and calories', unless people were suffering from specific conditions such as diabetes.[106] What was termed 'fatness' or 'adiposity' was not regarded as the product of hormonal imbalance, as some writers claimed, but was thought to stem simply from habitual overeating.

> Ordinarily you can make two assumptions about fatness. First – it
> is the result of the *habit* of over-eating; not occasional over-eating

but the regular habit of doing so. Second – the need to over-eat in these cases is essentially a psychological problem, and a common one; as common as obesity.[107]

On occasion, comments were less tolerant and more acerbic. People certainly recognized that overeating and obesity, like many other adult behaviour patterns and illnesses, were as likely to be triggered by difficult life circumstances as they were by the physiological and psychological changes of midlife and menopause. In addition, obesity – like juvenile delinquency – was often understood as the result of poor parenting, especially on the part of mothers.[108] Nevertheless, obese middle-aged men and women were personally blamed for ignoring clinical advice; adults became obese and ill because of smoking, excess consumption of food and alcohol, and a lack of exercise.[109] As middle-aged spread came to signify midlife complacency and stagnation, it also gained currency as a metaphor for the constitutional softness and moral flabbiness that appalled post-war politicians and self-help authors alike. Politicized concerns about the consequences of excess weight led to

Advertisement for Ayds slimming pills, 1940s.

126

health education campaigns warning the middle-aged to curb their appetites and exercise more, as well as the expansion of weight-loss groups such as Fatties Anonymous, Take Off Pounds Sensibly and Weight Watchers, aimed especially at women. They also encouraged the growth of a slimming industry marketing weight-loss diets, supplements and pills endorsed by celebrities such as Hedy Lamarr, Ann Sheridan and Zsa Zsa Gabor, and triggered the rising popularity of advice literature for those who considered themselves to be – or were told that they were – overweight.[110]

Obesity threatened physical health, but it also carried social implications – especially for women, whose value rested on their capacity to conform to conventions of feminine beauty and charm across the life course. In an article intended as a refresher course on obesity for general practitioners, published in 1951, the English physician A. H. Douthwaite suggested that overweight young women attending parties and dances could become depressed by the recognition that they were less attractive than their peers. Anxieties did not disappear, but perhaps deepened, during middle age. 'The married woman', Douthwaite wrote, 'who has "run to fat" after several pregnancies is assailed with fears that she will lose her attractiveness and thus her husband.'[111] Women who were worried about their appearance and the stability of their marriages were advised to use beauty products and self-care routines to preserve their complexions and figures through the travails of motherhood and menopause.[112] Medical and popular advice to women at midlife may have been intended to support isolated and lonely suburban housewives whose fatigue and family duties encouraged poor diets, but they also reinforced the stigma of obesity and strengthened contemporary associations between excess weight and lack of attractiveness in women. Gaylord Hauser's recommendations for maintaining a healthy weight and good looks ostensibly applied equally to men and women, but they betrayed contemporary preoccupations with the appearance of ageing wives and mothers. Although 'triple chins' and 'spare tyres' could afflict both sexes, Hauser's examples of celebrities who had 'achieved long life and agelessness' by training their appetites were all women. Beauty regimes designed to retain elegance and youthfulness were demonstrated by reference not to Fred Astaire, but to his mother. And the techniques and tricks that Hauser advocated to reduce weight were tailored to wives who wanted to fit into dresses that they had worn when they first met their husbands. In order to restore youth, health and beauty, Hauser argued, middle-aged women 'running away from their forties' needed to slow down, take time to enjoy life, forget trying to keep up with the Joneses and focus no longer on their children but on the pursuit of self-fulfilment.[113]

Like other self-help authors, Hauser advocated honest reflection if overweight middle-aged women were to avoid being submerged under 'rolls of unhealthy and un-beautiful fat' and retain the attention of their husbands.[114] For Marion Hilliard, it was pointless for a woman to use cosmetic products on her face and hair when 'she has a fine roll around the middle, which is where age really shows'.[115] The best way for middle-aged women and men to assess clearly the impact of age on their weight and figure was in the mirror. 'First of all', wrote the British general practitioner Dame Annis Gillie in her advice book on middle age published in 1969, 'have a very good look at yourself in a long mirror, stripped.'[116] The experience might not be pleasant, she warned, but it was necessary if the health hazards of obesity were to be avoided and relationships were to survive beyond middle age and menopause. Advice to women to avoid overeating and sustain physical attraction across the life course was often patronizing. According to Kenneth Hutchin, women were unable to understand the basic principles of profit and loss and were therefore incapable of balancing calorific intake with energy expenditure. It was a husband's responsibility, he believed, to direct his wife's diet and encourage her to consider housework as an opportunity to exercise in order to attain the degree of slimness dictated by cultural norms.[117] Such condescension did not exonerate women from blame if their husbands were unfaithful. According to some writers, it was a woman's expanding waist that was primarily responsible for the midlife crisis; not her own crisis, of course, but that of her husband who no longer found his middle-aged wife sexually attractive.[118]

Discussions of men's physique took on a different hue, partly because men were seemingly more concerned with their wealth than their health. Sinclair Lewis's hero George Babbitt proved to be the first in a long cast of twentieth-century men – both fictional and real – for whom material possession and civic status were more important than the damage caused by immoderate living. Indeed, for Babbitt, the ideal American citizen, in whose hands the future of the country would be safe, was the ambitious businessman or entrepreneur who certainly worked hard, but who also smoked, drank and played hard.[119] Warnings against ignoring the impact of overwork and overconsumption – perhaps the archetypal manifestations of Babbitry – were widespread in the middle decades of the twentieth century. 'For the neglect of our bodies,' wrote the Irish physical instructor Frederick Hornibrook in 1957, 'for over-indulgence, for laziness, we have all to pay the price one way or another, and that price is usually a heavy one.'[120] Hornibrook recommended appropriate exercises to improve posture and physical fitness, especially in men over forty whose health was compromised by sedentary living, emotional stress and overwork. Writers concerned about men's health paid limited attention to their figures. Of course, appearance did matter to men – a fact that was exploited in advertisements for Flora margarine or in later Health Education Campaigns across England and Wales.[121] And the overweight, middle-class, middle-aged middle manager – like Reggie Perrin – was as much an object of ridicule as the adipose woman of forty. But the major concern of doctors, employers, insurance com-panies and the state was the impact of excess weight on heart disease and the risk of premature mortality among the most affluent and influ-ential sectors of society – that is, among what Hutchin referred to in 1962 as 'the most valuable citizens' in both Britain and America.[122]

Concerns about a link between obesity and heart disease were not new in the post-war period. During the early decades of the twentieth century, writers such as Hornibrook and Leonard Williams had high-lighted how excess weight increased the risk of cardiovascular disease among middle-aged men.[123] After the Second World War, clinical and epidemiological studies, media reports and high-profile cases – such as the heart attack suffered by President Eisenhower in 1955 – raised the importance of tackling obesity in order to combat what appeared to be an epidemic of hypertension, high cholesterol and coronary artery disease, especially among stressed, competitive, goal-driven professionals and executives.[124] Across the 1950s and '60s, the majority of victims of heart disease in countries adopting Western lifestyles and diet were thought to be middle-aged men between 45 and 65 years old.[125] This did not mean that overweight younger men or middle-aged women were immune from heart attacks, but they were thought to be less commonly afflicted, at least until the late 1960s and '70s, when rates of heart disease also began to rise in these groups.[126] Other than obesity, the principal mediators of heart disease and premature death were thought to be stress, seden-tary occupations, smoking and overly rich diets. Such factors could be addressed by the adoption of appropriate dietary regimens to reduce the consumption of fat and carbohydrates, sufficient relaxation to dissolve tensions associated with the pace of modern living, and a programme of exercises – not dissimilar to those advocated by army widow Matilda Parsons – designed to restore the tone of the abdominal muscles and reduce middle-aged spread. The primary responsibility for ensuring that men followed this advice and survived their forties without significant problems lay – perhaps unsurprisingly – with their wives. In advice literature published across the post-war decades, it was women who were instructed – and expected – to act as custodians of their husbands' health, as well as the well-being of their children, much as they had been throughout the early decades of the twentieth century.[127]

Post-war emphasis on the figure of the adipose middle-aged woman and the heart of the middle-aged man – like dramatic accounts of menopausal misery – contributed to on-going beliefs that midlife was to be feared rather than embraced. Through the 1950s, '60s and '70s, clinicians, journalists, marriage guidance counsellors, novelists and presenters and producers of radio and television programmes referred dramatically to the 'problems', 'hazards', 'dangers' and 'challenges' of middle age.[128] Writers highlighted the multiple ways in which the passage of time changed men and women alike. Biological and social clocks began to slow. Occupational opportunities receded as employers sacrificed wisdom and experience for youth and speed in the workplace, leaving middle-aged men in particular diminished by redundancy. The death of friends and family members overshadowed personal appreciation of life. Domestic tensions unsettled marriages, leading to separation and divorce. And the cumulative effects of unrestrained materialism and immoderate consumption of food and alcohol left their mark on minds and bodies approaching the afternoon of life. If individual health and social stability were to be preserved, midlife crises could not be avoided simply by imitating youth or pursuing love and satisfaction elsewhere, but by investing in appropriate advice and support for middle-aged men and women struggling to cope with their jobs, marriages and age-related physical changes.[129] As the prime of life came and went, happiness was to be found in candidly 'facing the challenge of change in middle age', as American psychiatrist Lawrence Greenleigh put it in 1974.[130] Men and women at midlife should look to balance work and leisure more effectively, find new outlets for creativity and commit fully to the comforts – and discomforts – of home and family.

IN A 1977 issue of *Punch* edited by students, Nicholas Coleridge lamented the disappearance of the 'angry young man'. During the 1960s, he argued, political dissent and cultural rebellion had been widespread, particularly among young adults. But by the 1970s, righteous anger had been replaced by selfish complacency. In the face of what the English poet, painter and cultural critic Jeff Nuttall referred to in 1968 as the 'bomb culture' of the Cold War, advocates of peace and love had been superseded by 'dodos', who extolled the benefits of wholemeal bread and vegetarian shepherd's pie, and who travelled to America with 'a list of Daddy's "contacts" in their pockets rather than just "flowers in their hair"'.[131] The metaphor that Coleridge adopted to account for the transformation in attitudes was menopausal. 'The Angry Young Menopause of the 50s and 60s', wrote Coleridge,

> has given way – perhaps owing, in part, to the recession – to a tepid acceptance of the status quo, and the energy that was formerly directed towards a Fair Deal for the Third World has been tempered with a certain anxiousness about a Fair Deal for oneself in the 'Outside World'.[132]

Coleridge's use of the menopause to symbolize the rise and fall of cultural and political upheaval after the war reflected concerns about the demise of youthful activism. But it also constituted a critique of conservative attempts to restore traditional, less disruptive gender norms. His sardonic allusion to men was misleading. The prime casualties of post-war policies to restore social stability were not middle-class men overloaded by workplace pressures and fears of waning virility. Rather, it was women – once again confined to home and family – who struggled with the loss of the educational and occupational opportunities that had appeared within their grasp during the immediate post-war years. One of the 'enemies of promise', claimed the English writer Cyril Connolly in 1938 as he attempted to explain his own sense of failure at the age of thirty-five, 'was the pram in the hall'.[133] While post-war Western societies continued to stress the seemingly natural linkages between womanhood, wifehood and motherhood, menopause signified the onset of women's declining importance to society – and to their families.[134]

The change of life was not the only transition to impact on the health and behaviour of middle-aged men and women. One of the key

determinants of midlife malaise, especially in women, was the departure of children from the home and the dissolution of the nuclear family
– what became known as the 'empty nest syndrome'.[135] The concept and
significance of the empty nest had first been broached by the American
author Dorothy Canfield Fisher in 1914. In her study of mothers and
children, Fisher had emphasized that 'maternity is not the occupation
of a lifetime'.[136] Increased life expectancy meant that mothers lived well
beyond the moment when their children left home and the 'nest was
empty'. The result, Fisher argued, was that women who had invested
their energies in family life were now confronted with an 'empty shell',
as their home had become merely 'a meeting-place – no longer a place
where the family lives together'.[137] According to Fisher, the despair
experienced by women who had lost their maternal identity could be
addressed by enabling them to cultivate personal interests beyond the
home and by promoting greater social recognition of the value of older
women as grandmothers and teachers. Fisher's reflections – as well as
novels from the period – acknowledged that men were not immune
to feelings of inadequacy or a sense of detachment from home and
family in later life, but they were structured differently. Men's emptiness
was triggered by retirement from an active occupational and social life
while still relatively young, rather than by the sudden loss of parental
responsibility.

In 1915 the novelist Charlotte Perkins Gilman imagined an isolated community organized largely along the collective maternal lines
hinted at by Fisher. In the utopian novel *Herland*, Gilman contrasted
modern patriarchal societies – in which women's roles were largely
confined to motherhood and wifehood – with a society in which childbearing was possible without men and motherhood shared between
all women, ensuring that no woman was left 'alone with her empty
nest'.[138] Subsequent iterations of the 'empty nest' during the middle decades of the twentieth century continued to wrestle with the conflicting
images of maternity and the post-maternal years captured by Fisher
and Gilman. On the one hand, the 'empty nest syndrome' in women
constituted an undesirable state characterized by boredom, loneliness,
the loss of identity, the challenges of marital adjustment and the onset
of despair, a sequence of changes and emotions comparable to – and in
some narratives responsible for – the midlife crisis in men. 'Now, more
than ever,' wrote Lee and Casebier in 1973, 'the bored housewife feels
trapped and incarcerated in the split-level dream house.'[139] Negative

interpretations of post-maternity were politically charged. Whether women with children had worked beyond the home or not, the 'empty nest' served as a euphemism for the empty woman, whose abilities were no longer pertinent to the viability of the family, the health of her husband or the future of the nation. On the other hand, however, the exit of children from the home was cast as an opportunity for women, a reward for years of maternal service, a relief from the monotonous demands of domesticity and an opportunity to pursue creative pastimes. Not all women experienced this stage of life in terms of crisis; some experienced it in terms of an 'enriched sense of self and an enhanced capacity to cope'.[140] Adjusting to the demands and expectations of middle age required women to recognize that time was not yet running out, but extending constructively beyond the limiting horizons of the nuclear family. 'Time is, finally, your own,' wrote the American journalist Cynthia Bell in 1979.[141]

Images of the empty nest carried particular resonance during the post-war decades.[142] Across the 1950s, '60s and '70s, the emergence of a standardized individual and family life course ensured that many of the key transitions in the lives of family members coincided, creating the possibility for magnifying and multiplying crises. For middle-class couples who had married and started a family in their early twenties, a number of life stresses emerged in their forties and fifties to widen the gap between spouses and threaten marital stability. Children were experiencing the emotional turmoil of adolescence and moving away from home to work or marry. Women were approaching and passing through menopause. Parents were struggling with the increasing demands of work and the financial stress of keeping up with – or ahead of – the Joneses at a time when their energy was waning. Doubts and insecurities proliferated as the effects of age began to undermine confidence and self-esteem in a culture that valued youth and beauty. Elderly parents needed greater support as they aged – and then died, leaving their children grieving and alone. Although middle-aged men and women faced their own physiological and psychological crises, the personal pressures of midlife were aggravated by simultaneous transitions in the lives of those around them. Far from being an individual event, the midlife crisis was a family affair.

5

FAMILIES UNDER STRESS

'The price of the American dream of upward mobility may be
family disorganization and breakdown.'
REUBEN HILL, 1949[1]

If contemporary novelists and screenwriters are to be believed, no one
was happy after the Second World War. So many post-war novels, films
and television series were populated by disaffected middle-aged men,
disenfranchised women and delinquent children. The lives of fictional
characters reflected the worlds inhabited by their creators. Immediately
after the war, austerity constrained the freedom of individuals, couples,
families and communities as they struggled to cope with housing
shortages, unemployment, sickness and divorce. Unfamiliar forms of
communication, emergent models of corporate bureaucracy and new
technologies of production – most notably industrial automation –
placed unfamiliar physical and psychological demands on managers and
workers.[2] As the austerity of the 1950s was superseded by the affluence
of the 1960s, the expanding beauty, leisure and entertainment industries excited and exploited everyday dreams of material prosperity and
timeless youth. Western families were tempted by glamorous – but often
unattainable – distractions from the tedium of everyday life. Advertisers
promised stylish weddings, happy marriages, faster cars and larger
houses in the suburbs. But family fortunes across the post-war decades
continued to be unsettled by the Cold War, with its crises and catastrophes in Korea, Vietnam and Cambodia; by the Civil Rights movement;
by feminism and sexual liberation; by the growing expectations of freedom and autonomy among teenagers and young adults; and by the threat
of the nuclear age. The post-war world was itself in crisis.

The plotlines and emotional tenor of post-war midlife novels were
driven by narratives of personal distress. Worn down by the monotony
of making a living and raising children, middle-aged men and women
were drained of energy and ambition. Preoccupied with careers, civic

status and wealth, husbands and fathers were fractious and despondent at home – or simply absent, searching elsewhere for sexual arousal and satisfaction. Married women, often discouraged by their husbands from working outside the home, were neglected or trapped in the small towns and suburbs of Britain and America – supposedly vulnerable to the allure of alcohol or prescription medications for anxiety, insomnia and depression. Striving to define themselves in a world that remained in conflict long after the Second World War had ended, children were rejecting the domestic aspirations, political preferences and cultural values of their parents. Every character in the post-war fictional world was overstimulated, their appetites inflamed, their lives overloaded. As the collective American dream collapsed under the weight of individualism, family bonds were liable to fray and fracture.

The intensity of the malaise felt by middle-class, middle-aged men and women and their children in the decades after the war was most eloquently expressed by Joseph Heller, not only in *Catch-22* (1961) and *Good as Gold* (1976), which satirized the bureaucratic capriciousness of the American armed forces and federal government respectively, but more directly in *Something Happened* (1974), a bestseller that heartlessly exposed the banality of corporate and domestic life.[3] As was so often the case in midlife novels, the authorial voice in *Something Happened* belonged to a disillusioned man, whose unhappiness was matched by that of his wife and children. Bob Slocum's discontent was not merely a reaction to occupational stresses and domestic duties or a response to physical signs of ageing – although those certainly figured prominently in his self-obsessed digressions. Rather, it arose as an echo of the sick society in which he lived. 'I've got an unhappy wife to support', he reflects early in the novel,

> and two unhappy children to take care of. (I've got that other child with irremediable brain damage who is neither happy nor unhappy, and I don't know what will happen to him after we're dead.) I've got eight unhappy people working for me who have problems and unhappy dependents of their own. I've got anxiety; I suppress hysteria. I've got politics on my mind, summer race riots, drugs, violence, and teen-age sex. There are perverts and deviants every-where who might corrupt or strangle any one of my children. I've got crime on my streets. I've got old age to face. My boy, though nine, is already worried because he does not know what he wants

to be when he grows up. My daughter tells lies. I've got the decline of American civilization and the guilt and ineptitude of the United States to carry around on these poor shoulders of mine.[4]

Slocum was not alone in fearing the imminent disintegration of social order. Nor was he alone in the manner in which he chose to resolve – or at least quell – his midlife anxieties. Like the protagonists in Sloan Wilson's *The Man in the Gray Flannel Suit* (1955), Richard Yates's *Revolutionary Road* (1961) and David Ely's *Seconds* (1963), Bob Slocum sought solace from alienation and despair in infidelity – with colleagues, acquaintances and prostitutes – and in recurrent dreams of divorce. 'I want a divorce. I need a divorce. I long for it. I crave a divorce. I pray for divorce,' Slocum repeats to himself towards the end of the novel.

> I dream of divorce. All my life I've wanted a divorce. Even before I was married I wanted a divorce. I don't think that there has been a six-month period in all the years of my marriage – a six-*week* period – when I have not wanted to end it by divorce. I was never sure I wanted to get married. But I always knew I wanted a divorce.[5]

In fictional scenarios, personal and family crises were paraded as marital storms. Children appeared only tangentially in stories of domestic decay, which focused primarily on the pain and loneliness of unhappy marriages, sexual frustration and adultery. The disrupted nature of intimate relationships between partners – rather than those across generations – similarly dominated the advice offered to middle-aged men and women by marriage guidance counsellors, psychiatrists, psychologists, self-help authors and journalists. Over time, it was argued, couples became shackled by marriages that had grown stale or hostile, necessitating a re-evaluation of personal aspirations for married life. In arguing for greater consideration of the benefits of trial – or temporary – marriages, American journalist Alvin Toffler highlighted the odds against love enduring in a society in which husbands and wives followed divergent routes and traversed multiple identity crises across extended life courses. 'In conventional relationships,' according to one of Toffler's interviewees, 'time is a prison', one that allowed emotional distance, as well as intimacy, to flourish.[6]

Yet middle-aged men and women in crisis were not only rejecting the time – and love – that they had shared with their partners. They were also discarding their families. Self-help literature, media coverage and advertisements in magazines stressed that personal success was to be measured in terms of the ability not only to attract a spouse and craft a career, but to raise children, purchase houses and cars, and afford leisurely holidays for the whole family. These broader dimensions of midlife pressures and crises, extending beyond the marital dyad, were mirrored in some post-war novels. In *Good as Gold*, for example, Heller depicted the desire of middle-aged men not only to divorce their wives, but to jettison family responsibilities: 'Well, Bruce, to put it plainly,' explains a divorced friend to the novel's troubled hero Bruce Gold, 'I couldn't see much point in tying myself down to a middle-aged woman with four children, even though the woman was my wife and the children were my own. Can you?'[7] An academic in his late forties, Gold needed little encouragement to pursue a similar path. Deciding that his marriage was dead and family life tedious, he pursued a new government job in Washington, spent more time away from home and started an extramarital affair. Gold's callous justification for his behaviour echoed the thoughts of almost every fictional – and perhaps real – midlife man in the post-war years: 'If a man marries young,' Gold tells himself, 'it will likely be to someone near him in age: and just about the time he learns really to enjoy living with a young girl and soars into his prime, she will be getting old.'[8]

Cynical literary accounts of derelict marriages and broken families were possibly exaggerated. In his reflections on 'the happy family' in 1945, C. W. Topping, Professor of Sociology at the University of British Columbia, denounced novelists as 'Jeremiahs', their scathing views on family life 'tangential and pathological'. Academic surveys, Topping insisted, demonstrated that in spite of increasing rates of divorce and family disorganization in the United States and Canada, there was still a 'very high percentage of families in the middle and upper middle class who consider themselves to be happily married'.[9] In contrast to the doom-laden narratives of contemporary novelists, Topping believed that pathways to marital and domestic contentment could be taught, enabling partners and their children to adjust together to challenges and crises. But it is clear that novelists such as Heller were justifiably exposing the manner in which post-war families, whether dysfunctional or not, were under considerable stress. A lack of adequate housing, financial constraints, increased mobility, political instability and pressure to conform to models of companionate marriage and domestic happiness ensured that strains within the family surfaced with greater magnitude than before.

Understanding and mitigating the stresses on – and within – families lay at the heart of post-war studies of domestic life. In 1949 the American sociologist Reuben Hill examined how well families adjusted to periods of enforced separation and reunion. In particular, Hill's work helped to explain the readjustment of veterans to family life, the impact of loneliness on the mental health of women separated from their partners by military service, and the ways in which families adapted differently to stress.[10] For Hill, crises and conflicts within the family appeared in three dimensions: personal, marital and familial.

> The first dimension involves the individual, the crisis situation, and the individual's adjustment to that situation. The second dimension involves the pair (it may be an engaged pair, a married pair, a business partnership, or just room-mates), a crisis situation involving the pair, and the pair's adjustment to that situation. The third dimension involves the larger grouping of the family made up of parents, children, and any kin living within the closed system of the family unit; it involves a crisis situation defined by the family as a crisis; and it involves the family's adjustment to that situation *as a family*![11]

Given that individuals, relationships and families evolved at different rates across the life course, crises were more likely to emerge at particular moments in time – that is, in a fourth dimension – when pivotal transitions coincided. Middle age was often crowded with crises. Personal disappointments, marital tensions, infidelity, economic hardship, redundancy, relocation and declining health were not the only challenges faced by middle-aged couples after the war. Relationships between parents and adolescent children and across extended kinship networks were also fragile and liable to break down under mounting internal and external stresses – generating further fault lines within the family. Robin Williams's 1955 study of American society indicated that family instability was not merely the product of marital incompatibility, as some contemporaries claimed. It was also the result of greater pressures being placed on post-war families in the absence of adequate social support and the emergence of occupational structures that were 'incompatible with stable family life'. Modern families, Williams suggested, were ill-equipped to cope with the social and emotional burdens being placed upon them.[12] Under such conditions, intimacy had to be fought for rather than assumed.

In some cases, it was the gap between parents and children more than the emotional distance between partners that threatened the resilience of families – although, of course, they were not unrelated. According to E. E. LeMasters, Professor of Social Work at the University of Wisconsin and author of studies on courtship, parenting and working-class cultures, conflicts in relation to parental – rather than marital – roles often determined the degree of family disruption: 'parenthood (and not marriage)', he wrote in 1957, 'is the real "romantic complex" in our culture.'[13] In a child-centred world, crises within families were generated by the birth of children, the care of infants, the growing independence of adolescents, the departure of grown-up children from the home and the need to support ageing parents. As American gerontologist Thomas Desmond put it in 1956, neither the rewards nor the crises of midlife could be understood without taking family structures and dynamics into account: 'Middle age is family life.'[14]

'THE FUTURE OF marriage and the family', wrote David Mace in 1948, 'trembles in the balance.'[15] Written for a broad readership, Mace's thoughts on the future of the family restated contemporary concerns about the capacity of post-war families to cope with the expectations placed upon them, as well as government attempts in Britain and America to situate families at the heart of policies to restore social stability after the war. In his study of urban families carried out in the 1950s, Henry Dicks argued that the family was 'the irreducible unit of social organisation' and its protection essential for 'mental and communal health'.[16] In the midst of dramatic social, political and technological changes, work and family relationships were liable to be unsettled and marriages more inclined to break down, leaving children psychologically disturbed and likely to repeat their parents' behaviour in the next generation. Research by Dicks and his colleagues at the Tavistock Clinic indicated that marital stress and unresolved conflicts within a family consigned children to unrealistic expectations – or 'false idealisations' – of potential spouses, expectations that were soon thwarted by the realities of married life. Disappointed dreams of happy families emboldened husbands and wives to search for extramarital partners with whom they could find fulfilment – a strategy destined to fail if personal issues were not first resolved. According to Dicks, strains within families were exacerbated by economic hardship, men working longer hours, women working beyond the home, social isolation in the suburbs and the monotony of the 'quasi-mechanical routine' of everyday life that dashed hopes for self-expression and self-realization.[17] But whatever the cause, the predicament of the modern family in the decades after the war – and the midlife crisis that emerged within its battlements – can be traced to its social functions.

Dicks's emphasis on the importance of understanding the 'over-worked, over-charged, isolated social atom' that constituted the modern family was replicated elsewhere.[18] During the 1950s and '60s, political interest in the success and failure of families deepened on both sides of the Atlantic. In his address to the National Conference on Family Life held in Washington in 1948, President Truman emphasized the ways in which the stability of governments and the preservation of liberty depended on the welfare and security of the family as a unit.[19] Researchers and journalists stressed the need to understand more clearly the recipe for happy families, as well as the determinants of family breakdown and marital dissatisfaction. The sustainability of a family across the life course, they argued, was determined by cultural values that influenced age at marriage, the timing and number of children, the moment at which husbands and wives entered the workforce, the stage at which children left home, and the age of retirement and bereavement.[20] Sociological and psychological studies of family life – and the attendant challenges of middle age – focused on three related issues: the emergence and limitations of what became known as the 'nuclear family'; whether family life was in decline or crisis in the post-war years; and the role of the family as a stabilizing force in Western societies unsettled by war and austerity.

In the post-war period, the ideal – but not necessarily most common – configuration of the Western family was nuclear or, as Alvin Toffler put it, 'streamlined'.[21] Pre-industrial families had tended to be extended, incorporating grandparents, uncles, aunts and cousins, an arrangement that provided safeguards against economic hardship and ensured kinship – especially grandmotherly – support for working parents. As industrialization introduced the need for greater social mobility to meet shifting patterns of labour, the extended family was 'stripped down', resulting in a 'portable family unit consisting only of parents and a small set of children'.[22] Not only family size but the nature of relations within families changed. The authoritarian, patriarchal family of the Victorian period, with its clearly defined gender roles, was superseded by what researchers began to refer to as the 'democratic' or 'symmetrical' family in which domestic duties were more evenly shared – a transition that paralleled the trend towards companionate or conjugal marriages.[23] Contemporary writers were not convinced that this narrative of family evolution – from extended to nuclear, patriarchal to symmetrical – was entirely accurate, pointing out that pre-industrial families were not always extended and that the mid-century dominance of the nuclear family was by no means uniform across classes or cultures. Writing in 1970, sociologist Robert Winch argued that at least three different family types were identifiable in America: a nuclear family embedded in a network of extended kin; an isolated nuclear family; and a mother-child nuclear family, which sometimes included the maternal grandmother.[24] Differences in family structures were not arbitrary, but determined by religious, racial and regional traditions.[25]

Regardless of the heterogeneity of family configurations, it was the relatively isolated nuclear family of the urban middle classes that occupied the centrepiece of political plans to restore social cohesion after the war. In 1948 a collection of papers edited by the eugenicist and social reformer Sir James Marchant reflected on a number of facets of family life in Britain: patterns of parenthood; economic and social welfare; health and education; the influence of the war; and the spiritual foundations of the family. In his introduction, the English physician Lord Horder stressed the urgency of rebuilding family lives that had been 'shattered, broken or disorganized by the social upheaval of a second world war'.[26] Although subsequent chapters were written from a variety of professional perspectives, they shared a common belief that stable family units were essential for social reconstruction and the development of healthy, well-balanced children and adults. 'It is in the home and in family life,' wrote Sir Arthur S. MacNalty, formerly Chief Medical Officer of the Ministry of Health, 'that the future and happiness of this country rest.'[27] MacNalty's emphasis on promoting family life was echoed in America. In his address to the National Conference on Family Relations held in New York in 1938, Rabbi Sidney Goldstein had urged the United States federal government to take more seriously its responsibilities for strengthening marriage and family life by ensuring better housing, sufficient income and improved support for married couples.[28] Goldstein's challenge was taken up, if not fully met, after the war. The 1948 National Conference on Family Life stressed the 'importance of successful family life in the practice of democracy' and considered the environmental, community, educational and professional resources that were needed to ensure greater security for family members.[29] New approaches were needed for a new world. In the aftermath of global crisis, argued Grace Reeves in an issue of the journal published by the National Conference on Family Relations in 1945, 'new designs' were required to chart a fresh course for the post-war American family.[30]

The dynamics of family life became a key focus for sociologists, psychologists and anthropologists investigating the determinants of health and personality across the life course. Interest in the family as a site for education and socialization – and as a mediator between individuals and society – led to academic studies and the production of journals such as *Family Process*, which aimed to foster a 'science of the family.'[31] Although there was no consensus about what constituted 'normal' family life, it was the image of the happy nuclear family – usually two parents with two children – that dominated academic, clinical and popular literature across the post-war decades. In Britain the Marriage Guidance Council used what became the stereotypical nuclear family at leisure to convey its aspirations to stabilize marriages and promote the well-being of families in the face of dramatic cultural change. In novels and films, the nuclear family appeared as the backdrop to – and often by inference the cause of – midlife marital malaise.[32] Advertisers used images of nuclear families to sell suburban houses, electrical appliances, life insurance, furnishings, cars, medication, food and holidays.[33] Marketing strategies reflected – and shaped – popular beliefs and practices. Responses to a Mass-Observation survey of British lay attitudes suggested that, if housing and finances allowed, the 'ideal family' consisted of between two and four children, with boys and girls in even numbers. In reality, material factors often outweighed the supposed social and psychological advantages of large families, leaving parents generally unwilling to have more than two children.[34]

There was an irony in the normalization and commercialization of the Western nuclear family. Pressure to keep up with neighbours and friends by having an appropriate number of children, moving to a larger house, purchasing home comforts and investing in leisure activities necessitated men working longer hours and women joining the

Front cover of the Annual Report of the Marriage Guidance Council, 1966.

workforce. Although domestic luxuries – such as television – made homes more attractive and encouraged families to spend more time together, additional working hours separated spouses for longer periods, created greater distance between parents and children, limited time for social contacts and reduced involvement in local communities that were being transformed by the flight to the suburbs. Relationships within post-war families became strained as parents struggled to keep the family unit together in the face of occupational and educational stresses, peer pressure, rising standards of living and the growing expectations of teenage children for independence.[35] Rather than safeguarding marital and domestic contentment, caricatures of happy nuclear families on screen or in the media ran the risk of exacerbating feelings of inadequacy and frustration among middle-aged couples and their children, whose lives rarely matched those of their fictional counterparts. The dilemmas facing parents in a consumer culture were articulated by Margaret Mead in an interview in 1963.

> We tell people every day in the advertisements, on TV, over the radio: 'This is the kind of house you ought to have. This is the kind of car you ought to drive. Are you keeping your wife a prisoner because you only have one car? Are you making a slave of your wife because you've turned her into a dishwasher instead of buying a dishwasher?' As a result, we're forcing husbands into 'moonlighting'

– holding two jobs. And we're forcing wives into 'sunlighting' – that's a word I made up and I like it – which is having an extra job in the daytime.[36]

It is not difficult to find critiques of the nuclear family in the post-war years. The resilience of the nuclear family to changing occupational, economic and political conditions was questioned. In 1957 the Scottish social historian Oliver McGregor pointed out that the democratic nature of the model nuclear family was often double-edged: it might improve marital relations and stabilize families as partners shared economic and domestic responsibilities; or it might lead to the disintegration of family life as traditional buffers against internal and external stresses were withdrawn.[37] One particular area of concern was the impact of family conflict on juvenile behaviour. In his 1967 Reith Lectures, the English social anthropologist Edmund Leach reflected on whether 'youthful disorder' could really be attributed to a breakdown of family life, as some commentators were claiming, or whether the streamlined family that had emerged in the middle decades of the twentieth century was itself pathological. Leach's analysis of what he termed the 'monogamous neo-local nuclear family' of the post-war years emphasized the ways in which the loss of kinship networks laid greater stresses on parents and children.

In the past, kinsfolk and neighbours gave the individual continuous moral support throughout his life. Today the domestic household is isolated. The family looks inward upon itself; there is an intensification of emotional stress between husband and wife, and parents and children. The strain is greater than most of us can bear. Far from the basis of good society, the family, with its narrow privacy and tawdry secrets, is the source of all our discontents.[38]

For Leach, the insularity of the nuclear family – sometimes vaunted as one of its strengths – led to overly private spaces within which abuses could thrive: 'Privacy', he insisted, 'is the source of fear and violence.'[39] Leach was not alone. In the post-war years, the modern family came under increasing attack from those often wishing to abolish it entirely. As Ronald Fletcher pointed out in several studies published between the 1960s and the 1980s, concerns came from a number of quarters. Anti-psychiatrists such as R. D. Laing and David Cooper regarded the family as a breeding ground for neuroses and psychoses, as a socially imposed device for constraining individuality. For Marxist theorists, the family was a purveyor of bourgeois capitalist values. Feminists such as Betty Friedan, Kate Millett and Germaine Greer believed that allegiance to the family as the primary source of social stability obstructed women's rights and endorsed adultery as a justifiable male indulgence.[40] Rather than raising the status of women, post-war emphasis on marital partnerships – rather than segregated roles – within the family either doubled the burden on women by expecting them to work both within and beyond the home or consigned them more firmly to domestic duties.[41] The damage wrought extended beyond the immediate family. According to social historian Tamara Hareven, writing in 1976, the isolation of suburban families was responsible for the loneliness of elderly parents left living in the city or in retirement homes.[42]

Although writing from different perspectives, abolitionists insisted that the nuclear family not only stifled growth and self-fulfilment across the life course, but that it was incompatible – or at least in tension – with its professed social functions. In either case, idealized notions of the family – often 'heavily tinged with fantasy', as one member of the Association of General and Family Caseworkers put it in 1957 – were creating conditions for conflict and crisis.[43] Apologists for the family believed that such criticisms were overstated, arguing that it was external socio-economic factors, rather than psychodynamic transitions within the nuclear family, that were undermining domestic stability. According to Ronald Fletcher, families had been unsettled by the 'long tentacles of war', rising emphasis on individual rights and the secularization and de-moralization of society.[44] In his study of marital breakdown first published in 1968, Jack Dominian similarly suggested that marriage and family were under threat from a growing tendency for people to 'seek and attain a high degree of personal fulfilment'. While material aspirations could be realized relatively easily in periods of affluence, such as the 1960s when Dominian was practising as a psychiatrist, the 'emotional and spiritual' needs of parents and children were less likely to be met 'in a home situation which is frequently distant from the support and help of the other members of the family'.[45] For Fletcher, Dominian and others, the demands on individuals and relationships generated by seismic social change constituted an argument for strengthening, not abolishing, marriage and the family.

Families were vulnerable to multiple pressures after the war. According to the American psychiatrists Thomas Holmes and Richard

Rahe, stress was most often linked to the 'ordinary and personal trans-actions' generated by the 'social structure of the American way of life'. In particular, they claimed, stress appeared to be 'consonant with the American values of achievement, success, materialism, practicality, efficiency, future orientation, conformism and self-reliance' – that is, with the principles and aspirations embedded in the American dream.[46] Ronald Fletcher attributed family stress – and the personal crises of parents and children – more directly to social and political conditions. Mass communication, and especially the invasion of the home by tele-vision, had promoted appetite (lust) at the expense of sentiment (love), encouraged self-interest over the welfare of society as a whole, and overwhelmed men, women and children with news of disasters and catastrophes around the world. Individual and family crises were simply part of a wider crisis of identity infecting modern Western societies. Citing studies that revealed how concerns about the Cold War were impacting on attitudes to marriage and divorce, Fletcher concluded that it was perhaps '"nuclear war" far more than the "nuclear family" which threatens the order and quality of our human life'.[47] Under stress, the family was no longer 'a haven in a heartless world', as American histor-ian Christopher Lasch put it in 1977.[48] Rather, disputes within families mirrored the political divisions of a broken world, encouraging men and women – husbands and wives – to escape from what were felt to be the suffocating confines of conjugal marriage and the nuclear family.

'HAPPY FAMILIES ARE all alike; every unhappy family is unhappy in its own way.'[49] The opening sentence of Leo Tolstoy's *Anna Karenina*, pub-lished in 1877, set the tone for the rest of the novel, which contrasted Anna's reckless pursuit of personal gratification – evident in her affair with Count Vronsky – with her social responsibility to protect her mar-riage and family. The concept of the family lay at the heart of Tolstoy's vision. 'If a work is to be really good,' he told his wife Sofia, 'there must be one fundamental idea in it that one loves. So in *Anna Karenina*, I love the idea of the *family*.'[50] Elements of *Anna Karenina* – marital tensions, infidelity and family stress – echoed parts of the Tolstoys' own family life. Sofia was particularly explicit about the difficulty – perhaps impossibility – of women reconciling personal aspirations with their subservient roles as wives and mothers or closing the gap between the expectations of men and women. 'A woman wants *marriage* and a man wants *lechery*,' she wrote on 18 January 1891 in reference to her husband's 'casual debauch-ery' before they were married, 'and the two can never be reconciled.'[51] Although they should be read with caution, since their marriage was as intimate as it was troubled at times, Sofia's diaries presage the feelings of separation, loneliness and unhappiness that appeared to characterize many marriages and families across the twentieth century. 'Why am I not happy?', she asked herself on 25 July 1897.

> Is it my fault? I know all the reasons for my spiritual suffering: firstly it grieves me that my children are not as happy as I would wish. And then I am actually very lonely. My husband is not my friend; he has been my passionate lover at times, especially as he grows older, but all my life I have felt lonely with him. He doesn't go for walks with me, he prefers to ponder in solitude over his writing. He has never taken any interest in my children, for he finds this difficult and dull.[52]

Sofia's reflections on her domestic relationships were not dissimilar to Bob Slocum's lament about the unhappiness of his wife and children three-quarters of a century later. Yet the experiences of Slocum and his family – and indeed those of Sofia – ran counter to Tolstoy's opening pronouncement in *Anna Karenina*. For much of the twentieth century, the recipe for a happy family life remained elusive. By contrast, the ingredients of unhappy families were all too clear. Disappointments and ruptures in relationships could be traced to a familiar pattern of cir-cumstances and behaviours, and they generated a relatively consistent catalogue of symptoms. Under the stress of economic hardship, occu-pational pressures, social isolation and sickness, parents and children displayed a set of reproducible traits: rebellion against intimacy; disil-lusionment with work; alcohol abuse and violence; infidelity; juvenile delinquency; separation and divorce. Family disturbances were more marked during middle age when the multiple stresses associated with ill-health, work pressures, economic constraints, declining libido, fear of death, ageing parents and troubled teenagers overlapped. Western fam-ilies at midlife faced particular strains as fathers, mothers and children passed together through their own – and each other's – identity crises.[53]

According to sociologist Alice Rossi, children and parenting rarely figured directly in Anglo-American social science research on fam-ilies.[54] Rossi's claim was probably overstated – at least in relation to studies of role conflicts within families. Divorce law reformers certainly stressed the importance of taking into account the impact of marital disputes – as well as divorce – on the health and well-being of children, who were considered to be both causes and casualties of failing families.[55] Psychoanalytical explanations of the midlife crisis emphasized the ways in which tensions between parents and adolescents exacerbated the pressures on middle-aged men and women, who were facing their own existential problems. Studies of families in conflict highlighted the importance of analysing family discord in relational terms. Deborah Weinstein has shown how, in conditions of political uncertainty, American family life and therapeutic culture came together during the post-war years to shift clinical attention away from individual psychopathology towards an understanding of families as dynamic systems with the capacity to self-regulate, as well as self-destruct.[56] American family therapy was informed in part by the work of Melanie Klein and others at the Tavistock Clinic and Institute of Human Relations in Britain. In their publications on social casework, Kathleen Bannister and her colleagues pointed out in 1955 that marital problems should not be isolated from other aspects of family and social life.[57] Similar statements were made by American stress researchers. In 1957 John Spiegel suggested that families should be analysed as systems in which 'no role exists in isolation'.[58] Averting or coping with crises in dysfunctional families required parents and children to recognize and adjust to complementary roles as they evolved across the family life cycle.

Yet Rossi was right to draw attention to a lack of sustained academic or political interest in the children of parents riven by midlife marital discord. Marriage guidance counsellors, psychiatrists and self-help authors rarely ventured beyond the marital dyad in their explanations of the causes of domestic instability or their prescriptions for resolving personal and marital crises.[59] Destructive behaviour on the part of husbands and wives – such as violence and neglect – was attributed more often to personality defects and marital disputes than to conflicts between parents and children. The tendency for family researchers and psychologists to focus almost exclusively on couples is surprising given contemporary clinical interest in maladjustment and delinquency in children. Indeed, marriage counselling in Britain was partly based on the practices of child guidance clinics and the two systems often interacted. Psychologists and psychiatrists reproached mothers for rearing sick and maladjusted children. Couples were referred for marriage guidance by psychiatric social workers and probation officers who had been alerted to family problems by the courts dealing with juvenile delinquency.[60] And parenting – if not children *per se* – constituted a key focus for researchers seeking to understand families under stress.

Difficulties adjusting to parenthood became apparent in a number of ways. Women confined to home caring for young children were lonely, exhausted and frustrated, managing symptoms of anxiety and depression with sedatives and tranquillizers – or 'Mother's Little Helpers', as the Rolling Stones put it in 1966 – prescribed by their general practitioners.[61] Worried about job security, promotion and money, men resorted to alcohol or infidelity to escape the demands of home and work. As sexual intimacy within the marriage faded, alternative routes to happiness often appeared. According to Robert Lee and Marjorie Casebier, writing in 1973, 'the temptation is great for spouses having marital problems to have extra-marital consolations.'[62] The wider family impact of such parental behaviour was evident. The children of jaded, separated and divorced parents and step-parents became emotionally disturbed, their education suffered and they feared repeating the domestic conflicts experienced during childhood in their own adult relationships.[63]

These patterns of disruption and despair were evident in fictional accounts of families at midlife. Bob Slocum's self-absorbed malaise infected his wife and children, as well as his colleagues. 'My wife is unhappy,' Slocum admits.

> She is one of those married women who are very, very bored and lonely, and I don't know what I can make myself do about it . . . She thinks she has gotten older, heavier, and less attractive than she used to be – and, of course, she is right. She thinks it matters to me, and there she is wrong. I don't think I mind. (If she knew I didn't mind, she'd probably be more unhappy.)[64]

Slocum's teenage daughter was not immune to the family complaint – indeed, according to Slocum her adolescent rebellion was partly its cause.

> My daughter, who is past fifteen, is a lonely and disgruntled person . . . She is dissatisfied with us and dissatisfied with herself. She is a clever, malicious girl with lots of insight and charm when she isn't

morose and rude. She is often mean, often depressed. She resents my wife and me terribly and as much as tells us frequently that she wishes one or both of us were gone or dead.[65]

Slocum blames himself – rather piteously and insincerely – for the chronic resentment and acute crises that plague his family. Yet Heller's readers were left in no doubt that the anxieties of middle-aged men and their families were the product of wider social and economic factors. Post-war families were broken by pressures to consume, by the rhythms of suburban living and urban working that separated families, and by a growing appetite for doing, rather than being, together.

In 1963 Canadian sociologist Charles Hobart pointed out that although the family remained pivotal to social stability, it was under threat from conflicting social values and from the commodification of people and leisure. 'The family persists because people want and need the family,' Hobart wrote in his reflections on the future of the American family.

> The problem is that, having often lost the family in its meaningful sense as a primary commitment [in terms of companionship and the socialization of children], people want a fantasy; they compulsively seek security. They get disillusionment. Pulled apart by the value conflict of our society they want both personal loving involvement and social efficient achievement, and often they can commit themselves to neither. Thus straddling both ways of life, they can only distract themselves from their predicament.[66]

According to Hobart, safeguarding the future of the family and the health of its members required a 'value revolution in American society'. Commitment to success, efficiency, productivity and prosperity – all features of the American dream – needed to be replaced by 'more human oriented being, knowing, caring, loving values'. In this way, Hobart argued, home life would be enriched and any temptation to jeopardize marriage vows would be nullified by awareness of the pain that would be caused by infidelity.[67] However convincing it might have appeared to his readers, Hobart's conservative defence of family and fidelity skated over the complexity of family relations across the life cycle. Families could rarely isolate themselves from social pressures or avoid periods of dissatisfaction that threatened their stability. In the

1930s the American feminist sociologist Jessie Bernard had highlighted how marital satisfaction varied across the life course, dipping slightly between five and ten years, and plummeting dramatically just after twenty years. For men, but not so clearly for women, satisfaction also declined as the number of children increased.[68] Bernard recognized that her survey sample was too small and the variables too complex to fully unravel the determinants of happy families. But her general principle that children – as well as the passage of time – constituted a hazard to middle-class marital happiness and family stability continued to figure in scholarly and popular publications after the war.

Although children were regarded as an important source of satisfaction and pride for married couples, some post-war studies suggested that marital contentment reached its nadir in the years before children left home; that is, when children were teenagers and parents were likely to be in their late thirties or forties. This conclusion appeared to hold true for all areas of family life: management of finances, social activities, domestic tasks, companionship, sex, and relationships with the children. 'The adolescent stage,' wrote Wesley Burr, who later served as President of the National Council on Family Relations, 'as would be expected by the earlier research, is persistently more problematic.'[69] It was well known that adolescence constituted a pivotal transition in the life cycle, especially when educational opportunities and career prospects were more fluid and when rising affluence made new forms of rebellion more widely available. In the 1960s, wrote one correspondent to Mass-Observation, 'children's peer pressures – the drug scene and general freedom – added to parental strain'.[70] The crises of adolescence – and their impact on families – were recognized in public debates. In his third Reith Lecture on the 'Vicissitudes of Adolescence', delivered in 1962, George Carstairs highlighted some of the problems faced by teenagers and young adults striving for independence.

> At adolescence, however – and by this I do not mean simply the year of attaining physical puberty but the often long-drawn-out transition between childhood and adult life – comes the real challenge: is one ready to relinquish one's parents' support, to be independent? At this time all the anxieties which were aroused at the earlier stages tend to be reanimated, and most prominent now is what Erikson has called the 'crisis of identity', the pressing question: 'Who am I?' In their attempt to answer this question, adolescents frequently

try out various roles, identify themselves with gangs or indulge in hero-worship.[71]

One of the challenges of adolescence – for both children and their parents – lay in its timing. Adolescence was first identified as a distinct phase in the life course at the end of the nineteenth century, in the context of growing interest in child development, changing rhythms of education and occupation, concerns about the quality of family life and greater age-consciousness.[72] Like midlife, adolescence came to be regarded as a moment of potential crisis between major life stages, a transition that carried the capacity to unsettle emotions, relationships, aspirations, behaviour and identity. As it evolved across the twentieth century, the more tightly defined Western life course ensured that, by the post-war years, adolescence and midlife almost invariably coincided. The consequences could be disastrous. Collisions between the storm and stress of adolescence and the identity crises of middle age disrupted families. Teenagers and young adults expressed their individuality by turning to innovative fashion and music trends or by belligerently rejecting of any form of authority associated with their parents. Dissatisfied with their achievements, middle-agers struggled to accept their children's values, which seemed to lead only to delinquency, criminality, promiscuity and addiction.[73] And partners – already struggling with their own crises – argued about how best to manage their children's behaviour, placing marriages and families under further stress.[74] 'At no point is parental influence more sharply challenged than by these junior-adults,' wrote sociologists Robert and Helen Lynd in their analysis of middle-class American family life during the 1920s, 'so mature in their demands and wholly or partially dependent upon their parents economically but not easily submitting to their authority.'[75]

Differences and disagreements between middle-aged parents and their adolescent children represented a new form of discontinuity or rupture – one that appeared not within the life course of an individual, but between generations. In 1928 the German sociologist Karl Mannheim had argued that generations were becoming increasingly separated from each other as the result of the 'accelerated pace of social change' in the twentieth century – change that brought into relief the contrasting patterns of belief and practice adopted by those born at different periods in time.[76] The notion of the 'generation gap' attracted greater comment after the Second World War as the divisions of the life course became more standardized, nuclear families became increasingly isolated from cross-generational kinship networks, and cultural and technological change accentuated misunderstandings and discord between children, parents and grandparents.[77] For middle-aged men and women, the generation gap could be particularly painful since it worked in both directions, sandwiching them between the values and lifestyles of their parents and those of their children. Without effectively handling personal crises, the multiple challenges of midlife left many parents with a sense of loneliness that threatened to darken their own journeys towards death.[78]

Heightened by cultural differences between generations, marital tensions could lead to unhappy and broken families. Children suffered as much as – if not more than – their parents. A number of studies revealed the impact of marital breakdown and divorce on children's health. 'In the typical American family of today,' wrote Margaret Mead in 1929, 'divorce, like death, breaks up the home, cuts the child's universe in half if it does not shatter entirely.'[79] Mead's warning about the disastrous effects of divorce on children's sense of security informed subsequent understandings of the ways in which broken homes impacted on the personalities of children deep into adult life – often leading, it was feared, to a repetition of their parents' behaviour. Her concerns were echoed in the experiences and beliefs of families after the war. Remembering family life during the 1960s and '70s, respondents to Mass-Observation stressed the importance of safeguarding loyalty and stability within the family and highlighted the ways in which children suffered more acutely than their parents from marital breakdown. Divorce and remarriage rarely resolved tensions. Rather, couples tended simply to 'exchange one set of problems for the same set', while their children often remained dislocated and vulnerable.[80]

Not all families struggled to bridge the distance between generations or to reconcile interpersonal conflicts. Although parents and children were overloaded with competing roles and expectations, families were not always 'prisons of love' constraining individual growth and autonomy; they were often sites of safety and rescue from hazardous socio-economic conditions.[81] The nature and strength of family relationships also varied according to gender and class: Bob Slocum related very differently to his daughter to how he did to his sons; and parental authority may have persisted relatively unchallenged well beyond the Second World War in working-class families.[82] Nevertheless, balancing work and family commitments could be exhausting, particularly at midlife when time and energy were at a premium. In 1936 the author of an article in *Harper's Monthly Magazine* described their growing resentment at having to satisfy their children's demands for attention and support at the cost of their own health and happiness. After years of austerity, greater expectations of prosperity and freedom – at least among middle-class teenagers and young adults – had bred a selfish generation with 'little sense of personal obligation to others' and only limited respect for family unity or parental authority.[83] This lament articulated the ideological gap that existed between generations in the middle decades of the twentieth century.[84] But after the war, it came to reflect even more closely the reality for parents striving to fulfil the obligations of companionate marriage, keep up with the Joneses and endure the monotony and conformity of industrial and corporate life.

IN 1936, AT the age of 39, the American novelist F. Scott Fitzgerald wrote three autobiographical essays recounting his own midlife breakdown – or 'crack-up', as he put it. Creator of Jay Gatsby, one of the greatest fictional prophets and victims of the American dream, Fitzgerald had been diagnosed with tuberculosis earlier in his life. Damaged by the effects of heavy drinking and the stress of his wife's ill-health, in his late thirties Fitzgerald 'cracked like an old plate', feeling that his life was no longer worth preserving. 'I began to realize', he wrote in the first essay, 'that for two years my life had been drawing on resources that I did not possess, but I had been mortgaging myself physically and spiritually up to the hilt.'[85] Fitzgerald sought to recover through solitude and silence, during which he realized that in the pursuit of literary success his identity had been fragmented: 'So there was not an "I" any more – not a basis on which I could organize my self-respect – save my limitless capacity for toil that it seemed I possessed no more.' Survival, Fitzgerald realized, required a complete breach in normal patterns of behaviour. Merely running away from everything, as some midlife men tried to do, was not sufficient because it led only to being caught in another trap. A clean break, by contrast, was 'something that you cannot come back from; that is irretrievable because it makes the past cease to exist'. Searching for an alternative route to restoring his identity in what he regarded as a counterfeit world, Fitzgerald became convinced that happiness was a form of self-delusion. The 'natural state of the sentient adult', he argued, 'is a qualified unhappiness' that could only be made worse by a persistent determination to succeed as youth receded.[86]

Fitzgerald's image of the midlife man as a cracked plate was fitting. During the interwar and post-war years, middle-age crises appeared in the cracks between partners, between generations and between the office or factory and home. For men it was arguably working practices that constituted the major source of dissatisfaction. In part, occupational stress was linked to aspirations for domestic comforts and leisure, to opportunities to improve a family's standard of living – stress that was willingly embraced by many husbands and fathers. But there was a downside – or trap – to the American dream of upward mobility, as Joseph Heller pointed out in *Something Happened*. 'Most of the people around me seem to make more money than I do,' Bob Slocum acknowledges towards the end of the novel.

> Where I live now is perfectly adequate: and when I get my raise and move, it will again be among people who make more money than I do. This is known as *upward mobility*, a momentous force in contemporary American urban life, along with *downward mobility*, which is another momentous force in contemporary American urban life. They keep things stirring. We rise and fall like Frisbees, if we get off the ground at all, or pop flies, except we rise slower, drop faster. I am on the way up, Kagle's on the way down. He moves faster. Only in America is it possible to do both at the same time. Look at me. I ascend like a condor, while falling to pieces.[87]

The relentless rhythms of working life accentuated the sense of alienation felt by middle-aged men – the 'forgotten men', as Edmund Bergler described them in 1958 – who sought refuge from the rat-race in alcohol and adultery.[88] Critiques of the damaging effects of corporate life on health and happiness were not confined to novels and films. Sociological studies expressed similar concerns that, in a world struggling to cope with social, economic and political uncertainty, various facets of working life were constraining men's capacity for growth and self-expression. Commuting from the suburbs to the city dulled the senses and increased the distance between white-collar workers and their families, leaving them with little in common. Long hours, overwork and the intensity and pace of modern life disrupted psychological and physiological equilibrium, causing anxiety, ulcers, high blood pressure, high cholesterol and heart disease.[89] Without sufficient relaxation and self-discipline, by the time they reached midlife men were weighed down by work, family and social responsibilities – at which point they began to realize that life was no longer what it was 'cracked up to be', as Leslie Tizard and Harry Guntrip put it in 1959.[90] According to self-help authors, the solution to men's fragility was for wives to ensure that their husband's energies were not prematurely sapped or their hearts overloaded by the strain of professional and business life.[91] But the ministrations of an understanding wife were often not sufficient, it would seem. The remedy for physical ill-health, restlessness and emotional rebellion in middle-aged men frequently came in the form of a mistress, who promised – but almost invariably failed – to renew self-esteem and reinvigorate sexual confidence. 'In a somewhat similar state', wrote the British physician Ivor H. Mills in his analysis of why people sometimes failed to cope with life stresses,

> are the numerous middle-aged men whose work load is great and whose wives no longer strike them as exciting. The challenge of trying to win a much younger woman raises their arousal level and may restore their flagging potency. So long as the novelty lasts the increased arousal level makes them succeed. After a year or so the novelty decreases and sexual activity with the mistress becomes something to be expected rather than a challenge to be fought for; potency may once again flag.[92]

The undercurrents of male frustration and anger that ran through the pages of novels such as *Something Happened* were exposed more explicitly by post-war sociologists. In the preface to a reprint of *The Lonely Crowd*, which had been first published in 1950, David Riesman suggested that certain features of American social life, including the impact of affluence and mass media on private lives and personal relationships, were restricting the possible roles for young people. This 'shrinkage of alternatives', as Riesman put it, generated 'a solipsistic lack of concern for others'. More particularly, he argued, the relocation of meaning from work to home – sold by promoters of leisure and proponents of the nuclear family – carried costs for 'men trained in a work-driven age'.[93] 'In fact, we soon realized', Riesman wrote in 1960, that the burden put on leisure by the disintegration of work is too huge to be coped with; leisure itself cannot rescue work, but fails with it, and can only be meaningful for most men if work is meaningful, so that the very qualities we looked for in leisure are more likely to come into being there if social and political action fight the two-front battle of work-and-leisure.[94]

Although *The Lonely Crowd* was criticized at the time for over-emphasizing the alienation experienced by young Americans, when objective evidence indicated conversely that life had improved for much of the population, Riesman had captured some of the key features of male midlife despair: frustration with the 'career clock', against which success was measured; job insecurity; and the loss of autonomy in large corporations that had come to dominate the occupational landscape of men returning from the war, men who now expected freedom rather than confinement.[95] According to Riesman, aspirations for personal growth and self-fulfilment were being obstructed by the demands of 'forbiddingly powerful and efficient institutions', leaving workers with only two options: conformity or deviance.[96] In *The Organization Man*, published in 1956, American writer and urban analyst William Whyte pushed the argument further by suggesting that large corporations were – quite deliberately – stamping out men's capacity for individuality.[97] Whyte's concern was that organizations – and the growth of bureaucracy – required and expected men to blend in, put the company ahead of themselves and remain loyal throughout their lives if they were to realize their American dreams.[98] The result, according to Whyte, was not merely conformity, but also mediocrity.

Whyte's assessment of post-war occupational culture explained some of the patterns of male behaviour revealed in the clinics of marriage guidance counsellors and psychiatrists. Charles Hobart pointed out how Whyte's work indicated that 'organization men' would sacrifice 'success in marriage to career success, if forced to choose between them'.[99] This calculation was evident in responses to a Mass-Observation survey on the pace of life. One of the respondents, a 58-year-old retired man who had worked as a solicitor and bank director during the 1960s and '70s, reflected on how the tempo of his working day had impacted on his health and home life during his thirties and forties. Commuting usually took over one hour each way, but could be made worse by delays imposed by union strikes or IRA bomb scares. Whatever negative effects he felt as a result of 'continuous long hours', however, were compensated for by the affluence that it brought to his family. During middle age, when he was working for an international banking and finance group, life 'was so hectic that few must ever experience anything like it'. His salary allowed his wife to stay at home until the children were eighteen and he took little part in home life. 'As regards my children,' he recollected, 'I must say that I took little pleasure in them when very young – indeed few of my men friends have any interest in babies (and although I love my children dearly, I would not have minded had I had none).'[100] In relation to balancing work and family, the respondent's priorities – like those of many fictional men such as Tom Rath and Bob Slocum – were clear.

> I always insisted that, as I had a high responsibility to my Company, who remunerated me highly to the benefit of my family, then – within reason – the Company had to come first. Fortunately my wife shared this view. For example, it seemed likely that our son might be born on a day when it was crucial for me to be in the City at a very important meeting, so we prepared a contingency plan (for my sister-in-law to take my wife to hospital). In fact, that is what happened on the day, 9.4.63. I would not tolerate my employees phoning in, apologising for absence 'because my wife/husband has a migraine'. Friends should be called upon for help – the employer should not suffer. I am, incidentally, appalled at the idea of men taking 'paternity leave'.[101]

In 1964 American philosopher Herbert Marcuse – who acknowledged Whyte's influence – offered a more damning indictment of the suffocating conformity characteristic of post-war Western societies. In *One-dimensional Man*, Marcuse pointed to the ways in which the technological achievements of advanced industrial civilization were curtailing freedom, suppressing individuality and stifling dissent – a process referred to by Marcuse as the 'paralysis of criticism'.[102] Although 'the technological society' had helped to eradicate want, its mechanisms of control were totalitarian since they determined 'not only the socially needed occupations, skills, and attitudes, but also individual needs and aspirations'.[103] Various strains within Marcuse's critique of modern Western civilization were certainly shared by others during the 1960s and were portrayed neatly in contemporary novels. But middle-aged men appeared not only to be rebelling against the conformity imposed by one-dimensional lives. They were also struggling to cope with the multiple roles that they were now expected to fill – as faithful husbands, fathers and civic leaders, as well as loyal employees. Although corporate life provided many men with new forms of status and security, adjusting to competition within the workplace, domestic responsibilities and mass culture bred fatigue and despair. In deference to Betty Friedan's enunciation of the 'feminine mystique', which captured the impact of gendered domestic and occupational norms on women's health, American scholar Jessica Field Cohen referred to the hidden role conflicts that shaped middle-aged men's emotional well-being as 'the masculine mystique'.[104] Expectations to succeed in business – and inevitable failures along the way – coloured men's lives at home, leading them into alcoholism, poor health, marital instability and infidelity. It was these symptoms of the midlife crisis that prevented men from enjoying the successes that they had struggled so long to achieve or from sharing them with their families.[105]

In 1956 William Whyte explored in more detail the place of the organization man in the 'communities that have become his dormitories – the great package suburbs that have sprung up outside our cities since the war'.[106] Exodus from the city was not new after the Second World War. During the interwar years, extension of the Metropolitan Railway lines out from London allowed workers to live some distance away from the office, in newly built houses in 'Metro-land', a term that referred to the semi-rural commuter belt to the northwest of the city. Images of Metro-land were used to advertise not only railway companies, but building firms constructing housing estates that would allow families to enjoy the benefits of suburban living. As suburban development expanded after the war, some workers chose to move even further away from the city, well beyond the suburbs. In 1955 Auguste Spectorsky, a writer and associate publisher of *Playboy* magazine, described such men and their families as 'exurbanites', separated from each other by even greater distances and for longer periods of time.[107]

Spectorsky's reflections were more abstract than sociological and psychological studies of suburbia. They were also more critical, since he believed that, in the pursuit of false dreams to escape the rat-race, middle-class exurbanites were responsible for their own malaise: the exurbanites' problems, he argued, were largely self-contrived.[108] Spectorsky's portrayal of the challenges faced by men working at

Magazine
advertisement
for houses in
Metro-land, 1917.

HOUSES IN METRO-LAND

THE above is an illustration of some small

BARN ROOFED HOUSES

now in the course of completion at Wembley Park. They are erected in pairs and have more pleasing features.
The snug third sitting room is

GROWLERY

as Dickens would probably have termed it it is certainly something novel in homes of this size. The compactness
of all the rooms makes the work of the house quite a simple matter, a very important consideration in these
times of difficulty in obtaining domestic servants.
The gardens vary in size, some of the plots being as much as 200 feet long, and there is

A CARRIAGE OR MOTOR WAY

running at the back so all the houses so that a car can be kept and heavy goods as coal, etc., delivered
at the rear of the premises.
The houses all contain 3 sitting rooms, combined kitchen and scullery, 4 bedrooms, bathroom, linen closet
and excellent sanitary arrangements, and the prices are from £600 Leasehold and £730 Freehold.
No survey charges or legal charges (except out-of-pocket payments) are made.
Immediate possession given on payment of the deposit.
The number of trains daily between Wembley Park and Baker Street and the City is 77 each way. Journey
time of fast trains, 12 minutes.
Season Ticket rates, Wembley Park and Baker St., 3 months, 1st class, £3 0s. 6d.; 3 months, 3rd class, £1 7s.
*Illustrated lodges will be forwarded to an applicant, and appointment for their visit to be made in the first instance to Commercial
Manager, Metropolitan Railway, Baker Street Station, London, N.W.1, at the same time mentioning this advertisement.*

**POSSESSION CAN BE OBTAINED ON PAYMENT OF A DEPOSIT AND
THE BALANCE EXTENDED OVER A PERIOD OF YEARS AS RENT**

considerable distances from home were echoed by others. In 1960 psychiatrist Richard Gordon, social psychologist Katherine Gordon and writer Max Gunther claimed that modern families were 'commuting to disaster'.[109] Commuting certainly took its toll on men emotionally and physically, as long days and crowded smoke-filled carriages added considerable stress to the familiar challenges of maintaining a home, supporting a family and ensuring time for leisure. Some men attempted to cope with the strain of commuting and working – and delay returning to their families – by stopping off at 'the pub on the way home to unwind', as one Mass-Observation respondent put it.[110] The results of this lifestyle could be disastrous for the hopes and happiness of men at midlife. 'And riding to work,' Richard Yates wrote in *Revolutionary Road*, in reference to Frank Wheeler's time spent commuting, 'one of the youngest and healthiest passengers on the train, he sat with the look of a man condemned to a very slow, painless death. He felt middle-aged.'[111]

Suburban living brought other perils. William Whyte's impression of organization men at home in the suburbs focused on their rootlessness or transience. 'The man who leaves home', he argued in a passage that foretold the trajectory of many of his peers on both sides of the Atlantic in the post-war years, 'is not the exception in American society but the key to it.'[112] Men's opportunities were determined by their willingness to relocate in order to gain employment or to travel further between home and work. In these circumstances, suburbs constituted a new, relatively classless social institution, one that promised – even if it did not quite deliver – a communal way of life, a solution to economic realities and prospects of upward mobility. It was the organization man, argued Whyte, who set the tone for what he termed the 'inconspicuous consumption', competition and homogeneity that characterized suburban life: 'if he is as uncertain as any in keeping up with the Joneses, it is because he *is* the Joneses.'[113] Within a matrix of rapidly changing marital, family and occupational obligations, men could feel as trapped as their wives and children, unable to find an easy balance between the spirit of egalitarianism inherent in the suburbs and an equally strong imperative to achieve personal and material success. 'Somewhere in the middle', wrote Whyte, 'lies the good life, but like that elusive plateau they seek in The Organization, it vanishes as quickly as one finds it.' Overloaded and time-starved, men struggled to cope with the continual need to adapt, leaving them listless and depressed.[114]

According to Whyte, extramarital affairs were less common in the suburbs than in urban communities, because it was more difficult to conceal trysts from neighbours and because betrayal harmed not just two marriages, but the whole community.[115] Conversely, suburban living entailed long commutes and overnight stays away from home, which facilitated sexual infidelity. But attempts on the part of middle-class suburbanites to blame adultery – along with alcoholism, absence and abuse – on the demands of work and family or on the expectations of a consumer society were disingenuous. Men's sense of disaffection and anomie could be only partially explained in terms of post-war economic conditions, the pursuit of wealth or the norms of masculinity that continued to emphasize men's role as breadwinners. Social and cultural contexts were clearly important. But as contemporary novelists, psychoanalysts and marriage counsellors insisted, men's flight from commitment and confinement was also a manifestation of narcissistic impulses to pursue sexual gratification. The emotional misery and financial crises experienced by middle-aged men – and those around them – were self-inflicted.

The suburbs were not uniformly regarded – or experienced – as destructive. In 1969 the American scholar and newspaper editor Scott Donaldson challenged the popular myth, propagated by Whyte and others, that suburban life was merely 'silly and pretentious and conformity-ridden and homogeneous'.[116] According to Donaldson, suburbs were being blamed for a malady that was universal: a condition that was not confined to a single class, occupation or location, but was experienced by all families throughout America. Donaldson's point was pertinent. Contemporary stress researchers were similarly highlighting how focusing on the stresses of middle-class upwardly mobile suburbanites, or on executive stress in the business world, ignored the extent to which urban working-class families were struggling with the effects of low wages and high unemployment.[117] Wage-workers were clearly not immune to what Michael Young and Peter Willmott referred to as the 'career menopause' experienced by managers and executives as they reached the ceiling of promotion.[118] On the contrary, middle-aged blue-collar workers also feared being usurped by younger colleagues as their physical and mental capacity declined and work began to lose its appeal. 'Now that many executives in industry find themselves redundant or retired at a comparatively early age,' wrote the British author Frederick Le Gros Clark in 1967,

> the wage-worker in his fifties is looking more doubtfully at his prospects; and this makes him hesitate to compete with the younger voices he hears about him. He may at this stage withdraw his mind more and more from any part he once took on the labour side in the affairs of the works. The chances are that he would always go along with his group. But if he ever had dreams of promotion he knows that he has now reached about as far up the ladder as he is likely to. He concentrates on getting through with the jobs of which, after all, he is a complete master; such boredom as they entailed in the past has probably become dulled with long experience.[119]

As Le Gros Clark pointed out, many men working in collieries or building sites were middle-aged, and the majority of self-employed workers were 'beyond the age of thirty-five or forty'.[120] The families of older working-class men and women were particularly vulnerable to the stress of unemployment in times of austerity, leading to poverty, ill-health and marital breakdown even when extended kinship networks were available to support them. As their husbands became disillusioned with repetitive occupations or were unable to find employment, working-class mothers were forced to seek paid employment beyond the home, not as a source of self-fulfilment – as seemed to be the case for middle-class, suburban housewives – but simply in order to sustain family income. Although intended to reduce concerns about domestic finances, situations in which both men and women worked outside the home conversely created greater physical distance and longer periods of separation between parents and their children, adding expressly to the burdens already imposed on middle-aged wives and mothers, as well as on their husbands.

RESPONDING TO A Mass-Observation directive in 1992, a 74-year-old retired widow commented on the difficulties that women had faced when they worked within and beyond the home during the post-war decades. In 1966 she had experienced 'what was then called a "nervous breakdown" but is now called a mid-life crisis'.[121] Having raised two children and managed the family home, she was 47 years old, menopausal and working as a school secretary. Although dictated by the clock and requiring long hours in school, work was a source of satisfaction and pride. At home, by contrast, she lacked self-esteem and felt that her dual role as mother and wife was unappreciated. The family hired a 'grand-mother type of woman' to give her sons tea during the week until she came home. But, in addition to working all day, the respondent was nevertheless responsible for the housework, washing, ironing, cooking and gardening. Evenings were spent on further domestic duties.

> I would wash up after the evening meal, clean the cooker, and tidy the kitchen and join my husband in the sitting room (no help from him as he didn't like me working) and sleep the rest of the evening, later rousing just enough to fall into bed. I used to tell myself it was the television boring me, never acknowledging I was just plain tired out, for I would get no sympathy, only nagging.[122]

Recovery from exhaustion and depression involved finding new forms of manageable employment – as an orderly in a geriatric ward, then a secretary in a child guidance clinic – rather than through the customary routes open to women: medication, talking therapies and religion. In addition, the respondent began to reassess the values and practices that had led to her feeling overloaded. 'Instead of trying to reach the top of the tree through sheer drive and efficiency as I had in the past,' she wrote, 'I decided to use my efforts to keep down at the bottom,' where responsibilities were fewer, the fear of failure less pressing and happiness more easily attainable. The results were clear. As the urgency of life receded, her health improved and she achieved a degree of freedom to which she was unaccustomed: 'I feel I am now in control of my life having freed myself from a compulsion to work, a compulsion of which I was unaware when younger.'[123] In this sense, midlife crises in women were no different to those experienced by men. Driven by boredom and a sense of wasted time, middle-aged wives re-evaluated their husbands, as well as their work. With more time to 'see for the first time in years the man she married', wrote the marriage guidance counsellor Angela Reed in a book designed to help women through divorce, she 'wonders why on earth she ever did so, wonders how she can possibly endure his company now that they are once again alone together, facing each other like strangers across the breakfast table'.[124]

Post-war narratives of midlife breakdowns – or crack-ups – reveal the multiple layers of stress experienced by women as they grappled with the competing roles and expectations placed on them by husbands, children and society. For many women born in the interwar years, the original dream had revolved around marriage, home and family. But changing social conditions and cultural norms generated unexpected financial and emotional pressures on families after the war. During periods of economic depression and adversity, women sought paid work simply to boost the family income. In times of affluence, by contrast, additional earnings allowed families to afford houses in the suburbs, cars, domestic appliances, leisure activities and package holidays – that is, to keep up with, or ahead of, the Joneses. But aspirations of upward mobility left women trapped as political and commercial promises of happy families in ideal homes – safeguarded by wives and mothers – proved deceptive. The bind was neatly articulated by Marilyn French in *The Women's Room*. One of the central characters in the novel, Mira, reflects on how easily she had become seduced by the American dream of domestic contentment. Standing peacefully at the kitchen sink, preparing a meal and listening to the noise of children outside, she waited for her husband to return from work: 'It was happiness,' she believed momentarily.[125] Yet for Mira, domesticity – although rewarding – was double-edged, since it curtailed her pursuit of other forms of self-fulfilment, whether through work or creativity. The real post-war 'American Dream, female version', wrote French, was not harmony, but chaos; not certainty, but self-doubt; not companionate marriage within a symmetrical family, but continued dependence on men – whether they were husbands, fathers or employers.[126]

The notion that housewives were trapped – or that the image of contented domesticity portrayed in the media and advertisements was no longer credible – attracted the attention of social critics and family researchers during the 1950s and '60s. In *The Crack in the Picture Window*, published in 1956, the American writer John Keats reconstructed the experiences of an archetypal suburban family – John and Mary Drone and their children – living in one of the residential areas of 'identical boxes' that were 'spreading like gangrene throughout America'.[127] Keats did not hide his contempt for the conformity of the suburbs. 'In any one of these new neighbourhoods,' he wrote in his introduction, 'you can be certain that all other houses will be precisely like yours, inhabited by people whose age, income, number of children, problems, habits, conversation, dress, possessions and perhaps even blood type are also precisely like yours.'[128] The impact of homogeneity, which he traced to the greed of post-war housing developers and the limited vision of politicians, was clear to Keats.

If you buy a small house, you are assured that your children will leave you perhaps even sooner than they should, for at once they will learn never to associate home with pleasure. In short, ladies and gentlemen, we offer you here for your inspection facts relevant to today's housing developments – developments conceived in error, nurtured by greed, corroding everything they touch. They destroy established cities and trade patterns, pose dangerous problems for the areas they invade, and actually drive mad myriads of housewives shut up in them.[129]

Not everyone agreed. In 1969 Scott Donaldson argued that the tendency to mock the suburbs as collections of 'little boxes' that 'all look just the same' – as political activist Malvina Reynolds put it in a satirical song composed in 1962 – was misjudged.[130] But Keats's hyperbole was echoed by others, for whom the 'picture window' symbolized suburban emptiness and for whom the suburban home constituted merely another form of incorporation.[131] Based on research into the emotional problems experienced by families living in the suburbs of New York, the authors of *The Split-level Trap* argued that suburbia – or 'disturbia' as they referred to it – was responsible for many of the ailments suffered by post-war couples and their children. Split-level houses in post-war suburbs not only created distance between husbands who worked in the city and their wives who stayed at home, but separated parents from children as they occupied different levels and spaces within the house. While middle-aged men struggled to keep up with competition at work, their wives, ex-wives or widows – the 'nobodies' of suburbia – became isolated, mentally ill and suicidal. For both men and women, the 'golden plateau' of middle age had proved to be disappointing: 'Their years of backbreaking efforts, they now see, have gained them only a barren wasteland.'[132] As one review of *The Split-level Trap* pointed out, something had 'gone terribly wrong with the American dream' – for women perhaps more than men.[133]

During the 1950s and '60s, feminists denounced the ways in which reducing women to reproduction and domesticity rendered wives and mothers captive, unable to fulfil their ambitions or to realize their own happiness as they satisfied the needs of their families.[134] Tensions between young women's expectations of freedom, on the one hand, and the unequal distribution of duties within the household when they married and had children, on the other, led to anxiety and frustration. This dilemma was widely acknowledged. 'Resentful of the stresses imposed by their new liberty,' wrote George Carstairs in 1962, 'resentful and frustrated by the restriction placed on this liberty by the years of childbearing; anxious and guilty at this resentment, uncertain even of the division of parental responsibilities, such women begin to doubt whether femininity is indeed compatible with all the variety of roles they must play.'[135] But potential solutions to the isolation and frustration experienced by some women in the suburbs reinforced their subservience. Middle-aged women were encouraged simply to use medication or relaxation techniques in order to fulfil their duties as wives and mothers.[136]

In *The Feminine Mystique*, published in 1963, Betty Friedan urged women to rebel against the limited horizons offered to them by American culture: 'We can no longer ignore the voice within women that says: "I want something more than my husband and my children and my home."'[137] Preventing women from achieving 'full human identity' created the conditions for personal and relational crises, tempting women to have affairs for sexual and emotional satisfaction. Drawing on the work of Kinsey as well as on her own interviews, Friedan pointed out that in this respect the behaviour of middle-aged women was not unlike that of their husbands. After fifteen years or so of marriage – when couples were in their late thirties or early forties – extramarital sex provided an opportunity for wives to escape from the drudgery of family life and satisfy their fantasies. According to Spectorsky, the most common complaint made by women to their physicians was that their husbands were sexually inadequate, leading to adultery, separation and divorce.[138] The futility of adultery as a means of self-fulfilment was recognized. As Friedan and others pointed out, women – like men – rarely resolved their midlife crises by resorting to infidelity.[139]

For Friedan, there were more creative – or at least less destructive – ways in which women could evade the trap of wifehood and motherhood. She warned against searching for universal solutions that failed to take historical and cultural contexts into account. 'The identity crisis in men and women', she argued, 'cannot be solved by one generation for the next; in our rapidly changing society, it must be faced continually, solved only to be faced again in the span of a single lifetime.'[140] Nevertheless, Friedan believed that education and meaningful occupation would always be vital for women's self-realization. Attitudes to working wives and mothers were ambivalent when *The Feminine Mystique* first appeared. As the British social researcher Pearl Jephcott pointed out in her 1962 study of workers at a biscuit factory in Bermondsey in London, the married woman who went to work each day was a 'controversial figure in western society'. While some considered the working woman to be 'a symbol of freedom', others regarded her as 'the epitome of irresponsibility and neglect'.[141] This division of opinion was evident in contemporary commentaries on work and family. On the one hand, work was promoted as a means for married women to reduce suburban isolation, improve their mental health and enhance family income. On the other hand, a number of prominent British and American writers were concerned about the potential for working mothers to damage their children's health and undermine their husband's authority – simply by being absent from the home.[142] Friction was particularly apparent in middle age. As Le Gros Clark pointed out in 1963, the 'typical working woman' was no longer a young woman who was 'filling in time before she got married' – as it had been in the early twentieth century – but 'a married woman in her middle life'.[143] Crises clearly occurred throughout the life cycle, but middle age was particularly challenging for women caught between work and family.

Although often sympathetic to the increasing number of women seeking self-fulfilment and financial independence through paid employment, post-war researchers highlighted the potential hazards of mothers working while their children were still at home – including the fear that absent mothers produced delinquent children.[144] In spite of the rhetoric of symmetrical families, women's willingness to work outside the home was not necessarily matched by men's commitment to the family. According to the American psychologist Roland Tharp, husbands who valued mutual intimacy within the marriage might not be prepared to share household or child-rearing responsibilities.[145] As a result, working mothers became overloaded in new ways – particularly in their forties – as they struggled to balance competing demands on their energy and time.[146] In 1968 Alva Myrdal and Viola Klein argued that one solution to the double burden carried by wives and mothers was to reduce daily working hours to match school hours, allowing 'a complete renaissance of home life' in which both men and women could now participate.[147] Myrdal and Klein were overly optimistic when they claimed that the 'best of both worlds' was now within women's grasp.[148] Traditional social values and cultural norms were difficult to dislodge. Married women either continued to remain at home alone or worked – often unsupported – at some distance from their husbands and children, creating further cracks within which personal and marital crises emerged.

Balancing work, home and leisure was particularly problematic for 'dual career families'. In an article written while they were visiting the Tavistock Institute of Human Relations in 1965, American social scientists Rhona and Robert Rapoport emphasized the manner in which life stages affected relationships between work and home differently, as men's and women's career lines – as well as family roles – alternately diverged and converged across time.[149] Citing the work of Myrdal and Klein and Elliott Jaques, among others, the Rapoports subsequently argued that situations in which both parents pursued independent professional careers created 'overload dilemmas' at critical transition points in individual, career and family life cycles. The social organization of work had not yet evolved sufficiently to accommodate the changing emotional and economic needs of women – or indeed men.[150] The

Rapoports' concerns were taken up elsewhere. Growing expectations of gender equality within the household economy were incompatible with the traditional male-breadwinner model of family life. More equitable sharing of responsibilities between partners – as well as careers for women – could only be achieved, argued American sociologist Joseph Pleck in the 1970s, if there were substantial changes in attitudes to both employment and work-life balance that gave 'greater priority to family needs'.[151]

Dual-career families exemplified the ways in which social and cultural change after the war had forced additional modes of separation on couples and families, a situation parodied by the Romanian-French playwright Eugène Ionesco in *The Bald Soprano*, first performed in 1950. Believing that they had met each other before somewhere, two of the characters begin to exchange details of their lives, eventually realizing – absurdly – that they are in fact married.[152] But working-class parents, whose problems were exacerbated by economic need, were not immune to isolation and overload. Under sufficient stress, working women in their forties – as well as their husbands or partners – were prone to crises as career opportunities, family pressures and physiological changes coincided. By the 1960s many women were no longer prepared to accept constraints on their freedom and financial independence as they aged. With thirty years or so left to live, middle-aged wives and mothers sought to rewrite the midlife script or 'break the daisy chains' in order to make the most of the time available to them before death – with or without their husbands.[153]

'I ONCE THOUGHT', wrote F. Scott Fitzgerald in *My Lost City* in 1932, 'that there were no second acts in American lives'.[154] For people plagued by marital tensions, family disturbances and personal disappointments during the middle decades of the twentieth century, Fitzgerald's instinct was probably correct. After the war, self-help authors drew on personal and professional experience to warn middle-aged men and women that second chances were rare, if not impossible. Marriage guidance counsellors revealed the limits to reconciliation. And American and British novelists sketched out how breaking marriage vows and fragmenting families were unlikely to resolve midlife crises. Richard Yates's *Revolutionary Road* highlighted the risk of longing for renewal. Frank and April Wheeler had hoped to find a better life in the suburbs, but frustrated by the conformity and mediocrity of their neighbours they decide to emigrate to Europe. The Wheelers' sense of relief once the decision is made is clear. 'It's like coming out of a Cellophane bag,' insists Frank when they have agreed to leave. 'It's like having been encased in some kind of Cellophane for years without knowing it, and suddenly breaking out.' But their plans are in vain. Already undermined by infidelity, contempt and distrust, their marriage disintegrates and – like the dreams of so many fictional midlife couples – the Wheelers' ambitions for a life less tense end in tragedy.[155]

Set against the canvas of suburban life, the lure of second chances for happiness figured in many post-war texts. In 1963 David Ely set out a fresh vision of the American dream – one designed specifically for the middle-aged. Made into a film starring Rock Hudson in 1966, Ely's cult novel *Seconds* follows the fortunes of a middle-aged man at a moment of crisis in his life. A successful banker in his late forties, Mr Wilson earns a substantial salary, owns two homes and a boat, and has funded his daughter's private education. In spite of occupational success and material wealth, he is bored, anxious and disaffected. As a result, he accepts an offer from an organization referred to only as 'The Company' to provide him with a new identity in order to escape the tedium and disappointments of his life. Wilson expresses one of the sources of his unhappiness in familiarly misogynistic terms: 'Emily [his wife] was quite a pretty girl then,' he tells his potential saviours, 'but I had the suspicion that eventually she would grow fat, which proved to be the case.'[156] When questioned further about the fate of his youthful dreams, Wilson reveals not only the monotony of middle age, but the distance that had grown between him and his wife.

> 'You mean, do I like anything about the way I lived? Well, sir, I find that hard to answer. I was comfortable, I guess. I didn't think too much about things. I left my wife pretty much alone, and she did the same for me. We never quarreled, and in recent years we hardly ever – well, expressed much affection.'[157]

Although Wilson claims that he would not have committed adultery, he is nevertheless attracted by the prospect of looking and feeling younger, reinvigorating buried emotions and exploring new sensual opportunities. To his fellow fugitives, who have already undergone similar surgical procedures to alter their appearance and paid for the bureaucratic eradication of their identities, the benefits of physical renovation and freedom from the accumulated duties of corporate and domestic life are boundless:

> 'Look at it this way. You're living a dream. All those longings you had back in the old days – well, they've come true now. You've got what almost every middle-aged man in America would like to have. Freedom. Real freedom. You can do anything you want to. You've got financial security, you've got no responsibilities, and you've got no reason at all to feel guilty about what you've done. The company's taken care of everything. Right?'[158]

Ely's masterly narrative and its cinematic interpretation reveal the trap that middle-aged men – and women – were prone to falling into during the post-war decades. Like other men, Wilson's desperation for a new life is induced by the pressures of work and family. Unfortunately, he has miscalculated. Wilson eventually recognizes that personal freedom – much like the clean break that Fitzgerald had also yearned for – is illusory. Rather than holding him back, Wilson's wife and family have been the cornerstone of his stability and success, a source of comfort that he realizes – too late – he is reluctant to relinquish, at least to another man. 'Emily had been solid and loyal in her way,' he reflects, 'and certainly faithful; the idea of her being the wife of some stranger impressed him as being most inappropriate. Undignified in fact.'[159] Wilson's despair at not being able to turn back the clock to re-enter his old life – and his fear that he is fading into a 'two-dimensional representation of a man' – is tangible in the novel's closing pages. Ely makes it clear that if the interwar American dream of collective prosperity and upward mobility is no longer credible or sustainable, neither is the post-war narcissistic fantasy of self-fulfilment that has replaced it. Disillusioned with everyday habits and social conventions, Wilson has deceived himself into believing that simply changing his outer shell – or swapping partners – will transform his inner life and enable him once more to find love and happiness.[160]

Midlife dreams of fresh starts and clean breaks were not confined to the fictional world. They also surfaced in post-war studies of the hazards and opportunities of middle age. In 1967 the British psychiatrist Anthony Storr reflected on the manner in which the years between 35 and 45 constituted 'a time of crucial importance in the development of the individual'.[161] Instability and despair were common at midlife; but middle age was also a period in which 'new possibilities emerge and new patterns of living are explored'.[162] Rather than regarding mature adulthood as stagnant, Storr argued that it was important to acknowledge what Jung had already pointed out in the 1930s; namely, that around the age of 37 important challenges emerged. At midlife, emotional upheavals were more common; divorce rates peaked; the incidence of severe depression rose; and alcoholism and 'transient infidelities' began to destroy work and personal relationships. In part, these reproducible patterns of behaviour were triggered by an awareness that youthful dreams had evaporated. But for Storr, the ubiquity of these symptoms suggested that midlife restlessness was 'a vital part of living', one that indicated that personal growth continued well beyond adolescence and early adulthood. Given that artistic creativity often changed direction at midlife, Storr suggested that the years around forty should be regarded as a revised edition of adolescence, a springboard for personal renaissance rather than decline. Although changing sexual partners at midlife was a high-risk strategy, a change of direction at midlife would be accepted more readily, Storr argued, if second marriages were allowed to become 'the norm rather than the exception'.[163] The middle-aged should not be downhearted at the prospect of ageing and death, but optimistic about their futures.

> Whatever solutions society may ultimately approve, the fact remains that this second adolescence period is not one in which regret for the past need be a main feature, unless it be in the case of those unfortunates whose self-esteem is totally linked with physical prowess. Rather it is an age at which men and women can affirm their identities and look forward to new and enriching possibilities of future development.[164]

Storr's writing reflected the moment. The sexual freedom, political uncertainty and economic fluctuations of the 1950s and '60s created the conditions for individual and family crises of confidence, alongside nascent hopes for the future. 'This is an age', wrote the American social psychologist Kenneth Keniston in 1960, 'that inspires little enthusiasm. In the industrial West, and increasingly now in the uncommitted nations of the East, ardor is lacking; instead men talk of their growing distance from one another, from their social order, from their work and play, even from the values that in a perhaps romanticised past seem to have given their lives cohesiveness and direction.' The symptoms that Keniston regarded as indicative of post-war disaffection were recognizable to those already alarmed by the collapse of relationships and the breakdown of families: indifference and alienation were signs of the 'increasing distance between men and their former objects of love, commitment, loyalty, devotion and reverence'.[165] There were of course 'pockets of enthusiasm', as Keniston put it, amid an ocean of jaded marriages and social apathy. But accelerating cultural and technological change, excessive regulation of the workplace and allegiance to the power of the suburban nuclear family generated concerns about the demise of individuality, freedom and autonomy. Escaping the stranglehold of midlife occupational and marital conformity demanded either the sublimation of destructive impulses or – worse – the wilful reassertion of personality. In either case, rebellion proved futile. Although the pursuit of self-fulfilment after midlife was embraced as an antidote to the mundane world of institutionalized endeavour, it threatened paradoxically to destroy the dreams that it was intended to revive.

6

IN SEARCH OF A SOUL

'We see that in this phase of life – between thirty-five and forty –
a significant change in the human psyche is in preparation.'
CARL JUNG, 1933[1]

Born in 1265, Dante Alighieri was in the midst of his own midlife uncertainty when he wrote *The Divine Comedy*, a poetic masterpiece that portrayed a pilgrim's journey through hell, purgatory and paradise. The poem was in part an account of a middle-aged man's search for moral and spiritual meaning in the face of a personal crisis, but it was also a commentary on the political, economic and theological rivalries and tensions of the time. In 1301, at the age of 36, Dante had been exiled from his native Florence, a city divided by dynastic struggles for power between emperors and popes in a civilization dominated by commercialism and greed. Dante's first significant work, the *Vita nuova*, completed around 1294, was one of a number of early poems preoccupied with the figure of Beatrice, Dante's youthful courtly love who had died in 1290. While often retaining romantic allegiance to the image of Beatrice, who appeared as the narrator's saviour in *The Divine Comedy*, the poems composed by Dante while in exile adopted a more troubled, but no less expectant, tone. After witnessing the terrors and trials of hell and purgatory, the pilgrim's eventual sight of heaven allowed him to recognize the beneficence of God.[2]

At the start of the *Inferno*, the narrator – a middle-aged everyman – stands at a crossroads in his life. Hesitating at the entrance to hell, he is unsure how he has arrived at the scriptural midpoint of his life in a state of such despair.

> In the middle of the journey of our life, I came to myself in a dark wood, for the straight way was lost.
> Ah, how hard a thing it is to say what that wood was, so savage and harsh and strong that the thought of it renews my fear!

It is so bitter that death is little more so! But to treat of the good that I found there, I will tell of the other things I saw.

I cannot really say how I entered there, so full of sleep was I at the point when I abandoned the true way.[3]

The narrator's subsequent journey through the nine concentric circles of the inferno is facilitated by the poet Virgil, who acts – at Beatrice's request – as guide and mentor. With Virgil's assistance, Dante's hero witnesses the emptiness experienced by those living in limbo for their lack of faith, as well as the terrors inflicted on sinners guilty of lust, gluttony, greed, violence and treachery. Pilgrimage through the multiple layers of hell ends with hope and certitude. In the closing tercets of the *Inferno*, Virgil and his student leave the forest, ascending safely to the world that they had left behind: 'My leader and I entered on that hidden path to return to the bright world; and, without taking care for rest at all, up we climbed, he first and I second, until I saw the beautiful things the heavens carry, through a round opening. And thence we came forth to look again at the stars.'[4]

Dante's figure of the midlife seeker became a touchstone for twentieth-century writers hoping to understand and navigate the challenges and crises of middle age. In particular, it appealed to those who regarded midlife as a pivotal moment in the search for spiritual growth and identity. Elliott Jaques's interest in the psychology of midlife was triggered by reading the 'beautiful lines at the start of the *Inferno*', which melded with his 'own inner experiences of the midlife struggle with its vivid sense of the meaning of personal death'.[5] It was not only Jaques who drew private and professional inspiration from the narrator's transcendental passage through the inferno. Dante's opening lines were either cited directly – often as an epigraph – or paraphrased by psychologists, psychiatrists, self-help authors and journalists through the post-war years. In *Memories, Dreams, Reflections*, first published in German in 1961, Carl Jung recounted the early stages of his own midlife crisis at the age of 38 – and his eventual emergence 'from the darkness' five years later – in terms redolent of Dante's descent into, and journey through, the abyss.[6] Reflecting on the ordeals of adult development, academic and popular writers used Dante's depiction of a crisis of faith – as well as Jungian models of personality – as a reference point for comprehending the creative potential, as well as destructive power, of midlife transitions. According to the Jungian psychoanalyst Murray

Stein, writing in 1983, midlife was a liminal period – perhaps a rite of passage – marked by traumatic separation from earlier, outmoded identities and eventual reintegration of various facets of the self into a mature whole.[7] Ten years later, James Hollis emphasized the manner in which the 'Middle Passage', as he referred to it, not only triggered waves of despair that surfaced in infidelity and the disruption of relationships, but led to a greater sense of freedom, meaning and self-expression.[8] In such discussions, the midlife crisis was a moment of inner psychological rupture, largely independent of external circumstances.

Novelists and poets also appropriated Dante's literary style and iconography. In *The Waste Land* and *East Coker*, T. S. Eliot borrowed Dante's representation of the personal and relational crises of middle age as a means of depicting a period of life and a moment in historical time – *l'entre deux guerres* – in which there was no longer any 'secure foothold'. Eliot also sought to 'establish a relationship between the medieval inferno and modern life', the purgatorial fires of which were to be endured in order for health to be restored.[9] The allure of Dante's imagery was not restricted to writers concerned primarily with religious conventions or the spiritual significance of midlife uncertainties in the face of ageing and death. Partially stripped of its divine elements, the structure and rhythm of the 'thirteen-thousand-faceted form' of *The Divine Comedy*, as the Russian poet Osip Mandelstam put it in 1933, also inspired postmodern expressions of the midlife quest for meaning.[10] The French-Norwegian poet Caroline Bergvall collated 47 versions of the opening tercet of the *Inferno*, recording them – with a 48th variation revealed through the reading – and publishing them in 2005 as 'Via: 48 Dante Variations'.[11] Bergvall's work in turn motivated the American poet Mary Jo Bang to create an idiosyncratic translation of the *Inferno* tailored to the mentality of the twenty-first century.[12]

It was the passage of time – rather than death itself, perhaps – that figured most prominently in modern assimilations of the allegorical power of the *Inferno*. Poised 'in the balance of time', as American novelist Will Levington Comfort had put it in his autobiographical reflections at midlife, men and women dreaded the loss of subjective time, as well as the passing of biological, family, social and historical time – little of which remained and none of which could be recaptured.[13] As Carl Jung pointed out in *Modern Man in Search of a Soul*, first published in 1933, it was not 'at bottom the fear of death' that led to midlife despondency, but the fact that the middle-aged were largely unprepared for the specific psychological tasks associated with ageing through the evening or autumn of life. For those who struggled to accept that youthful dreams would remain unfulfilled, taking stock at midlife could be ruinous. No longer sustained by belief in life after death, modern populations should always look forward, Jung argued, and 'live the second half of life with as much perseverance and aim as the first'.[14] Jung's prescription for serenity in older age was incommensurable with the values – and doubts – of the Western world, in which achievements and self-worth were measured by the capacity to fill time, win the race against time or defy the tooth of time. Endeavouring to cheat time was futile, particularly in cultures where decline and death dominated narratives of ageing, and where lives were treasured in terms of whether – and when – personal aspirations for material success had been realized. While Western populations strove so earnestly to find time, they inevitably lost it – as the English novelist James Hilton intimated in 1933.[15]

Post-war studies of personality development across the adult life course were coloured not only by Western perceptions of time, but by aspects of the American dream. According to the psychologist Daniel Levinson – sometimes regarded as the architect of the male midlife crisis – one of the key tasks of early to mid-adulthood involved forming and living out 'the Dream', a self-identified vision of the future that generated 'excitement and vitality'.[16] Formulating a dream in their early twenties enabled young adults to create a basis for later life, to build a 'provisional life structure' that shaped career decisions and their choice of partners.[17] Without the creation of a new dream more appropriate to later life, the bankruptcy of youthful ambitions during middle age generated disappointment, particularly in relation to work and love. Occupations became mundane and relationships failed to provide the stability and support necessary for both partners to become autonomous, but mutually dependent, adults. The development of adult identity through articulation and attainment of the 'Dream' was not merely an individual task, but one shaped by intimate personal relationships.

> A couple can form a lasting relationship that furthers his development only if it also furthers hers. If his sense of her as the special woman stems mainly from his wishful projections and hardly at all from her own desires and efforts, sooner or later the bubble will burst and both will feel cheated. If in supporting his Dream

she loses her own, then her development will suffer and both will later pay the price. Disparities of this kind often surface in transitional periods such as the Age Thirty Transition or the Mid-Life Transition.[18]

Levinson's conception of the midlife crisis incorporated earlier insights into the trials of middle age. His work drew on studies that had already highlighted how – if unaddressed – emerging disparities between partners through the middle years could lead to bitterness, conflict and betrayal as couples attempted to settle down, raise a family and grow together into older age. At midlife, perhaps more than at any other stage in the life course, decisions had to be made about whether to recommit to existing choices or chart a different course – with a younger partner, a previously untried pastime or a new job – towards personal growth and self-satisfaction.[19] There were casualties of the narcissistic search for identity at midlife, evident most notably in the disruption of social conventions, the breakdown of families and the alienation of partners and children. The collapse of personal dreams and their replacement with novel aspirations for the future were products of individual choice. But, like the original dream, fresh starts and second chances at midlife were shaped by the epigenetic nature of the life course, as American developmental psychologist Erik Erikson referred to it in 1950 – that is, by interactions between psychological attributes, historical circumstances and cultural context.[20]

IN HIS MID-THIRTIES, Carl Jung began to distance himself from the work of Sigmund Freud, a decision that contributed to Jung's midlife crisis, led to the loss of friends and acquaintances, and shaped the remainder of his career. Only his family sustained him.[21] In part, Jung's rejection of Freudianism was based on his conviction that Freud had over-emphasized child and adolescent development at the expense of understanding the psychological tasks inherent in creating and sustaining identity across the second half of life. Jung was right to point to the absence of contemporary interest in the problems of adjusting to adulthood. While care of children and the elderly flourished during the early decades of the twentieth century, little attention was paid to the health of those between the ages of twenty and sixty, unless it impacted either on reproductive potential and aptitude for child-rearing or on the capacity of the middle-aged to contribute to the economy in the ways encouraged by Walter Pitkin in the 1930s.[22] In *The Integration of the Personality*, published in English in 1940, Jung emphasized other fault lines in studies of personality across the life course. Contemporary models of psychological development tended to disregard the connections – and indeed the cracks that appeared – between conscious and unconscious components of the self or to recognize the importance of effective adaptation to external conditions as a means of healing fractured identities.[23]

One of the most influential theories of development across the life cycle – including discussion of the crises of middle and later life – was elaborated by Erik Erikson, a psychologist renowned for his work on the evolution of identity in childhood and youth. In *Childhood and Society*, first published in 1950 as a textbook for doctors, psychologists and social workers, Erikson reflected on whether psychological disturbances could be attributed primarily to individuals or to the societies in which they lived. For Erikson, whose work was strongly influenced by Margaret Mead, the answer was clear. Health and illness, as well as anxieties about loneliness and death, were products of interpersonal relations and socio-cultural conditions as much as they were manifestations of inner psychological processes or biological pathways.[24] Erikson regarded post-war experiences of the life course and contemporary articulations of the challenges of middle age – and indeed other life stages – as historically and culturally specific. Crises did not emerge in a vacuum. They were the product of interactions between individuals and their environment, both in the past and the present.

Drawing on his work as a child analyst in Vienna and subsequently at various American clinical and research institutes, Erikson divided the human life cycle into eight stages, each marked by a distinctive psychosocial crisis. The first five stages related to the evolution of identity during infancy, childhood and adolescence. Across early life, conflicts emerged sequentially between trust and mistrust; autonomy, shame and doubt; initiative and guilt; industry and inferiority; and identity integration and role confusion in relation to work and love. The linguistic and conceptual framework within which Erikson sketched out the emergence of psychological maturity reflected the social conventions that constituted the American identity. Healthy adjustment to the emotional dilemmas of childhood and adolescence was measured in terms of the acquisition of respect for law and order, commitment to industry and enterprise, and willingness to temper ideological extremism – whether communist or capitalist – through self-restraint and the protection of autonomy and equality. As Erikson pointed out, these were the principles and qualities admired and marketed by architects of the American dream.[25] Psychological maturity, secure relationships and financial independence were congruent with – indeed, necessary for – the political and economic stability of the corporate world. Understanding the factors that shaped the development of mature personalities would help to address the apparent collapse of communities and the supposed crescendo of 'identity problems in the youth of the sixties', as Erikson put it.[26]

Identity formation persisted well beyond adolescence, extending deep into the second half of life, and continued to be marked by interactions between psychodynamic, economic and social processes. Young adults needed to decide whether to remain isolated and self-absorbed or to commit themselves to intimate 'affiliations and partnerships' such as marriage, which carried the likelihood of 'significant sacrifices and compromises' linked to the loss of self-identity.[27] While intimacy might only be achieved at a cost, Erikson regarded it – as did Freud – as a prerequisite for mature love and work. Intimacy was a social rather than an individual task, one that was shaped by 'a culture's style of sexual selection, cooperation, and competition'.[28] The period of middle age that followed young adulthood was characterized by conflicts between generativity and stagnation. For Erikson, generativity involved – but was not limited to – producing and guiding the next generation. Reflecting contemporary concerns about crises in marriage and family life, Erikson believed that failure to achieve psychosexual and psychosocial productivity resulted in personal impoverishment, pseudo-intimacy and excessive self-concern. Beyond middle age, successful navigation of the conflicts and crises of adulthood was rewarded by a sense of 'ego integrity', by acceptance of the human life cycle as finite and accidental but nevertheless meaningful. 'In such final consolidation,' wrote Erikson, 'death loses its sting.'[29] Inadequate ego integration in later life, however, was accompanied by fear of death and a feeling of despair that 'time is now short, too short for the attempt to start another life and to try out alternate roads to integrity'.[30]

Erikson set out his model of the life course in the form of a provisional 'epigenetic chart', a representation of ageing that recognized the

	1	2	3	4	5	6	7	8
VIII Maturity								Ego integrity vs despair
VII Adulthood							Generativity vs stagnation	
VI Young adulthood						Intimacy vs isolation		
V Puberty and adolescence					Identity vs role confusion			
IV Latency				Industry vs inferiority				
III Locomotor-genital			Initiative vs guilt					
II Muscular-anal		Autonomy vs shame, doubt						
I Oral sensory	Basic trust vs mistrust							

'An epigenetic chart', Erik H. Erikson, *Childhood and Society* [1950] (1963).

continual interplay between personality, social context and cultural norms. Although presented as a matrix of discrete compartments, the chart was not intended to be prescriptive; nor was it meant to indicate that crises were inevitable. Rather, it signified only that development proceeded by 'critical steps – "critical" being a characteristic of turning points, of moments of decision between progress and retrogression, integration and retardation.'[31] Erikson acknowledged that there would always be 'variations in tempo and intensity' according to individual and cultural differences.[32] The timing and manifestations of crises varied according to gender, structuring midlife trajectories differently for men and women.[33] Erikson also admitted that much remained unknown. Empty boxes in the chart were intended to provoke reflection on the precursors and consequences – or 'basic virtues' – of transformations in personality.[34] Some years later, partly in response to the continued lack of psychoanalytical interest in adult development, Erikson provided a more detailed epigenetic chart, as well as a worksheet that set out links between identity crises, personal relations, social order, psychosocial modalities and psychosexual stages.[35]

Erikson's use of the term 'epigenetics' to capture the complexity of psychological adaptation and personal development was not new. In 1942 the British biologist Conrad Waddington, whose work on evolutionary ethics was known to Erikson, had introduced the concept of epigenetics to convey how genes interacted with environments to produce observable physical and behavioural attributes.[36] Nor was Erikson the first to emphasize the complex interrelations between human identity, life events and psychological well-being. In the interwar period, the Swiss-born psychiatrist Adolf Meyer had adopted the 'life-chart' as a means of visualizing links between biological development, behavioural patterns, personal experiences and mental health.[37] Similarly, in the 1930s, the American physician George Draper had highlighted the manner in which illness resulted from collisions between environmental pressures and personality. In *Disease and the Man*, Draper suggested that health and sickness were determined by extrinsic stressors, such as overwork and over-worry, operating in conjunction with components of a patient's personality.[38] Together, these external and internal factors shaped, and were shaped by, what Draper referred to as 'the circus' of a person's life – an unfolding drama that anticipated the stage and crisis model of human development conceived by Erikson and others after the war.

Concerns about the harmful impacts of social disintegration and cultural change accelerated after the Second World War, promoting approaches to medicine that emphasized links between the health of populations and the environmental conditions in which they lived. Proponents of psychosomatic medicine regarded the increased prevalence of chronic diseases – as well as falling birth rates and rising levels of criminality and absenteeism – as the product of a 'sick society', as the Scottish physician James Halliday referred to it in 1948.[39] According to Halliday, the deprivation, frustration and strain triggered by economic competition, military conflict and social unrest led to peptic ulcers, rheumatism and heart disease.[40] But it was in the emergent field of stress research that links between environmental pressures, personality and early life experiences became most prominent. Across the 1950s and '60s, the work of Hans Selye and other prominent stress researchers indicated how the ability to adapt to stressful life events, such as bereavement, marriage, divorce, unemployment and retirement, was determined by innate biological and psychological factors operating in tandem with learned behaviour and socio-economic conditions. Stress researchers also revealed the neuroendocrine mechanisms through

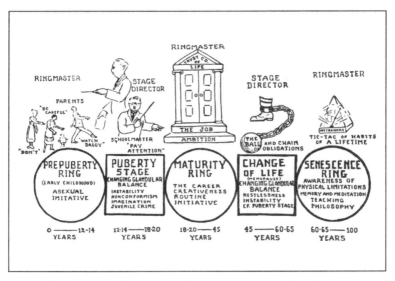

George Draper, 'The Circus of Life: Three Rings and Two Stages',
in Draper, *Human Constitution* (1928).

which emotions could destabilize – and eventually restore – physiological and psychological equilibrium, particularly during the liminal
periods of adolescence and the change of life.[41]

Although he shared the interests of stress researchers in the processes of adaptation to emerging challenges across the life course,
Erikson took his lead not from studies of stress, but from Freudian
understandings of child development and anthropological accounts
of the cultural determinants of health. As a result, his work focused
neither on unforeseeable major life events nor on the mundane stresses
and strains of everyday living that were linked to the 'social structure of
the American way of life', as psychiatrists Thomas Holmes and Richard
Rahe put it in 1967.[42] Instead, Erikson's framework for understanding
psychological health highlighted the more predictable pattern of crises
and transitions across the life course. Each of Erikson's stages of psychosocial development carried the potential for crisis, particularly during
periods of rapid cultural, scientific and political change. Uncertainties
and anxieties generated by industrialization, global communication,
centralization and mechanization – that is, by the technological and
bureaucratic forces of the consumer-led corporate world – rendered it
more difficult to attain and maintain durable adult identities. Failure to
reach psychological maturity in childhood and adolescence surfaced in
adult crises, appearing in the form of neuroses and destructive defence

mechanisms that threatened the stability of personal and social relations.[43] Successful resolution of conflicts at the appropriate stage in the
life course, however, provided the foundations for psychological growth
and a secure identity.

Erikson subsequently extended his account of adult development
in a variety of directions, most notably in relation to fidelity, which he
regarded as the 'cornerstone of identity' in both men and women.[44]
Fidelity was not a moral trait, he argued, but a human characteristic
acquired in adolescence as the result of interactions between individual
and social factors. Neither fidelity nor diversity – its polar opposite –
were restricted to personal relations, but also applied to attitudes to work
and play. The youthful search for variety and occupation could result
in being 'always on the go' or 'tearing after something' in an attempt to
identify more stimulating and rewarding forms of activity, recreation
or political involvement.[45] During adolescence, the construction of a
stable ego identity required balancing fidelity with diversity. 'Here again
diversity and fidelity are polarized,' Erikson wrote in 1962, 'they make
each other significant and keep each other alive. Fidelity without a sense
of diversity can become an obsession and a bore; diversity without a
sense of fidelity, an empty relativism.'[46]

While friction between fidelity and diversity peaked during youth,
it often re-emerged in 'the crises of later years', according to Erikson,
moulding midlife susceptibility to seduction and triggering the pursuit
of sexual novelty.[47] Seen within this frame, the conflicts of adolescence
constituted a rehearsal for the midlife crisis, and the midlife crisis
emerged as a revised edition of adolescence. Both were characterized by
idealistic rejection of conformity, a tool of social control that was integral to the success of industrial and increasingly individualist Western
democracies.[48] By the 1960s, technology was superseding ideology as
the driver of identity, generating – and reflecting – tensions between
'the American dream and the Marxist revolution', as Erikson put it.[49]
What mattered in this new competitive landscape, he argued, was 'what
man, on ethical grounds and without moralistic self-destruction, must
decide *not* to do, even though he could make it work – for a while'.[50] In
this critique of Western hedonism, Erikson had identified the ways in
which the life histories of individuals, couples and generations after the
war intersected with deeper historical processes to create the conditions
for crisis – and how the crises of middle age were as much the product
of power as they were of personality.

'DIAGRAMS', ERIKSON CLAIMED in 1959, 'have a quiet coerciveness all their own.'[51] Erikson's visualization of the stages and crises of life certainly proved persuasive, providing the primary point of reference for scholarly and popular accounts of the identity crises of adolescence and adulthood. Along with the work of Carl Jung and Elliott Jaques, Erikson's theory of psychological development across the life course offered a provisional framework for post-war discussions of adult growth and midlife transitions on both sides of the Atlantic.[52] Erikson's subsequent studies across the 1960s and '70s drew together insights from scholars working in disparate disciplines – including sociology, history, anthropology and psychiatry – to consider how experiences of ageing and adulthood were shaped by the changing form and functions of the family.[53] By bringing his own perceptions of the life cycle into conversation with those of psychologists and psychiatrists writing on family structures and marital tensions, Erikson played a pivotal role in promoting historically sensitive studies of the emotional crises and social challenges of middle age.

Interest in the relationship between experiences of adulthood and American culture deepened across the post-war years. According to sociologist Janet Zollinger Giele, revolutionary changes in sex roles, the availability of contraception, demographic shifts and alterations in work and family life in Western societies had created the conditions for new patterns of adult identity formation. Although she acknowledged the merits of stage-crisis models of adult development, Giele placed greater emphasis on continuities, rather than discontinuities, in identity across time. In line with Erikson's concept of the 'epigenetic unfolding of personality', Giele argued that the American life course should no longer be envisaged as a series of discrete age-dependent stages, but as a process of linkage and crossover – between stages, individuals, partners and generations – in which transitions and crises were determined by gender, class and culture.[54] In this context, one concern of contemporary scholars was that theories of adulthood that highlighted distinct life stages were too often built on observations of a 'privileged upper-middle-class and professional elite', as Giele put it.[55] Some empirical studies suggested that lower-middle-class or blue-collar workers, who aged more rapidly and arguably carried lower expectations of occupational and material success, did not experience clearly differentiated stages or crises in the same way.[56] As a search for meaning in the modern world, the midlife crisis – like other adult transitions – was regulated by socio-economic conditions and cultural norms.

Post-war analyses of adult growth assumed that psychological maturity was expressed ideally not through narcissism, but always 'within a context of relatedness' – that is, through loyalty to family, community or church.[57] Contemporary novelists painted a bleaker picture of American masculinity in particular. American culture idealized the autonomous man, one for whom marriage constituted a trap and work a loss of freedom. 'The emerging love ethic' of the post-war years, wrote cultural sociologist Ann Swidler in 1980, had reemphasized 'the rebellious, free, individualistic side of the love myth', in which fidelity, intimacy and care were no longer 'heroic, meaningful achievements'.[58] The result was the emergence of tensions between choice and commitment, rebellion and attachment, self-realization and self-sacrifice, and sexual expression and restraint. Renegotiation of the balance between these possibilities was transforming adulthood and the values attached to marriage, work and family. At the same time, it generated new ambiguities. While people were expected to marry for love, the language of love was also used to justify rebellion against normative notions of companionate marriage and the nuclear family – rebellion that was manifest in adultery or the rejection of dreary occupations.[59] According to Swidler, cinematic and literary studies of marital dynamics and family life, including Ingmar Bergman's *Scenes from a Marriage* (1973) and Joseph Heller's *Something Happened* (1974), validated adulthood as 'a period of continuing crisis, challenge, and change'. Since the 1960s, permanence and commitment had become dangerous, attachment a form of failure, and men's egotistical escape from the 'entangling demands' of women and society – or from 'congealed domesticity' – an act of self-affirmation.[60] But, echoing Edmund Bergler's study of the restless middle-aged man, Swidler was in no doubt that searching for self-fulfilment by switching partners or jobs was futile: 'There is nowhere for rebellion to go', she wrote, 'without again becoming binding attachment.'[61]

The work of Daniel Levinson highlights the manner in which post-war psychologists adopted and adapted Erikson's approach to the development of personality and identity during middle age. In a series of publications through the 1970s, Levinson and his colleagues at the Research Unit for Social Psychology and Psychiatry at Yale University set out an amended version of Erikson's life stages and psychosocial crises, focusing exclusively on men. Male adult development, they argued, proceeded through a number of discrete periods, each characterized by a particular challenge. 'Getting into the adult world' between the early and late twenties involved separating from the family of origin and setting up independently in a new home. A period of 'settling down', beginning in the early thirties, was marked by greater investment in work and family and the pursuit of stability, security and control. In their mid- to late thirties, men began to feel constrained by the expectations of others, struggled to achieve affirmation at home or work and experienced isolation and stagnation as they strove to become their 'own man'. In their late thirties and early forties, whether or not they had realized their dreams, men experienced a midlife transition, a turning point in which fear of bodily decline and death, along with a loss of masculinity, encouraged them to seek new relationships in an attempt to reinvigorate feelings of self-worth and attain a renewed sense of stability.[62]

In subsequent studies, Levinson interviewed men in the 'mid-life decade' – that is, between the ages of 35 and 45 – to understand transitional moments in the adult life course. Each stage of life, Levinson argued, was separated from the next by a specific transition: an early adult transitional phase between seventeen and twenty-two; an age thirty transition; a midlife turning point around the age of forty; and a late adult transition between sixty and sixty-five. Drawing on the work of Jung, Erikson and Jaques, Levinson suggested that for approximately 80 per cent of men the midlife transition constituted 'a time of moderate or severe crisis'. In middle age, men questioned almost every aspect of their lives, leading to conflicts with their wives, children, parents, colleagues and employers, as well as rejection of 'the implicit web of social conformity' that appeared to obstruct self-development and self-fulfilment.[63] Marriages in particular were often reappraised, as a 'fog of illusion' lifted to reveal unrecognized or suppressed difficulties in the relationship.

> Suddenly he feels free for the first time to see his wife as a person and to understand the nature of their relationship. New realizations – each with its own admixture of real insight, distortion, and self-justification – assail him: there is no excitement between them; he cannot share his main interests and concerns with her; she regards him more as one of the children than as a friend and lover; she is

disappointed over his failure to accomplish their early goals; she is resentful over his successes that have involved him in a world she cannot enjoy or share.[64]

As they passed through midlife, men needed to make decisions, primarily about whether to improve their marriage or enter a new relationship. But if either pathway was to be effective, Levinson warned, men needed to accept responsibility for their own contributions to marital tensions and family breakdowns, rather than blame their wives and children. Otherwise, they risked remaining in stagnant marriages that were 'destructive to both partners'. Or they embarked on new marriages that simply repeated the 'old hurtful themes with new variations'.[65] Like Bergler, Levinson intimated that the revolt of middle-age men was driven as much by psychological immaturity and self-deceit as it was by the constraints imposed by marriage, work and family.

Levinson's initial focus on men at midlife was not unusual. In most post-war scholarly studies – as well as novels – it was the rebellion of the middle-aged man that constituted the archetypal identity crisis. Indeed, the most extensive post-war examinations of adult development were the longitudinal Grant Study of male Harvard college students and the parallel investigation of disadvantaged men living in inner-city neighbourhoods in Boston, both of which were coordinated by American psychiatrist George Vaillant.[66] Preoccupations with men – and indeed with metaphors of crisis and decline – were increasingly challenged by feminist authors, who sought to retrieve the lost identity and agency of middle-aged women. During the 1950s, '60s and early '70s, Betty Friedan, Hannah Gavron, Germaine Greer, Susan Sontag and others exposed the double standards of sex and ageing that shaped attitudes to men's and women's behaviour at midlife. But it was arguably the American journalist Gail Sheehy who led the feminist assault on obsessions with the midlife crisis as a male prerogative. Sheehy's interest in adult transitions was triggered by an incident in her mid-thirties that brutally exposed her to 'the arithmetic of life' – a stark reminder of her own mortality as well as that of others.[67] In the wake of that experience, she began to challenge men's ownership of the midlife crisis and to focus attention on women's midlife transitions. In contrast to many other studies, Sheehy emphasized the ways in which critical turning points in the life cycle were not only foreseeable but necessary, enabling individual growth even in the face of traumatic life transitions.

Sheehy's framework for understanding and coping with the 'predictable crises of adult life' – set out in her bestselling book *Passages* in 1976 – was indebted to the work of Margaret Mead, Erik Erikson, Daniel Levinson and others. It also drew on interviews with 115 educated middle-class Americans between the ages of eighteen and fifty-five. According to Sheehy, adulthood could be divided into recognizable stages, each characterized by its own challenges. After the trials of adolescence, men and women entered the 'trying twenties', when they struggled to 'shape a Dream' or to balance the need for security and intimacy with the 'urge to explore and experiment'.[68] By thirty, Sheehy's interviewees felt that their lives had become constrained as the pressures of work and family generated discontent between partners.[69] Although the early thirties were relatively stable, satisfaction with marriage declined as energies were focused on career progression and raising young children. The result was that in their mid-thirties women and men arrived at a crossroads, the halfway point – or meridian – in their lives when they became aware of the loss of youthful vitality, the failure of their dreams, and a sense of spiritual emptiness. The 'deadline decade' that followed was marked by urgent reappraisal of aspirations and achievements. 'Each of us stumbles upon the major issue of midlife', Sheehy wrote, 'somewhere in the decade between 35 and 45'.[70] Recognizing the limits of time, women became more assertive as they began to look for a new future once their last child had started school, a future that might entail infidelity and divorce or re-entering the workforce. Whether successful or not, men started to feel 'stale, restless, burdened, and unappreciated', envious of their wives' energy and freedom, stifled by managerial responsibilities, eager to pursue novel – often destructive – forms of self-gratification.[71]

Although her analysis charted familiar territory, Sheehy anticipated that her attempt to systematize adult transitions, to identify commonalities between men and women, and to focus on inner growth rather than external recognition across the life course would provoke dissent.[72] But the controversy caused by *Passages* was striking. In 1975, shortly before the book was published, American psychiatrist Roger Gould, whose expertise Sheehy had drawn on during her research, accused Sheehy of plagiarizing his work without giving him sufficient credit and complained that she had not honoured an agreement to co-author the book and share any royalties. Sheehy subsequently amended the manuscript, removing many of the references to Gould, and argued that her ideas had been shaped not by Gould's work but by Erikson's earlier theory of life stages. Largely because she could not afford legal representation, Sheehy's accountant recommended offering Gould 10 per cent of all royalties, which he accepted.[73] Gould was not the only scholar to challenge Sheehy. Academic reviews of *Passages* were sometimes scathing. In 1977 American sociologist Michael Kimmel criticized the book on a number of grounds: it oversimplified adult development; it assumed too readily that crisis was necessary for growth; and it disregarded evidence that many people did not experience crises during middle age. More critically, Kimmel argued that Sheehy had failed to consider the 'pain and frustration of adult life in the United States in structural terms' – that is, in terms of the social forces that exerted stress on individuals, couples and families. 'What the reader gains from *Passages*', he wrote,

> is not, therefore, an analysis of the individual attempting to understand the structural underpinnings of alienation. Rather we are presented with a solipsistic vision of individual dynamics. Rather than an understanding of our adult passages, Sheehy has delivered a palliative to the upper middle class; a well-written assurance that we are not alone in our pain and fear. That misery seems still to require the company of a book which tells us that basically we're all OK.[74]

Although some reviewers acknowledged the relevance and popularity of Sheehy's work, they were often no less caustic than Kimmel. Sheehy was criticized for over-generalizing, resorting to arbitrary and tasteless catchphrases, skirting over the destruction wrought by middle-aged men and women – on family life, for example – as they selfishly pursued their own renewal, and failing to recognize that growth was not an option for many middle-aged men and women living more exigent lives than Sheehy's 'rather privileged subjects'.[75] She had 'done about as much', wrote one reviewer contemptuously, 'as a good journalist can do'.[76]

Susanne Schmidt has rightly pointed out that Sheehy was treated harshly by leading male academics, who used their professional status to dismiss what they considered to be a superficial and sensationalist approach to adult life crises.[77] Yet it is also clear that Sheehy's language, conceptual framework and arguments were often derivative and that she appropriated or paraphrased the words and ideas of other writers, frequently without citation. Her description of the conflict between 'aliveness' and 'stagnation' during the deadline decade mirrored Erikson's emphasis on the need to balance the forces of stagnation and generativity during adulthood. References to first shaping and later 'de-illusioning the Dream' repeated phrases used by Levinson throughout the 1970s. Sheehy's allusion to midlife as an 'apostrophe in time' echoed Bernice Neugarten's description of transitional points in the life course as 'punctuation marks'. And her characterization of midlife despair blended the opening lines of Dante's *Inferno* with Elliott Jaques's formulation of the contradictions inherent in reaching the prime of life.[78] Sheehy's tendency to borrow or imitate was sometimes less overt, but no less significant. In an illustrative case history, she referred to a traditional family of 'dreamers of the American dream' as the Babcocks – emulating Sinclair Lewis's fictional account of the Babbitt family and subsequent use of the term Babbitry to convey the materialistic pretensions of middle-class, middle-aged Americans.[79]

In spite of reservations at the time about her style and originality, Sheehy's work was nevertheless influential. The term 'passages' – which she later used also to capture experiences of menopause (the 'silent passage'), to understand the life course of men, and to frame her autobiography – introduced a less loaded and more positive description of midlife change. Rather than heralding inevitable crisis and decline, midlife disruption offered opportunities for psychological and spiritual growth.[80] Her incorporation of the midlife experiences of women helped to shift academic, literary and public attention away from clichéd discussions of middle-aged men crumbling under intimations of their own mortality. Men had too often been 'the salted peanuts of the social sciences', Sheehy wrote in a 1978 review of Phyllis Chesler's book *About Men*.[81] By including women as subjects for analysis, *Passages* identified commonalities between the experiences of men and women at a time when most sociological and psychological studies of identity formation, stress and adaptation were concerned almost exclusively with masculine norms.[82] It also highlighted, however, the ways in which men and women matured at different rates, leading to what Sheehy referred to as the 'sexual diamond' – an image that was intended to capture the manner in which male and female sexual life cycles diverged at midlife. As women's sexuality peaked, their husbands' energy began to fade, a situation that encouraged both partners – not just men – to look for a 'change-of-life affair'. In spite of Kimmel's criticism that she had neglected structural factors in favour of inner psychological changes, Sheehy was aware that the emergence of gaps between spouses was contingent on social conditions. 'Growing in tandem is virtually impossible in a patriarchal society, as ours has been,' she wrote.

> Only one-half of the couple has the use of that remarkable support system known as a wife. Added to this basic determinant of tempo is the rate of social change. Even in a relatively stagnant society, the odds are minimal that any couple can enjoy matched development. Subscribing to that view in his book *Future Shock*, Alvin Toffler goes on to point out that the odds take a nose dive when the rate of social change accelerates, as is happening in America.[83]

Originally conceived as a study of 'midlife as a crisis time for couples', *Passages* evolved into a wider analysis of adulthood.[84] But Sheehy's sensitivity to the problems faced by middle-aged couples was evident elsewhere in her writing. In *Lovesounds*, a novel published in 1970, Sheehy traced the disintegration of the marriage of a couple in their early thirties. As the 'dailiness of domesticity' drained intimacy, the husband's infidelity shattered trust. Read through the alternating voices of Gwyn and Michael, *Lovesounds* reveals how marital betrayal and separation were legitimated by political values and the double standard of ageing and sexuality. Husbands and wives were being pulled apart – emotionally and economically – by male anxieties about the loss of youthful dreams, by the denigration of 'wifeliness', and by men's sense of entitlement to self-gratification during middle age and beyond. Unrestrained pursuit of the American dream in the 'age of self' left women isolated, leading dull lives, lost in 'unstructured time', fearful of getting older while their dresses got bigger. But the novel ends in hope for Gwyn, as she revives her creativity, rediscovers her self-esteem and reaffirms her identity. 'I am moving back into myself,' she reflects as she starts a new life with her young daughter in San Francisco. 'I think I will like it here now.'[85]

Sheehy's emphasis on midlife opportunities for women attracted the attention of daily newspapers and magazines such as *Chatelaine*, and *Passages* remained on the *New York Times* bestseller list for three years.[86] The popularity of Sheehy's work can be traced partly to the rise of feminism and growing interest in the health of middle-aged women, particularly in relation to menopause. But her argument also resonated with contemporary divorce-law reform and the growth of self-help literature for women contemplating or facing marital separation.[87] Although it failed to dislodge the language of crisis from discussions of midlife, *Passages* shaped the attitudes of a generation anxious to empower middle-aged women – and, to a lesser extent, men. Interest in the midlife crisis blossomed after the publication of Sheehy's book – as well as the work of Vaillant, Gould and Levinson shortly afterwards.[88] More specifically, Sheehy motivated women who were already inspired by feminist critiques of wifehood and domesticity to pursue 'the midlife search for self' that American sociologist and therapist Lillian Rubin referred to in 1979.[89] Drawing on her own crisis at the age of 38, as well as on 160 interviews with women aged between 35 and 54, Rubin exposed the ways in which attitudes to marriage and motherhood were changing in response not only to biological and demographic factors, but to shifting customs and expectations. In the process, she challenged the 'long burden of guilt' carried by working and creative mothers, dispelled myths about sexual decline and the empty nest, and encouraged women to achieve their own dreams within the years left to live. It was time 'finally, for me', wrote one 48-year-old housewife interviewed by Rubin. 'Time to find out who I am and what I want. Time to live for me instead of them. All my life I've been doing for others. Now, before it's too late, it's time for me.'[90]

Other writers offered inspirational models for midlife women. Academic studies explored definitions of midlife, representations of midlife women in fiction and techniques for improving well-being during and beyond middle age. They also addressed the dilemmas faced by wives and mothers striving for careers, returning to work or looking to achieve a healthier work-family balance.[91] At the heart of this literature lay a conviction that middle-aged women could – and should – release themselves from the shackles of social expectations of wifehood and motherhood. Psychologists, doctors and self-help authors inspired women in their forties and fifties to leave stifling marriages, embrace new forms of intimacy, and identify fresh occupational and creative challenges to enrich their lives – that is, to make the most of their time before death. Although they encouraged middle-aged women to defy conventional restrictions on personal relationships and occupational opportunities, feminist novelists acknowledged that women faced obstacles to freedom and risked succumbing to exhaustion and resignation. While Simone de Beauvoir depicted a woman destroyed by her husband's infidelity, novels by Marilyn French and Doris Lessing provided post-war women with alternative, but often still bleak, trajectories through the labyrinth of midlife.[92]

Appropriation of the midlife crisis by – and for – women was short-lived. Prominent male psychologists used their publications to launch an anti-feminist critique of Gail Sheehy's work.[93] Often adopting a confessional tone, male authors reinforced earlier formulations of the midlife crisis as a justifiable masculine rejection of the boredom and frustrations of corporate and family life, blaming women – as Kenneth Hutchin and others had done in the 1960s – for men's declining potency, low self-esteem and infidelity.[94] Through the late 1970s and '80s, popular magazines reverted to analysing and glamorizing the male midlife crisis, publishing stories of middle-aged men yearning to be young, breaking free from socially prescribed roles and responsibilities at home and work, and chasing their own fulfilment without thought for the devastation inflicted on partners and families.[95] Always set within a heteronormative marital framework, advice literature encouraged women to understand and cope better with their husbands' crises, rather than their own.[96] When Daniel Levinson eventually turned his attention to the 'seasons of a woman's life' in 1996, the timings and details of women's dreams, achievements and crises were measured against patterns of adult male development.[97] By then, the needs of women at midlife had been side-lined once more by men's self-obsessed search for personal meaning, inner contentment and emotional fulfilment.

SURVIVING THE CRISES of middle age and sustaining spiritual growth and identity through later life were not straightforward tasks. According to Daniel Levinson, men's midlife crises emerged from an awareness that the more creative aspects of their personality had become muted in the process of establishing a career and supporting a nuclear family. 'In the Mid-life Transition', he wrote, 'these neglected parts of the self urgently seek expression.'[98] Middle-aged men became increasingly disgruntled: they grieved wasted opportunities, were outraged by the duplicity of others, regretted the ways in which they had betrayed the trust of their partners and families, and mourned the loss of identity. 'A man hears the voice of an identity prematurely rejected,' wrote Levinson in 1978, 'of a love lost or not pursued; of a valued interest or relationship given up in acquiescence to parental or other authority;

of an internal figure who wants to be an athlete or nomad or artist, to marry for love or remain a bachelor, to get rich or enter the clergy or live a sensual carefree life – possibilities set aside earlier to become what he is now.'[99]

The roots of post-war interest in nurturing self-identity across the second half of life lay in Jung's emphasis on the significance of 'individuation', a psychological, but also quasi-religious, process that involved making a 'human being an "individual" – a unique indivisible unity or "whole man"'.[100] While Jung focused primarily on the individual psyche, he was aware of the collective and relational dimensions of achieving psychological maturity, particularly in the context of marriage and the crises faced by those in the middle decades of life. Relationships at this stage of life were challenged by the fact that partners differed temporally in their realization of the extent to which 'surprise and discovery' had become 'dulled by custom', passion replaced by duty. Adapting to contrasting rhythms of 'spiritual development', as Jung referred to it, often led to marital, as well as personal, crises during middle age.[101] Jung was conscious that the capacity for ego-integration in later life was shaped by historical, political and social conditions. In a revised edition of *Modern Man in Search of a Soul*, published in 1945, he argued that personal attempts to address spiritual impoverishment and psychological disintegration were threatened by the catastrophe of the Second World War, the loss of metaphysical certainty, the rapid tempo of American life and the potential for scientific and material progress to create new forms of mass destruction. The post-war search for inner psychological and spiritual harmony was driven by a craving for security that was no longer satisfied by the external world.[102]

Jung stressed the importance of balanced self-reflection in order to survive a midlife crisis. He also emphasized the value of creativity to individuals and the societies in which they lived.[103] Erikson too used the 'creative confusion' of male artists and writers – such as George Bernard Shaw and William James – to reveal key features of adult identity crises and to highlight the role of creativity in preventing 'a pervading sense of stagnation and interpersonal impoverishment' during middle age.[104] It was his interest in the artistic creativeness of prominent male poets, painters and composers that shaped Elliott Jaques's account of the midlife crisis in 1965. For Jaques, midlife constituted a potential tipping point in the life course, a pivotal moment when artistic expression was liable to deepen, decline or shift in style or focus. Since midlife crises were manifest in new forms of creative expression, he argued, personal anxieties about decline and death could conversely be addressed in a therapeutic setting by working creatively through infantile experiences of love and loss. Carefully sculpted creativity facilitated the sublimation of destructive impulses and made it possible to accept the imperfections and finiteness of life. Just as Jaques's formulation of the midlife crisis had been inspired by Dante's descent into hell, so too his resolution of the crisis invoked Dante's closing words of *Paradiso*, the third and final book of *The Divine Comedy*: 'But now my desire and will, like the wheel that spins with even motion, were revolved by the Love that moves the sun and other stars.' It was the attainment of this spirit of cosmic creativity and serenity, Jaques believed, that allowed men and women to overcome the crises of midlife and become resigned to, but not defeated by, death.[105]

Perhaps the archetypal artistic crisis at midlife was that of the French painter Paul Gauguin, who in his mid-thirties left his wife and children, gave up his job as a stockbroker and began to pursue a career as a painter.[106] But it was not only men who experienced dramatic eruptions or disruptions of creativity at midlife. The early work of Canadian artist Helen Lucas in the 1960s and '70s was bleak. In her own words, her paintings consisted of religious icons with 'the colors stripped away'; 'life-size single nudes in black paint, again with eyes closed, which I called Sleep'; and 'very black, very contained and stiff' charcoal drawings – known as 'The Diary Series' – recording Lucas's 'daily turmoil and growth'. From the late 1970s, when she was in her forties, Lucas's work became more affirmative and gradually more colourful: figures of women with 'their life and sexuality confirmed'; or a crucifix 'overrun by luscious red flowers'. The transition in Lucas's creativity was symbolic of a deeper spiritual victory. 'Life has won over death', she insisted as her paintings of large flowers began to burst with colour, 'life has won over wasted life'.[107] Lucas's art was also political, speaking to feminist aspirations to ensure the survival, liberation and independence of women. 'Looking back over the past twenty-four years,' she wrote in 1982, 'black and white reflected the restrictive environment; color glories in its freedom. The new paintings say "Here I am, a woman, with a new-found sense of joy, confidence, sexuality and love." Each painting now is a joyous affirmation of these new truths.'[108]

As well as representing a spiritual and political journey, the transition from sadness to joy evident in Lucas's work around midlife reflected her changing circumstances. 'The Diary Series' narrated the breakdown of her marriage and recovery from divorce. 'My life was so connected to these drawings', she wrote, 'that what was happening to me personally showed up on paper.'[109] The explosion of colour in her work from the early 1980s coincided with meeting a new partner, who made her 'happy to be healthy and in love again', as she put it in a documentary about her life and work directed by Donna Davey in 1996.[110] But artistic expression was not available to everyone. Without creative options, many middle-aged men and women simply consigned themselves to 'the isolation of an unloving marriage', according to the psychotherapists Jane Pearce and Saul Newton, writing in 1963.[111] Women were especially vulnerable at midlife and beyond. Having given up careers to support their husbands and children, women's opportunities for creativity and growth were limited by social prejudices that prevented them from establishing new relationships after divorce or from pursuing certain occupations. Similarly, concerns about creativity did not figure so clearly in the midlife crises of blue-collar workers. According to the American psychiatrist Robert Butler, no one should be 'frozen into rigid roles that limit one's self-development and self-expression', but anxieties about creativity and integrity were the privilege of middle-class intellectuals.[112]

The recovery of creativity – and spirituality – lost during early adulthood constituted a key feature of attempts to reconcile middle-aged men and women struggling with individual disappointments and marital tensions. In 1962 the marriage guidance counsellor J. H. Wallis suggested that infidelity resulted from the eruption of the 'sudden, disruptive, compelling power of the neglected side of our nature'.[113] Couples who had focused for fifteen or twenty years on the practical business of living together and raising a family had lost the poetic or spiritual element of their relationship, leaving both partners bitter and abandoned. As April Wheeler realized too late in *Revolutionary Road* (1961), the belief that couples should resign from real life and settle down once they had a family was a delusion, 'the great sentimental lie of the suburbs'.[114] But the consequences of the suburban fallacy were real. The empty spaces that appeared once the marital magic had faded were loaded with midlife affairs. In response, counselling focused on enabling partners to appreciate, rather than ignore, the ways in which they had suppressed the magical or spiritual elements of their lives. Searching externally for substitutes to replace lost love, lost time and lost youth would lead eventually to indifference and the death of intimacy. It was more important to seek self-knowledge, to look inwards as well as outwards, to evaluate emotional reactions as well as attachments to material success, to challenge the conformity and triviality of mass culture, and to find fresh meaning in leisurely artistic endeavours rather than in unrelenting competitiveness and greed.[115] Midlife was the moment to 'abandon the last vestiges of narcissism', as the British psychologist William Brown had put it in 1938, and to recognize more inclusive values, 'those that are super-temporal, beyond time, the good, the beautiful, and the true'.[116]

Guidance on how to address midlife angst through the sublimation – or redirection – of destructive impulses into creative expression walked a fine line between encouraging individual and family stability, on the one hand, and undermining relationships, on the other. Pursuing pathways to self-realization could prevent or resolve marital tensions by allowing partners to express themselves without the compulsion to destroy relationships at home and work. But self-expression could be detrimental if self-fulfilment outweighed self-sacrifice, if the fear of losing meaning and identity prioritized personal survival over the survival of others. According to Edmund Bergler, the revolt of the middle-aged man was marked by an increasingly insistent sense of 'duty to self', leading to the betrayal and neglect of partners and children.[117] In Joseph Heller's *Something Happened*, Bob Slocum – like so many mid-century fictional middle-aged men – justified displays of brutality against his family by emphasizing the necessity of defending himself against occupational and domestic pressures, without much thought for the impact of his actions on others. The search for identity and meaning – for a sense of self that transcended time, as the existential psychologist Rollo May put it in 1953 – was necessary to ensure survival at midlife.[118] But too often the quest to heal the lost, undeveloped or divided self was transformed into a form of narcissism that provided a flimsy basis for enduring love.[119]

Post-war critics regarded narcissism as an obstacle to achieving personal maturity, marital contentment and social harmony. While British divorce law reformers and marriage counsellors cited self-interest as a key driver of marital and family breakdown, partners undergoing therapy cited each other's selfishness as a cause of tensions within the marriage. In an extended essay in *New York Magazine* published in 1976, the American novelist Tom Wolfe referred to the 1970s as the '"Me" decade', the culmination of post-war social, demographic and economic changes that had energized the pursuit of self-realization. The new alchemical dream, he argued, was 'changing one's personality – remaking, remodelling, elevating, and polishing one's very *self*... and observing, studying and doting on it'.[120] At one point, the capacity to self-fulfil had been a middle-class prerogative. But care of the self – the rediscovery of lost identity – was being democratized. Once restricted to the affluent classes, obsessions with self or with talking about oneself – manifest in novel forms of therapy, leisure and religion – were now available to everyone, at least in modern Western countries. 'But once the dreary little bastards started getting money in the 1940s,' Wolfe wrote, 'they did an astonishing thing – they took their money and ran. They did something only aristocrats (and intellectuals and artists) were supposed to do – they discovered and started doting on *Me*!'[121]

According to American historian Christopher Lasch, writing in 1978, the 'culture of narcissism' threatened the ability of couples to achieve lasting love through midlife and beyond.[122] The logic of individualism, at times lauded as a route to economic survival in capitalist consumer societies, had become 'a narcissistic preoccupation with the self', leading middle-aged men and women to take flight from commitment, as Barbara Ehrenreich put it in 1984, or to blame internal despair on external circumstances: a partner's indifference; troublesome adolescents; financial constraints; occupational pressures; or social unrest.[123] One of the dangers of self-obsession, Lasch argued, was a lack of interest in either the past or the future, leaving people unable 'to create a store of loving memories' with which to face the latter part of life.[124] Lasch's critique of post-war American dreams went further:

> Our culture's indifference to the past – which easily shades over into active hostility and rejection – furnishes the most telling proof of that culture's bankruptcy. The prevailing attitude, so cheerful and forward-looking on the surface, derives from a narcissistic impoverishment of the psyche and also from an inability to ground our needs in the experience of satisfaction and contentment.[125]

The hollowness of modern Western culture and the failure of the radical politics of the 1960s had created 'the sense of an ending' – or at least a sense of crisis. People across all layers of society began to focus only on themselves, to seek self-satisfaction and to adhere to self-help regimes designed to improve personal health and wealth in order to insulate themselves against social injustices in the world around them. Self-preoccupation stemmed not from complacency, Lasch argued, but from desperation.[126]

Narcissism was incompatible with lifelong marriage and family stability. According to Ulrich Beck and Elisabeth Beck-Gernsheim, an ego-epidemic had brought the interests of individuals, families and society into conflict, presenting people with stark choices between mutual love and personal freedom, between dependency and autonomy, between proximity and separation. Middle-aged couples struggling to live together while retaining distinct identities were by no means alone. What appeared to be 'an individual struggle to break free and discover one's true self', Beck and Beck-Gernsheim claimed, conformed to a 'general imperative'.[127] As Alvin Toffler had pointed out in 1970, the 'throw-away' post-war society was characterized by transient attachments not only to things, places, organizations and information, but to people.[128] Under these conditions, 'relationships were lived as if they were interchangeable': people married for love, had affairs for love, and divorced and remarried – sometimes several times – for love.[129] The midlife crisis constituted a manifestation of the struggle to survive as an individual within a matrix of shared lives, a yearning to escape from 'symbiotic entanglement', an expression of anxieties about how to rediscover youthful aspirations stifled by marriage and to emancipate souls destroyed by conformity.[130] As men and women at midlife reflected on failed dreams and lost opportunities, the urge to find 'time for me' – or to realize unfulfilled creative and spiritual potential – was incompatible with the romantic ideal of a loving, monogamous relationship that remained intact until it was interrupted by death.

IT WAS JOHN Updike – more than any other post-war author – who gave the lie to claims that adult crises could be explained or justified in terms of a philosophical search for meaning in a troubled world. In *Rabbit, Run*, published in 1960, Jack Eccles – an Episcopalian minister – admonishes Rabbit Angstrom for abandoning his wife and child for another woman. Eccles is unwilling to accept Angstrom's assertion that he is on a spiritual quest. 'It's the strange thing about you mystics,' Eccles insists in response to Angstrom's refusal to admit his adultery, 'how often your little ecstasies wear a skirt.'[131] Updike's cynicism is more evident in *A Month of Sundays*, first published in 1974. The novel comprises

the month-long diary of Thomas Marshfield, a 41-year-old priest sent
to a retreat for 'errant clerics'. Marshfield's reflections on midlife angst
comprise a mixture of egotism and self-deprecation, of honesty and
deceit. Every Sunday, Marshfield writes a sermon, each addressing in
different ways 'those flanking menaces to the fortress of the household –
adultery and divorce'.[132] Made possible by 'insatiable egos and workable
genitals', he argues in the first sermon, adultery is integral to the human
condition, a necessary tool for valuing and stabilizing the self.

> Wherein does the modern American man recover his sense of
> worth, not as dogged breadwinner and economic integer, but as
> romantic minister and phallic knight, as personage, embodiment,
> and hero? In adultery. And wherein does the American woman,
> coded into mindlessness by household slavery and the stupefying
> companionship of greedy infants, recover her powers of decision,
> of daring, of discrimination – her dignity, in short? In adultery . . .
> We are an adulterous generation; let us rejoice.[133]

Marshfield treats men and women equally, with both respect and
revulsion. He recognizes that women's urge to break free from a world
made by men is as powerful as men's desire to escape from the burdens
of work and domesticity. Although his testimony is dominated by his
own midlife crisis, Marshfield reflects on the patterns and meanings
of adultery across the life course. The 'adultery of the freshly married',
he wrote, 'is a gaudy-winged disaster' prompted by the revelation that
'a life-swallowing', but not irredeemable, mistake has been made. In
the thirties, he insists, the adultery of 'hopelessly married' partners
with 'slowly growing children and slowly dwindling mortgages' is a
'more stolid and more domestic creature, a beast of burden truly, for
this adultery serves the purpose of rendering tolerable the unalterable'.
The adultery of men and women in their forties, by contrast, 'recovers
a certain lightness, a greyhound skittishness and peacock sheen'. Here,
Updike's imagery captures the situational and psychological drivers – as
well as tragic endpoints – of the midlife crisis.

> Children leave; parents die; money descends; nothing is as difficult
> as it once seemed. Separation arrives by whim (the last dessert
> dish broken, the final intolerable cigar-burn on the armchair) or
> marriages are extended by surrender. The race between freedom

and exhaustion is decided.[134]

It is only towards the end of his month in retreat that Marshfield acknowledges his cruelty to his wife; but even then, he seeks to justify a man's prerogative to desert a marriage in pursuit of missed opportunities. 'When is it right for a man to leave his wife?', Marshfield asks. 'When the sum of his denied life overtops the calculated loss of the children, the grandparents if surviving, the dog, and dogged *ux.*, known as Fido, residual in himself.'[135] In the world created by Updike, the midlife crisis constitutes not just a tipping point between past and future, but a precarious balancing act between committing to others and saving oneself – a moment to decide not only what to do, but what not to do, as Erikson had put it some years earlier.[136]

Updike's casual banality conceals the many tragedies of midlife. Other late twentieth-century novelists treated the crises of middle age in more sincere terms. Two short stories by Doris Lessing reveal the appalling consequences of failing to cope with the turbulence of marriage and family life in middle age. In 'To Room Nineteen', first published in 1963, Lessing captures the ways in which middle-aged wives and mothers felt – and became – invisible during the post-war period. Having worked for twelve years, Susan Rawlings's career has been interrupted by marriage and children. From 'the moment I became pregnant for the first time', she reflects, 'I signed myself over, so to speak, to other people'.[137] Susan's descent into despair, accelerated by her husband's confession that he has been unfaithful, is marked by a sense of emptiness and isolation: 'They were living side by side in this house like two tolerably friendly strangers.'[138] Seeking solace, Susan rents a room – Room Nineteen – in a small hotel in London, where she sits alone on weekdays while the children are at school, a pattern of existence that enables her to continue playing her part as wife and mother in the matrimonial home. Retreat into solitude proves to be an effective buffer against desolation – at least for a short period of time. But relief from the crisis does not last. Lying on the bed in Room Nineteen one day, Susan 'made sure the windows were tight shut, put two shillings in the meter, and turned on the gas'.[139]

If Susan Rawlings is the archetypal middle-aged, middle-class woman struggling to find a way through the suffocating loneliness of family life, Jack Orkney demonstrates another side of the midlife coin. In 'The Temptation of Jack Orkney', published initially in 1972, Lessing presents the male protagonist's existential crisis as a reaction to domestic stress, a troubled marriage, the manner in which his wife has been transformed by motherhood into an 'obsessed, complaining woman', boredom with his work as a journalist, ideological distance from his three children, the death of his father and a collapse of faith.[140] Jack explains his midlife malaise in temporal terms familiar to his contemporaries – and indeed to the generations that have followed.

> Terror was not the word. Nor fear. Yet there were no other words that he knew for the state he found himself in. It was more like a state of acute attention, as if his whole being – memory, body, present and past chemistries – had been assaulted by a warning, so that he had to attend to it. He was standing, as it were, at the alert, listening to something which said: Time is passing, be quick, listen, attend.[141]

Jack treads a different path from that taken by many middle-aged men who resort to adultery, alcohol or aggression to resolve their midlife crises. Much like J. G. Ballard's 'overloaded man', who learns to dissolve into his surroundings in order to free himself from 'the nausea of the external world', Jack Orkney vows simply to suppress his identity.[142] Faced with a choice between freedom and submission – between infidelity and impotence – Jack chooses the latter. At the age of fifty or so, he becomes a man 'whose pride and strength had to come from a conscious ability to suffer, in silence, the journey into negation'.[143] Lessing's message is unequivocal. As Reggie Perrin soon discovers, whatever or whoever men and women are running from at midlife, there is nowhere and no one to run to.

POSTSCRIPT

The death of Reginald Iolanthe Perrin can be attributed – quite frankly – to his creator, David Nobbs. One of the finest British comedy writers of the late twentieth century, Nobbs published *The Death of Reginald Perrin* in 1975, when he was forty years old, at precisely the midpoint of his life – although he was not to know that at the time, of course. The novel had been conceived initially as a thirty-minute play about a 'businessman driven berserk by the pressures of the rat race and the absurdities of conspicuous capitalist consumption'.[1] When his proposal was rejected by the BBC, Nobbs developed the characters and ideas into a series of novels, which were subsequently adapted for television with Leonard Rossiter in the title role. According to Nobbs, inspiration for *The Death of Reginald Perrin* came from a variety of sources. He had been alerted to the tediousness of corporate life by a newspaper article about the efforts of staff at Morton's Jam Factory to create a new product. A 'nauseous advert for a mortgage company', showing 'two smug parents in matching sweaters with two smug children in matching gear', had drawn his attention to the suburban conceit against which Reggie was rebelling. And Reginald Maudling, the Conservative Member of Parliament for Barnet – the London suburb where Nobbs lived through the 1970s and '80s – provided a blueprint for Reggie himself.[2]

Yet *The Death of Reginald Perrin* was more than a fictional tale of midlife masculine discomfort. The figures of Reggie, his wife and their children were drawn from everyday scenes of family and working life after the Second World War. Raised in the 1930s and '40s and reaching adulthood in the '50s, Reggie – like his creator – belonged to a cohort of expectant middle-agers who had been sold a vision of lifelong marriage, happy families and steady jobs. Failure to realize dreams of success – or to do so by a certain time – led to despair. Amid the cultural, socio-economic, political and technological upheavals of the post-war years, the cracks that appeared between partners, between generations, between home and work, and between contradictory elements of personal identity were filled with the doubts, anxieties and insecurities that fed the midlife crisis sketched out by Elliott Jaques in 1965. In Reggie's eyes, his wife was dull, his marriage jaded; his job was tiresome, his younger colleagues intimidating; his nest was empty, his children distant; his past was lost, his future bleak. Searching for meaning, Reggie found emptiness. 'He was a man', wrote David Nobbs in his autobiography, 'trying to find an individual way through a corporate world. It was implicit that he was without religious faith. He was searching for value, for moral certainty, and he was restricted by habit, routine, discipline and all the forces of conformity.'[3]

While indulging his midlife fantasies, Reggie wilfully disregarded the feelings and frustrations of his wife and children. Here too, Nobbs deftly – perhaps inadvertently – captured the asymmetries of middle age after the war. Women were not immune to midlife dissatisfaction. On the contrary, wives and mothers in particular were trapped by childcare and domesticity, drained by marital tensions, separation and divorce, struggling with the double burden of family and work, and equally resentful of lost dreams. In spite of attempts to empower women to break the chauvinistic chains that confined them to supporting roles, it was the tribulations of middle-aged men that continued to dominate Western accounts of the midlife crisis. Like Elizabeth Perrin, middle-aged women remained largely tangential to the midlife plot, whether fictitious or real. In art, as in life, women were concealed in the gaps between scenes and sentences, often unwitting casualties of male cravings for second – more pneumatic – chances at life and love. Children – at least from a first marriage – were even more clearly invisible. Their destiny – whether in fact or fiction – was to witness, inherit and repeat their parents' behaviour.

Letters that David Nobbs received after *The Fall and Rise of Reginald Perrin* was first aired in 1976 led him to believe that the series had become successful because 'it had defined a despair that wasn't Reggie's alone but was present in the zeitgeist.'[4] In *The Man in the Gray Flannel Suit II*, published in 1984 but set in 1963, the principal character, Tom Rath, claims that terms such as 'midlife crisis', 'male menopause' and 'the dangerous years' serve only to denigrate middle-aged passion, to dismiss midlife infidelity 'as a disease or symptom of the inevitable disintegration of the body'.[5] Yet even Rath's irritation reveals the popularity of the concept of the midlife crisis as a vehicle for capturing the emotions and experiences of middle-aged men and women across the second half of the twentieth century. It is perhaps for this reason that – like Tom Rath, Frank Wheeler and Bob Slocum in America – Reggie Perrin became a British icon, a cult hero who lightened the complexion of midlife despondency. Eager to escape lives of quiet desperation, middle-aged men dreamed of 'doing a Reggie' – of leaving their clothes on a beach and starting a new life, as the Labour Member of Parliament John Stonehouse had done in November 1974.[6] Reggie's legacy survived well beyond 1979, when the final episodes of the third television series were aired. *The Legacy of Reginald Perrin*, which charted the efforts of his family and friends to spend his fortune following his (actual) death, was broadcast in 1996. In 2009 the series was revived with Martin Clunes playing Reggie. The British media continued to reflect on Nobbs's classic work well into the twenty-first century. And the flawed 'emancipatory strategies' of Reginald Perrin provided material for earnest analyses of the 'contradictions inherent in capitalism'.[7]

David Nobbs's heartening resolution to Reggie Perrin's bout of midlife malaise – in which he returns to his former life and wife with no ill consequences – is deceptive. Attempts to turn back the clock, recover lost time, recapture a youthful past and create a firmer future have always been more likely to multiply than resolve the existential problems associated with ageing, family and work. Historical evidence – and vicarious experience – suggests that pursuing a new relationship or occupation in middle age might relieve certain burdens, open up new vistas and renew self-esteem for a short while. But, as novelists, marriage guidance counsellors, self-help authors and psychologists have repeatedly stressed over the last half-century or so, avoidance of internal conflicts and external pressures is a high-risk strategy at midlife, one that leads almost invariably to personal disenchantment and guilt, as well as the destruction of marriages, families and friendships. Left unattended, our midlife delusions will continue to ruin lives long after we have gone.

REFERENCES

1 ANATOMY OF A CRISIS

1 Elliott Jaques, 'Death and the Midlife Crisis', *International Journal of Psychoanalysis*, 46 (1965), reproduced in Elliott Jaques, *Work, Creativity, and Social Justice* (London, 1970), pp. 38–63, at p. 48.
2 David Nobbs, *The Death of Reginald Perrin* (London, 1975). Subsequent books in the series were *The Return of Reginald Perrin* (1977), *The Better World of Reginald Perrin* (1978) and *The Legacy of Reginald Perrin* (1996).
3 Nobbs, *The Death of Reginald Perrin*, pp. 10–11. The words are those of the company doctor. Reggie's symptoms of anxiety and insecurity associated with middle age – 'he's going mad' – reappear later in the novel, when his secretary expresses concern about his behaviour – see p. 134.
4 Ibid., p. 69.
5 John Braine, *Life at the Top* [1962] (London, 1973), pp. 18–19. *Life at the Top* was a sequel to Braine's *Room at the Top* (London, 1957).
6 Nobbs, *The Death of Reginald Perrin*, p. 73.
7 Ibid., p. 179.
8 The television series, which starred Leonard Rossiter as Reggie, ran for three series between September 1976 and January 1979. It was followed by a single Christmas sketch aired in 1982 and a far less successful follow-up series, *The Legacy of Reginald Perrin*, in 1996. In 2009 the programme was reprised with Martin Clunes in the title role.
9 Nobbs, *The Death of Reginald Perrin*, p. 285.
10 Rupert Cross, 'Final Report of the Denning Committee on Procedure in Matrimonial Causes', *Modern Law Review*, 10 (1947), pp. 184–92, at p. 185.
11 Ronald Fletcher, *Britain in the Sixties: The Family and Marriage* (Harmondsworth, 1962), p. 175; H. Mainwaring Holt, 'The Decay of Family Life', *Health Education Journal*, 9 (1951), pp. 181–5.
12 Alvin Toffler, *Future Shock* (London, 1970).
13 The British historian Eric Hobsbawm labelled the twentieth century – or at least the period between 1914 and 1991 – 'the age of extremes'. Having witnessed a series of global economic disasters, ethnic cleansing, two world wars, the foundation and fall of the Soviet Union, and the dismantling of pernicious empires – which were often replaced by insular and inequitable nation-states – Hobsbawm saw the twentieth century as devoid of balance, ravaged instead by the failed ideologies of nationalism, imperialism,

communism, capitalism, fascism and liberalism. See Eric Hobsbawm, *The Age of Extremes: The Short Twentieth Century, 1914–1991* (London, 1994).

14 Marie Carmichael Stopes, *Enduring Passion* [1928] (London, 1936), p. 2. Interwar fears of decay are explored in Richard Overy, *The Morbid Age: Britain Between the Wars* (London, 2009).

15 For discussion of longitudinal studies that shaped understandings of midlife, see Alice S. Rossi, 'Life-span Theories and Women's Lives', *Journal of Women in Culture and Society*, 6 (1980), pp. 4–32.

16 Margaret Morganroth Gullette, *Declining to Decline: Cultural Combat and the Politics of the Midlife* (Charlottesville, VA, 1997).

17 See the discussion of Churchill's pledge in Sir William H. Beveridge, *The Pillars of Security* (London, 1943), pp. 187–91.

18 The 'revolt of the middle-aged man' was a term used by Edmund Bergler in his analysis of the emergence and resolution of conflicts in middle age: Edmund Bergler, *The Revolt of the Middle-aged Man* (London, 1958).

19 Elliott Jaques, 'Social Systems as a Defence against Persecutory and Depressive Anxiety', in *New Directions in Psychoanalysis*, ed. Melanie Klein, Paula Heimann and R. E. Money-Kyrle (London, 1955), pp. 478–98. See also Susan Long, 'Organizational Defenses against Anxiety: What has Happened since the 1955 Jaques Paper', *International Journal of Applied Psychoanalytic Studies*, 3 (2006), pp. 279–95.

20 Elliott Jaques, *The Changing Culture of a Factory* (London, 1951); Elliott Jaques, *Equitable Payment: A General Theory of Work, Differential Payment, and Individual Progress* (London, 1961); Wilfred Brown and Elliott Jaques, *Glacier Project Papers* (London, 1965). Overviews of Elliott Jaques's life and work were published by colleagues and peers shortly after his death in a special issue of *International Journal of Applied Psychoanalytic Studies*, 2 (2005). For an idiosyncratic account of Jaques's influence, see Russell John Connor, *It's About Time: An Introduction to Elliott Jaques; A Galileo for the Social Sciences* (Fleet, 2012).

21 Elliott Jaques, *The Form of Time* (London, 1982); Elliott Jaques, 'On Trust, Good, and Evil', *International Journal of Applied Psychoanalytic Studies*, 2 (2005), pp. 396–403; Elliott Jaques, 'Psychotic Anxieties and the Sense of Justice', in Jaques, *Work, Creativity, and Social Justice*, pp. 181–99.

22 Janet Sayers, *Mothering Psychoanalysis: Helene Deutsch, Karen Horney, Anna Freud and Melanie Klein* (London, 1992), pp. 257, 289.

23 Douglas Kirsner, 'The Intellectual Odyssey of Elliott Jaques from Alchemy to Science', *Free Associations*, 11 (2004), pp. 179–204. Kirsner's account draws on conversations with Jaques.

24 Jaques, 'Death and the Midlife Crisis', pp. 47–8. For psychoanalyst Erik Erikson, our lives are a 'one-way streets to success – and sudden oblivion': Erik H. Erikson, *Insight and Responsibility* (London, 1964), p. 132.

25 Jaques, 'Death and the Midlife Crisis', p. 59.

26 Ibid.

27 Ibid., pp. 51–6. The term 'patient' was used by Jaques himself.

28 Ibid., p. 56.

29 Ibid., pp. 39–45.

30 Paul H. Rohmann, 'The Gauguin Syndrome', *Antioch Review*, 13 (1953), pp. 341–50.

31 Piotr K. Oleś and Monika Kłosok-Ścibich, 'The Gauguin Syndrome – Change of Identity or Myth', *Psychologia Rozwojowa*, 14 (2009), pp. 9–25; Piotr K. Oleś, 'The Paul Gauguin Syndrome: A Great Life Change', in *The Palgrave Handbook of Social Creativity Research: Palgrave Studies in Creativity and Culture*, ed. I. Lebuda and V. Glǎveanu (London, 2018), pp. 317–34; Ronnie Mather, 'Narcissistic Personality Disorder and Creative Art: The Case of Paul Gauguin', *PsyArt* (20 May 2007).

32 Charlotte Bühler, 'The Curve of Life as Studied in Biographies', *Journal of Applied Psychology*, 18 (1935), pp. 405–9; Walter B. Pitkin, *Life Begins at Forty* (New York, 1932), pp. 73–5. On the history of ageing, geriatrics and anti-ageing therapies, see Thomas R. Cole, *The Journey of Life: A Cultural History of Aging in America* (Cambridge, 1992); Kay Heath, *Aging by the Book: The Emergence of Midlife in Victorian Britain* (New York, 2009); Hyung Wook Park, *Old Age, New Science: Gerontologists and their Biosocial Visions, 1900–1960* (Pittsburgh, PA, 2016); James F. Stark, *The Cult of Youth: Anti-ageing in Modern Britain* (Cambridge, 2020).

33 G. Stanley Hall, 'The Dangerous Age', *Pedagogical Seminary*, 28 (1921), pp. 275–94, at p. 290; G. Stanley Hall, *Senescence: The Last Half of Life* (New York, 1922).

34 C. G. Jung, *Modern Man in Search of a Soul* (London, 1933); C. G. Jung, *The Integration of the Personality* (London, 1940).

35 Jung, *Modern Man in Search of a Soul*, p. 120.

36 Jaques, 'Death and the Midlife Crisis', p. 59.

37 Ibid., p. 38.

38 Jaques, *Equitable Payment*, pp. 149, 182.

39 R. Doll and F. A. Jones, *Occupational Factors in the Aetiology of Gastric and Duodenal Ulcers* (London, 1951); B. S. Dohrenwend and B. P. Dohrenwend, *Stressful Life Events: Their Nature and Effects* (New York, 1974).

40 Fred Kerner, *Stress and Your Heart* (New York, 1961), p. 76.

41 Dorothy Canfield Fisher, *Mothers and Children* (London, 1915), p. 245.

42 Jaques has almost invariably been credited as the originator of the term in popular newspapers, magazines and books on the midlife crisis. See for example Pamela Druckerman, 'How the Midlife Crisis Came to Be', *The Atlantic* (29 May 2018); Kieran Setiya, *Midlife: A Philosophical Guide* (Princeton, NJ, 2017).

43 Carl Frankenstein, *The Roots of the Ego: A Phenomenology of Dynamics and of Structure* (Baltimore, MD, 1966), p. 184; Kenneth Soddy and Mary C. Kidson, *Men in Middle Life* (London, 1967), pp. 55–6; Marjorie Fiske Lowenthal and David Chiriboga, 'Transition to the Empty Nest: Crisis, Challenge, or Relief', *Archives of General Psychiatry*, 26 (1972), pp. 8–14. It should be noted that Jaques was not always credited with introducing the term in these texts.

44 Rhona Rapoport and Robert N. Rapoport, 'The Dual Career Family', *Human Relations*, 22 (1969), pp. 3–30, at p. 14. See also references to Jaques's work in Orville G. Brim, Jr, 'Theories of the Male Mid-life Crisis', *Counseling Psychologist* (1 March 1976), pp. 2–9.

45 Henry V. Dicks, *Marital Tensions: Clinical Studies towards a Psychological Theory of Interaction* (London, 1967), pp. 223–5.

46 Barbara Fried, *The Middle-age Crisis* (New York, 1967); Hermann Schreiber,

Midlife Crisis: Die Krise in der Mitte des Lebens (München, 1977); Henry Still, *Surviving the Male Mid-life Crisis* (New York, 1977); Nancy Mayer, *The Male Mid-life Crisis: Fresh Starts After Forty* (New York, 1978).

47 Martha Weinman Lear, 'Is There a Male Menopause?', *New York Times* (28 January 1973), pp. 10, 57–8, 61, 64–6, at 65.

48 John Updike, *Rabbit, Run* (New York, 1960); John Updike, *Rabbit Redux* (New York, 1971); John Updike, *Rabbit Is Rich* (New York, 1981); John Updike, *Rabbit at Rest* (New York, 1990); Sloan Wilson, *The Man in the Gray Flannel Suit* (New York, 1955); Sloan Wilson, *The Man in the Gray Flannel Suit II* (New York, 1984); Richard Yates, *Revolutionary Road* (Boston, MA, 1961); Simone de Beauvoir, *The Woman Destroyed* [1967] (New York, 1979); Ingmar Bergman, *Scenes from a Marriage* (AB Svensk Filmindustri, 1973). For discussion of some of these literary and cinematic treatments, see Margaret Morganroth Gullette, *Safe at Last in the Middle Years: The Invention of the Midlife Progress Novel* (Berkeley, CA, 1988); Julie Levinson, *The American Success Myth on Film* (Basingstoke, 2012). 'I can't believe I forgot to have my midlife crisis' was a Pop art illustration by Lou Brooks.

49 Cited in Jaques's obituary in *Business Wire*, www.businesswire.com, 14 March 2003.

50 See, for example, the rising frequency of references to the midlife crisis in English-language books through the 1980s and '90s in Google NGram Viewer, accessed 21 July 2017.

51 Susanne Schmidt, 'The Feminist Origins of the Midlife Crisis', *Historical Journal*, 61 (2018), pp. 503–23. As Schmidt shows elsewhere, feminist perspectives on midlife transitions were also contested by psychologists: Susanne Schmidt, 'The Anti-feminist Reconstruction of the Midlife Crisis: Popular Psychology, Journalism and Social Science in 1970s USA', *Gender and History*, 30 (2018), pp. 153–76; Susanne Schmidt, *Midlife Crisis: The Feminist Origins of a Chauvinist Cliché* (Chicago, IL, 2020).

52 Linda Wolfe, 'A Time of Change', *New York Magazine* (5 June 1972), pp. 68–9.

53 Susan Sontag, 'The Double Standard of Aging', *Saturday Review* (23 September 1972), pp. 29–38.

54 Schmidt, 'The Feminist Origins'.

55 J. H. Wallis, *The Challenge of Middle Age* (London, 1962), p. 89; Jane Pearce and Saul Newton, *The Conditions of Human Growth* (New York, 1963), pp. 131–5.

56 Jaques, 'Death and the Midlife Crisis', p. 62.

57 Ibid., p. 38.

58 Ibid., p. 47.

59 Nigel Burke, 'Grumpy Old Men', *Daily Express* (21 June 2010), p. 13. For reference to the introduction of the term 'midlife' in 1895, see Steven Mintz, *The Prime of Life: A History of Modern Adulthood* (Cambridge, MA, 2015), pp. 300–301.

60 Jaques, 'Death and the Midlife Crisis', pp. 47–8.

61 According to Gullette, it is the symbolism of entering middle age that traditionally 'anchors the midlife crisis': Gullette, *Declining to Decline*, pp. 171–3.

62 Thomas C. Desmond, 'America's Unknown Middle-agers', *New York Times* (29 July 1956), pp. 5, 42–3.

63 See, for example, D. B. Bromley, 'Middle Age: An Introduction', in *Middle Age*, ed. Roger Owen (London, 1967), pp. 7–21.

64 William Osler, 'The Fixed Period', in *Aequanimitas* (Philadelphia, PA, 1910), pp. 389–411. Osler's work formed one of the starting points of G. Stanley Hall's studies of ageing – Hall, 'The Dangerous Age'.

65 For reference to middle age as 'a state of mind, a way of feeling and thinking about oneself and one's position in the world', see Bromley, 'Middle Age', p. 9.

66 Julie-Marie Strange, *Fatherhood and the British Working Class, 1865–1914* (Cambridge, 2015).

67 Margaret Lock, 'Deconstructing the Change: Female Maturation in Japan and North America', in *Welcome to Middle Age! (And Other Cultural Fictions)*, ed. Richard A. Shweder (Chicago, IL, 1998), pp. 45–74, at p. 45.

68 Heath, *Aging by the Book*; Patricia Cohen, *In Our Prime: The Invention of Middle Age* (New York, 2012); John Benson, *Prime Time: A History of the Middle Aged in Twentieth-century Britain* (London, 1997); Mintz, *The Prime of Life*; Ben Hutchinson, *The Midlife Mind: Literature and the Art of Ageing* (London, 2020).

69 Margaret Lock, *Encounters with Aging: Mythologies of the Menopause in Japan and North America* (Berkeley, CA, 1993); Margaret Morganroth Gullette, *Aged by Culture* (Chicago, IL, 2004).

70 Margaret Morganroth Gullette, 'Midlife Discourses in the Twentieth-century United States: An Essay on the Sexuality, Ideology, and Politics of "Middle-ageism"', in *Welcome to Middle Age!*, ed. Shweder, pp. 3–44.

71 Benson, *Prime Time*, pp. 8–12. For contemporary reference to middle age as the years between 35 and 50, see Active 54, 'The Middle-aged Man and the War', *Lancet* (5 September 1914), pp. 667–8. In 1920 a report in the *Lancet* suggested that much 'misery and ill-health' could be avoided by compulsory medical examination for those around the age of forty, that is, 'half-way through what we all hope will be our span of life': 'A Medical Survey at Middle Age', *Lancet* (1 May 1920), p. 974. A correspondent to the same journal agreed that 'the downward curve of life' began after the age of 35 or 40: Aetas, 'Age and Pensions', *Lancet* (12 February 1921), pp. 249–50.

72 The manufacturers of Phyllosan promised readers that they would 'feel younger as they grow older' – 'Forty-phobia (fear of the forties)', *The Times* (28 April 1938), p. 19. For discussion of advertisements and the growing use of terms such as 'middle-aged spread', see Benson, *Prime Time*, pp. 9–10, 17–18.

73 Jaques, 'Death and the Midlife Crisis', p. 38.

74 Lock, *Encounters with Aging*; Elizabeth Siegel Watkins, 'The Medicalisation of the Male Menopause in America', *Social History of Medicine*, 20 (2007), pp. 369–88; Hans-Georg Hofer, 'Medicine, Aging, Masculinity: Towards a Cultural History of the Male Climacterium', *Medizinhistorisches Journal*, 42 (2007), pp. 210–46; Hans-Georg Hofer, 'Men in the Critical Age: Kurt Mendel and the Controversy over the Male Climacteric', *Urologist*, 50 (2011), pp. 839–45; Judith A. Houck, *Hot and Bothered: Women, Medicine, and Menopause in Modern America* (Cambridge, MA, 2006).

75 Richard A. Shweder, 'Introduction: Welcome to Middle Age', in *Welcome to Middle Age!*, ed. Shweder, pp. ix–xvii. The economic significance of the middle-aged during a period of depression was most clearly expressed in Walter B. Pitkin, *Life Begins at Forty* (New York, 1932).

76 On performative aspects of the self, see Erving Goffman, *The Presentation of the Self in Everyday Life* (Edinburgh, 1956).

77 Lock, 'Deconstructing the Change'.

78 Ulrich Beck and Elisabeth Beck-Gernsheim, *The Normal Chaos of Love*, trans. Mark Ritter and Jane Wiebel (Cambridge, 1995), pp. 52–6.

79 Lock, 'Deconstructing the Change', pp. 60–61, 65–8.

80 Hall, 'The Dangerous Age', pp. 275, 287.

81 On the origins of Hall's approach, see Thomas R. Cole, 'The Prophecy of *Senescence*: G. Stanley Hall and the Reconstruction of Old Age in America', *Gerontologist*, 24 (1984), pp. 360–66.

82 Karin Michaëlis, *The Dangerous Age: Letters and Fragments from a Woman's Diary* (New York, 1911), p. 25.

83 André Tridon, 'Author of the Latest "Daring" Novel is in America', *New York Times* (16 July 1911), Magazine Section, p. 9.

84 Karin Michaëlis, 'Why are Women Less Truthful than Men?', *Munsey's Magazine* (May 1913), pp. 185–8; Karin Michaëlis, 'Why are Women Less Truthful than Men?', *Munsey's Magazine* (June 1913), pp. 343–5. Michaëlis continued to enrage American women in particular with her views on their 'selfish, vain and arrogant' personalities – Anon., 'Insults American Women: Articles by Mme. Michaelis called "International Scandal"', *New York Times* (2 August 1914), p. 11. According to Hall, Michaëlis was regarded 'as a traitor to her sex': Hall, *Senescence*, p. 29.

85 Rose Macaulay, *Dangerous Ages* (London, 1921). For a comparison between the works of Michaëlis and Macaulay, see Phyllis Lassner, 'Women's Midlife and the Crisis of Writing: Karin Michaëlis's *The Dangerous Age* and Rose Macaulay's *Dangerous Ages*', *Atlantis*, 4 (Spring 1989), pp. 21–30.

86 Newell Dwight Hillis, 'The Dangerous Age in Man', *Good Housekeeping Magazine*, 54 (1912), pp. 537–40. The peculiar challenges of middle age also figured in medical commentaries exploring the role of diet and exercise in maintaining health through midlife. See Anon., 'Middle Age and Old Age', *British Medical Journal* (10 July 1915), p. 57, an article reviewing S. Taylor, *Health for the Middle-aged* (London, 1915).

87 Will Levington Comfort, *Midstream: A Chronicle at Halfway* (New York, 1914), p. 293. Helen Keller, an American author and political activist, used the same metaphor to narrate her life: Helen Keller, *Midstream: My Later Life* (New York, 1929).

88 Winston Churchill, *The World Crisis*, 6 vols (London, 1923–31). Churchill's hopes for a peaceful world were expressed in the final chapter of vol. IV, *The Aftermath, 1918–22* (1929).

89 Hall, *Senescence*, pp. 30–31, citing H. G. Wells, *The Salvaging of Civilisation: The Probable Future of Mankind* (New York, 1921). Contemporaries also used the notion of salvage to describe approaches to improving the lives of the elderly – see Lillien J. Martin and Clare de Gruchy, *Salvaging Old Age* (New York, 1930).

90 See Goetz A. Briefs's review of P. A. Sorokin's *The Crisis of Our Age* (1941), in *Review of Politics*, 4 (July 1942), pp. 315–26.

91 On the American dream, see Sarah Churchwell, *Behold, America: A History of America First and the American Dream* (London, 2018). The dream shaped attitudes not only in the West, but in China. In the

decades after the Second World War, the Chinese philosopher Tang Junyi – exiled in Hong Kong – expressed the tensions between communism and capitalism and between 'the ideal purity of an imagined homeland (e.g. The American Dream) and the frustration and alienation of daily life in our place of residence': see Hok Yin Chan, 'A Critique of Colonialism and Capitalism: Tang Junyi's Views on Plurality and Openness', in *Confucianism for the Contemporary World: Global Order, Political Plurality, and Social Action*, ed. Tze-ki-Hon and Kristin Stapleton (New York, 2017), pp. 167–80.

92 William G. Carleton, 'Our Post-crisis World', *American Scholar*, 33 (Winter 1963–4), pp. 27–44, at p. 44. On the growth of crisis studies, see Lydia Rapaport, 'The State of Crisis: Some Theoretical Considerations', *Social Service Review*, 36 (1962), pp. 211–17; Rhona Rapoport, 'Normal Crises, Family Structure and Mental Health', *Family Process*, 2 (1963), pp. 68–80. On the political work achieved by the rhetoric of crisis, see Janet Roitman, *Anti-crisis* (Durham, NC, and London, 2014).

93 Michael Crichton, *The Andromeda Strain* [1969] (London, 1993), p. 18.

94 Ibid., pp. 17–19.

95 Ibid., pp. 18–19.

96 See, for example, Arthur M. Schlesinger, Jr, 'The Crisis of American Masculinity', in Arthur M. Schlesinger, Jr, *The Politics of Hope* (Boston, MA, 1963), pp. 237–46; Earl Lomon Koos, 'Middle-class Family Crises', *Marriage and Family Living*, 10 (1948), pp. 25 and 40; Irving Tallman, 'Working-class Wives in Suburbia: Fulfillment or Crisis', *Journal of Marriage and Family*, 31 (1969), pp. 65–72.

97 Josie McLellan, *Love in the Time of Communism: Intimacy and Sexuality in the GDR* (Cambridge, 2011), pp. 77–81; Harald Fuess, *Divorce in Japan: Family, Gender, and the State, 1600–2000* (Stanford, CA, 2004), pp. 144–66.

98 Beck and Beck-Gernsheim, *The Normal Chaos of Love*, p. 4.

99 Ibid., p. 1. For their reflections on marriage and the midlife crisis, see ibid., pp. 66–72.

100 Tom Wolfe, 'The "Me" Decade and the Third Great Awakening', *New York Magazine*, 23 August 1976, https://nymag.com.

101 Zygmunt Bauman, *The Individualized Society* (Cambridge, 2001), p. 157.

102 Zygmunt Bauman, *Liquid Modernity*, 2nd edn (Cambridge, 2012), pp. viii, 31; Zygmunt Bauman, *Liquid Love: On the Frailty of Human Bonds* (Cambridge, 2003).

103 *Report of the Royal Commission on Marriage and Divorce*, pp. 7–8.

104 Bauman, *The Individualized Society*, p. 153.

105 Jane Lewis, *The End of Marriage? Individualism and Intimate Relations* (Cheltenham, 2001), p. 11; Barbara Ehrenreich, *The Hearts of Men: American Dreams and the Flight from Commitment* (New York, 1984).

106 On Perrin as a 'suburban everyman', see Jonathan Freedland, 'Reggie Perrin – A Suburban Everyman who Captured the Essence of His Era', *The Guardian*, www.theguardian.com, 14 August 2015. The term 'crisis of confidence' became a prominent expression of concerns about a decline in the restorative potential of traditional American values after President Jimmy Carter's speech on 15 July 1979, www.millercenter.org, accessed 15 December 2020.

107 Beck and Beck-Gernsheim, *The Normal Chaos of Love*, p. 67. See also

Michael C. Kearl and Lisbeth J. Hoag, 'The Social Construction of the Midlife Crisis: A Case Study in the Temporalities of Identity', *Sociological Inquiry*, 54 (1984), pp. 279–300.

108 Robert Morison, Tamara J. Erickson and Ken Dychtwald, 'Managing Middlescence', *Harvard Business Review* (2006), https://hbr.org, accessed 7 May 2017.

109 James R. Ciernia, 'Myths about Male Midlife Crises', *Psychological Reports*, 56 (June 1985), pp. 1003–7; Winifred Gallagher, 'Midlife Myths', *The Atlantic* (1993), www.theatlantic.com, accessed 18 September 2018; Alexandra M. Freund and Johannes O. Ritter, 'Midlife Crisis: A Debate', *Gerontology*, 55 (2009), pp. 582–91; Jenny Chanfreau, 'Hard Evidence: Is the Midlife Crisis Real?', *The Conversation* (2013), http://theconversation.com, accessed 18 September 2018; Anne Tergesen, 'The Myth of the Midlife Crisis', *Wall Street Journal*, www.wsj.com, 12 October 2014.

110 Elaine Wethington, 'Expecting Stress: Americans and the "Midlife Crisis"', *Motivation and Emotion*, 24 (2000), pp. 85–103.

111 For quasi-metaphorical use of the term, see Betty Glad, 'Reagan's Midlife Crisis and the Turn to the Right', *Political Psychology*, 10 (1989), pp. 593–624.

112 For details of the rules and aims of the game and images of the board and game cards, see https://boardgamegeek.com, accessed 28 December 2018; and Alicia Hinkle, 'The Midlife Crisis Is Just a Game: Want to Play?', *The Back Forty*, https://aliciahinkle.wordpress.com, 15 December 2016.

113 J. A. Hazeley and J. P. Morris, *The Ladybird Book of the Mid-life Crisis* (Loughborough, 2015).

114 Joe Ollmann, *Mid-life* (Montreal, 2011).

115 David A. Hamburg and Beatrix A. Hamburg, 'Occupational Stress, Endocrine Changes, and Coping Behaviour in the Middle Years of Adult Life', in *Society, Stress, and Disease*, vol. IV: *Working Life*, ed. Lennart Levi (Oxford, 1981), pp. 131–44.

116 J. H. Wallis, *Someone to Turn To* (London, 1961), p. 34.

117 Cited in Cynthia Port, '"Ages are the Stuff!": The Traffic in Ages in Interwar Britain', *NWSA Journal*, 18 (2006), pp. 138–61, p. 43.

118 Alexandra Robbins and Abby Wilner, *Quarterlife Crisis* (London, 2001).

119 Joseph Heller, *Something Happened* (London, 1974).

2 LIFE BEGINS AT FORTY

1 George Ryley Scott, *The Quest for Youth* (London, 1953), p. 8.

2 Gayelord Hauser, *Look Younger, Live Longer* (London, 1950). On Hauser's impact, see Catherine Carstairs, '"Look Younger, Live Longer": Ageing Beautifully with Gayelord Hauser in America, 1920–1975', *Gender and History*, 26 (2014), pp. 332–50.

3 Scott, *The Quest for Youth*, title page and inside front cover. 'Quest for Youth' was also the title of a 1935 film, made by the Tees-side Cine Club, highlighting the dangers of rejuvenation experiments.

4 Scott, *The Quest for Youth*, p. 21.

5 Ibid., p. 8. Italics in original. For a focus on middle-age as 'a habit' and the importance of people staying young even as they age, see Anon., 'The Prolongation of Youth', *Spectator* (12 September 1935), p. 5.

6 Scott, *The Quest for Youth*, p. 21.

7 Ibid., pp. 54–7, 152.

8 Ibid., pp. 57–8.

9 James Truslow Adams, *The Epic of America* (Boston, MA, 1935), pp. 415–28.

10 Erik H. Erikson, *Childhood and Society* [1950] (New York, 1963), p. 269.

11 Jane Pearce and Saul Newton, *The Conditions of Human Growth* (New York, 1963), p. 134.

12 John Updike, *Rabbit at Rest* [1990] (London, 2006), p. 24.

13 Susan Sontag, 'The Double Standard of Aging', *Saturday Review* (23 September 1972), pp. 29–38, at p. 31.

14 Bernice L. Neugarten, 'Adaptation and the Life Cycle', *Counseling Psychologist*, 6 (1976), pp. 16–20, at p. 18.

15 G. Stanley Hall, 'The Dangerous Age', *Pedagogical Seminary*, 28 (1921), pp. 275–94. Similar sentiments were expressed in the late nineteenth century in Henry James's depiction of Dencombe's recognition that the 'infinite of life had gone' and that he was nearing 'the limit of his course': Henry James, 'The Middle Years', originally published in *Scribner's Magazine* (May 1893), reproduced in *Henry James: Complete Stories, 1892–1898* (New York, 1996), pp. 335–55.

16 For post-war references to taking stock, weighing life in the balance or altered perceptions of time and timing at midlife, see Eric Berne, *Games People Play: The Psychology of Human Relationships* (London, 1964), pp. 38, 44, 50; Anon., 'The Pleasures and Perils of Middle Age', *Time*, 29 July 1966, http://time.com; Bernice L. Neugarten, 'Continuities and Discontinuities of Psychological Issues into Adult Life', *Human Development*, 12 (1969), pp. 121–30; Robert Lee and Marjorie Casebier, *The Spouse Gap: Weathering the Marriage Crisis During Middlescence* (London, 1973), pp. 73–80; B. H. Peterson, 'The Age of Ageing', *Australian and New Zealand Journal of Psychiatry*, 7 (1973), pp. 9–15, at p. 13; Hermann Schreiber, *Midlife Crisis/Die Krise in der Mitte des Lebens* (Munich, 1977); Michèle Thiriet and Suzanne Képès, *Women at Fifty* (New York, 1987), pp. 11–18.

17 *Ikiru*, directed by Akira Kurosawa (Toho Company Limited, 1952), at 3:24 to 3:40 (minutes and seconds). For discussion of *Ikiru*, see Sanford R. Weimer and Francis G. Lu, 'Personal Transformation through an Encounter with Death: Cinematic and Psychotherapy Case Studies', *Journal of Transpersonal Psychology*, 19 (1987), pp. 133–49; Francis G. Lu and Gertrude Heming, 'The Effect of the Film *Ikiru* on Death Anxiety and Attitudes toward Death', *Journal of Transpersonal Psychology*, 19 (1987), pp. 151–9; and Francis G. Lu, 'Personal Transformation through an Encounter with Death: A Study of Akira Kurosawa's *Ikiru* on its Fiftieth Anniversary', *Journal of Transpersonal Psychology*, 37 (2005), pp. 34–43.

18 *Ikiru*, at 1:24:46.

19 Evelyn Waugh, *The Ordeal of Gilbert Pinfold* [1957] (London, 1967), pp. 9–157; Samuel Beckett, *Krapp's Last Tape*, a one-act play first performed on 28 October 1958.

20 John Braine, *Room at the Top* (London, 1957), p. 131.

21 Adams, *The Epic of America*, p. 417.

22 Bernice L. Neugarten, 'Dynamics of Transition of Middle Age to Old Age:

Adaptation and the Life Cycle', *Journal of Geriatric Psychiatry*, 4 (1970), pp. 71–87. For reflections on Neugarten's contributions, see Robert H. Binstock, 'In Memoriam: Bernice L. Neugarten', *The Gerontologist*, 42 (2002), pp. 149–51.

23 Neugarten, 'Dynamics of Transition', p. 72.

24 Ibid.

25 Tamara K. Hareven, 'Aging and Generational Relations: A Historical and Life Course Perspective', *Annual Review of Sociology*, 20 (1994), pp. 437–61. On demographic shifts in the last two decades of the twentieth century, see Dieter Demey et al., 'The Changing Demography of Midlife, from the 1980s to the 2000s', *Population Trends*, 145 (2011), pp. 1–19.

26 Michael Anderson, 'The Emergence of the Modern Life Cycle in Britain', *Social History*, 10 (1985), pp. 69–87. Similar points have been made in relation to American adulthood by John Modell, Frank F. Furstenberg, Jr, and Theodore Hershberg, 'Social Changes and Transitions to Adulthood in Historical Perspective', *Journal of Family History*, 1 (1976), pp. 7–32.

27 George Carstairs, 'Lecture 4: The Changing Role of Women', *This Island Now*, Reith Lectures, 3 December 1962.

28 Richard Titmuss, *Essays on 'The Welfare State'* [1958] (London, 1963), pp. 91–3.

29 Anderson, 'The Emergence of the Modern Life Cycle', pp. 73, 69.

30 Ibid., p. 76.

31 Benita Eisler, *Private Lives: Men and Women of the Fifties* (New York, 1986), pp. 11–12.

32 Howard P. Chudacoff, *How Old Are You? Age Consciousness in American Culture* (Princeton, NJ, 1989); Howard P. Chudacoff, 'The Life Course of Women: Age and Age Consciousness, 1865–1915', *Journal of Family History* (Autumn 1980), pp. 274–92. Hareven refers to homogenization of the life course as 'age uniformity in the timing of life transitions': Hareven, 'Aging and Generational Relations', p. 445

33 Susan J. Matt, *Keeping Up with the Joneses: Envy in American Consumer Society, 1890–1930* (Philadelphia, PA, 2003), pp. 1–10.

34 Mass-Observation, 'Keeping Up with the Jones", File Report 3088 (February 1949).

35 Chudacoff, *How Old Are You?*, pp. 3–8, 132–7. More recent strategies for 'commodifying the decade' are discussed in Justine Coupland, 'Time, the Body and the Reversibility of Ageing: Commodifying the Decade', *Ageing and Society*, 29 (2009), pp. 953–76.

36 Steven Mintz and Susan Kellogg, *Domestic Revolutions: A Social History of American Family Life* (New York, 1988), pp. 178–9.

37 A point made by Tamara K. Hareven, 'Family Time and Historical Time', *Daedalus*, 106 (Spring 1977), pp. 57–70.

38 In spite of differences, there were also shared cross-cultural approaches to shaping and measuring the life course: Charlotte Ikels et al., 'Perceptions of the Adult Life Course: A Cross-cultural Analysis', *Ageing and Society*, 12 (1992), pp. 49–84.

39 George Orwell, 'The Art of Donald McGill', *Horizon* (September 1941). For a discussion of class differences in ageing across time, see Pat Thane,

'Social Histories of Old Age and Aging', *Journal of Social History*, 37 (2003), pp. 93–111.

40 Orwell, 'The Art of Donald McGill'.

41 Kiyomo Morioka, 'Life Cycle Patterns in Japan, China, and the United States', *Journal of Marriage and the Family*, 29 (1967), pp. 595–606. As Chapter Three explores, divorce levels were nevertheless high in Japan: Harald Fuess, *Divorce in Japan: Family, Gender and the State, 1600–2000* (Stanford, CA, 2004).

42 Morioka, 'Life Cycle Patterns'.

43 Sudhir Kakar, 'The Search for Middle Age in India', in *Welcome to Middle Age!*, ed. Richard A. Shweder (Chicago, IL, 1998), pp. 75–98. See also Susanne Hoeber Rudolph and Lloyd I. Rudolph, 'Rajput Adulthood: Reflections on the Amar Singh Diary', in *Adulthood*, ed. Erik Erikson (New York, 1976), pp. 149–71.

44 Mintz and Kellogg, *Domestic Revolutions*, pp. 141–4.

45 Steven Mintz, *The Prime of Life: A History of Modern Adulthood* (Cambridge, MA, 2015), pp. 135–40.

46 Thomas S. Weisner and Lucinda P. Bernheimer, 'Children of the 1960s at Midlife: Generational Identity and the Family Adaptive Project', in *Welcome to Middle Age!*, ed. Shweder, pp. 211–57, at p. 216.

47 On historical models of ageing, see Thomas R. Cole, *The Journey of Life: A Cultural History of Aging in America* (Cambridge, 1992).

48 Hall, 'The Dangerous Age', p. 275.

49 See Cole, *The Journey of Life*, pp. 120–27, 239–51; Mark Jackson, *The Age of Stress: Science and the Search for Stability* (Oxford, 2013), pp. 42, 54.

50 Margaret Morganroth Gullette, *Aged by Culture* (Chicago, IL, 2004); Margaret Morganroth Gullette, *Declining to Decline: Cultural Combat and the Politics of the Midlife* (Charlottesville, VA, 1997); and Margaret Morganroth Gullette, *Ending Ageism, Or How Not to Shoot Old People* (New Brunswick, NJ, 2018).

51 Margaret Morganroth Gullette, *Safe at Last in the Middle Years: The Invention of the Midlife Progress Novel* (Berkeley, CA, 1988).

52 Ibid., pp. 59–84.

53 John Updike, *Rabbit Is Rich* [1981] (London, 2006), p. 208.

54 For examples of women's fictional writings about midlife, see Simone de Beauvoir, *The Woman Destroyed* [1967] (London, 1969); Doris Lessing, *The Summer Before the Dark* (London, 1973). For a male perspective on women at midlife, see also Angus Wilson, *The Middle Age of Mrs Eliot* (London, 1958).

55 Daniel J. Levinson et al., *The Seasons of a Man's Life* (New York, 1979); Daniel J. Levinson, *The Seasons of a Woman's Life* (New York, 1996). See also Hilda L. Smith, '"Age": A Problematic Concept for Women', *Journal of Women's History*, 12 (2001), pp. 77–86.

56 Julia Kristeva, 'Women's Time', *Signs: Journal of Women in Culture and Society*, 7 (1981), pp. 13–35.

57 Margaret Morganroth Gullette, 'Midlife Discourses in the Twentieth-century United States: An Essay on the Sexuality, Ideology, and Politics of "Middle-ageism"', in *Welcome to Middle Age!*, ed. Shweder, pp. 3–44, at p. 22.

58 Ikels et al., 'Perceptions of the Adult Life Course', pp. 61–2.
59 Lynne Segal, 'Temporal Vertigo: The Paradoxes of Ageing', *Studies in Gender and Sexuality*, 15 (2014), pp. 214–22, 217–18.
60 Ibid., pp. 218–19, citing Greer.
61 Ibid. Segal is referring especially to autobiographical works by Simone de Beauvoir and Doris Lessing.
62 There are some studies of relationships in both heterosexual and same-sex couples in the late twentieth and early twenty-first centuries, most notably those emerging from Jacqui Gabb's ESRC-funded research project 'Enduring Love?': Jacqui Gabb and Janet Fink, *Couple Relationships in the 21st Century* (Basingstoke, 2015). See also the brief discussion of Erik Erikson's theories on adult personality development in relation to 'homo-sexuality' in Raphella Sohier, 'Homosexual Mutuality: Variation on a Theme by Erik Erikson', *Journal of Homosexuality*, 12 (1986), pp. 25–38. For a provocative analysis of how women's life stories were shaped by family and society, see Lynn Abrams, 'Liberating the Self: Epiphanies, Conflict and Coherence in the Life Stories of Post-war British women', *Social History*, 39 (2014), pp. 14–35.
63 Alice S. Rossi, 'Life-span Theories and Women's Lives', *Signs: Journal of Women in Culture and Society*, 6 (1980), pp. 4–32, at pp. 5–6.
64 Marjorie Fiske Lowenthal, Majda Thurnher and David Chiriboga, eds, *Four Stages of Life: A Comparative Study of Women and Men Facing Transitions* (San Francisco, CA, 1976), p. x.
65 Rossi, 'Life-span Theories', p. 7.
66 Charlotte Bühler, 'The Human Course of Life in its Goal Aspects', *Journal of Humanistic Psychology*, 4 (1964), pp. 1–18, at p. 1; Charlotte Bühler, 'The Curve of Life as Studied in Biographies', *Journal of Applied Psychology*, 19 (1935), pp. 405–9.
67 John Benson, *Prime Time: A History of the Middle Aged in Twentieth-century Britain* (London, 1997), pp. 32–6.
68 Thomas C. Desmond, 'America's Unknown Middle-agers', *New York Times* (29 July 1956), pp. 5, 42–3.
69 Clark Tibbitts, 'Life Begins at 50', *Buffalo Courier Express* (15 May 1960).
70 Anon., 'The Pleasures and Perils of Middle Age'.
71 William Osler, 'The Fixed Period', in *Aequanimitas* (Philadelphia, PA, 1910), pp. 391–411, at p. 398.
72 Ibid., p. 399.
73 Anthony Trollope, *The Fixed Period* [1882] (London, 1997).
74 Osler's words continued to incite debate about the relative merits of middle age through the twentieth century: 'Skill and Old Age', *Lancet* (4 August 1951), pp. 210–11; G. Stanley Hall, *Senescence: The Last Half of Life* (New York, 1922), pp. 3–31. On the diversity of opinions on Osler's work, see Laura Davidow Hirschbein, 'William Osler and *The Fixed Period*: Conflicting Medical and Popular Ideas about Old Age', *Archives of Internal Medicine*, 161 (2001), pp. 2074–8.
75 Edmund Leach, *A Runaway World? The Reith Lectures 1967* (London, 1968), p. 74.
76 Richard E. Varner, 'The Organized Peasant: The *Wakamonogumi* in the Edo Period', *Monumenta Nipponica*, 32 (1977), pp. 459–83, at p. 465.

77 Cicely Hamilton, *Marriage as a Trade* (New York, 1909), Chapter XVIII,
    https://digital.library.upenn.edu, accessed 2 August 2019.
78 Mary Scharlieb, *The Seven Ages of Woman: A Consideration of the
    Successive Phases of Woman's Life* (London, 1915), pp. vi, 264.
79 Ibid., pp. 264–5.
80 Erik H. Erikson, *Childhood and Society* [1950] (New York, 1963), p. 273;
    Erik H. Erikson, *Identity and the Life Cycle* [1959] (New York, 1994), p. 129.
81 Jean Frumusan, *Rejuvenation*, trans. Elaine C. Wood (London, 1923).
    Frumusan, whose book had been published first in French in 1922, also
    believed that it was a mistake to ascribe the age of a person merely to the
    'almanac': ibid., p. 34.
82 On middle age as a stage of mind, see D. B. Bromley, 'Middle Age: An
    Introduction', in *Middle Age*, ed. Roger Owen (London, 1967), pp. 7–21,
    at p. 9. On the need to pay greater medical attention to the problems of
    middle-aged men and women, see Leslie J. Tizard and Harry J. S. Guntrip,
    Middle Age (London, 1959).
83 Bernice L. Neugarten, 'The Awareness of Middle Age', in *Middle Age and
    Aging*, ed. Bernice L. Neugarten (Chicago, IL, 1968), pp. 93–98, at p. 97. For
    historical discussion of this notion, see Mintz, *The Prime of Life*; Patricia
    Cohen, *In Our Prime: The Invention of Middle Age* (New York, 2012).
84 The disengagement model of adult ageing originated in the Kansas City
    Study carried out in the 1950s and '60s: Robert J. Havighurst, Bernice L.
    Neugarten and Sheldon S. Tobin, 'Disengagement and Patterns of Aging', in
    Middle Age and Aging, ed. Neugarten, pp. 161–2; Jon Hendricks, 'Revisiting
    the Kansas City Study of Adult Life: Roots of the Disengagement Model in
    Social Gerontology', *The Gerontologist*, 34 (1994), pp. 753–5.
85 Marjorie Fiske Lowenthal and David Chiriboga, 'Transition to the Empty
    Nest: Crisis, Challenge, or Relief?', *Archives of General Psychiatry*, 26
    (1972), pp. 8–14; Carl G. Jung, *The Integration of the Personality*
    (London, 1940).
86 On forty as the 'nightmare birthday', see Benson, *Prime Time*, p. 10, citing
    a 1930 article in *John Bull*.
87 Pearce and Newton, *The Conditions of Human Growth*, p. 135.
88 Cited in Benson, *Prime Time*, p. 25.
89 Jim Tomlinson, 'Inventing "Decline": The Falling Behind of the British
    Economy in the Postwar Years', *Economic History Review*, 49 (1996),
    pp. 731–57.
90 On the challenges – and implications – of receding hairlines, see 'Need
    Men go Bald?', *Family Doctor*, 3 (August 1953), pp. 443–4. On the post-war
    crisis of masculinity, see James Gilbert, *Men in the Middle: Searching for
    Masculinity in the 1950s* (Chicago, IL, 2005).
91 According to Cohen, one of the drivers of understanding midlife in
    terms of decline was the introduction and dissemination of Taylorism or
    scientific management: Cohen, *In Our Prime*, pp. 34, 36.
92 Cited in Jeanne Brooks-Gunn and Barbara Kirsh, 'Life Events and the
    Boundaries of Midlife for Women', in *Women in Midlife*, ed. Grace Baruch
    and Jeanne Brooks-Gunn (New York, 1983), pp. 11–30, 11.
93 Erikson, *Identity and the Life Cycle*, pp. 98–9.
94 Lee and Casebier, *The Spouse Gap*, p. 80.

95 Ibid., pp. 75–6.

96 Alva Myrdal and Viola Klein, *Women's Two Roles: Home and Work* [1956] (London, 1968), p. 39.

97 Nixola Greeley-Smith, 'Now Is the Time for All Women to Train for the Duties that War Time May Bring', *Pittsburgh Press* (10 April 1917), p. 20.

98 Mrs Theodore Parsons, *Brain Culture through Scientific Body Building* (Chicago, IL, 1912). Parsons later published an abridged version for 'use in homes, schools and colleges': Mrs Theodore Parsons, *Making the Body Think* (New York, 1926).

99 Greeley-Smith, 'Now Is the Time'.

100 Forbes Lindsay, 'The Man of Fifty', *Harper's Weekly*, 53 (16 October 1909), pp. 15–16.

101 James F. Stark, *The Cult of Youth: Anti-ageing in Modern Britain* (Cambridge, 2020); Aimee Medeiros and Elizabeth Siegel Watkins, 'Live Longer Better: The Historical Roots of Human Growth Hormone as Anti-aging Medicine', *Journal of the History of Medicine and Allied Sciences*, 73 (2018), pp. 333–59. 'Middle-aged spread' became a popular term in the 1930s: Benson, *Prime Time*, pp. 17–19.

102 Anon., 'So Often . . . Life Begins at Forty', *Tatler* (27 June 1934), p. 605. Gayelord Hauser was nutritional director of Elizabeth Arden's 'beauty farm' in Maine: Carstairs, '"Look Younger, Live Longer"', p. 338.

103 'Forty-phobia (fear of the forties)', *The Times* (28 April 1938), p. 19; 'Fortyphobia', *Maclean's*, 1 April 1938, http://archive.macleans.ca, accessed 18 February 2019.

104 Mass-Observation Project, Winter 2009, 'Mid-life transitions', Respondent B.1180, p. 1.

105 On concerns about body weight and heart disease in working men, see Jane Hand, 'Marketing Health Education: Advertising Margarine and Visualising Health in Britain from 1964–c. 2000', *Contemporary British History* (2017), pp. 477–500; Jane Hand, '"Look After Yourself": Visualising Obesity as a Public Health Concern in 1970s and 1980s Britain', in *Balancing the Self: Medicine, Politics and the Regulation of Health in the Twentieth Century*, ed. Mark Jackson and Martin Moore (Manchester, 2020), pp. 95–124.

106 Sontag, 'The Double Standard of Aging', p. 35.

107 Ibid., p. 31.

108 Walter B. Pitkin, *Life Begins at Forty* (New York, 1932). Pitkin's work was regularly and widely reported in the local press across North America. See, for example, 'Life Begins at 40', *Daily News* (15 April 1938), p. 105.

109 Pitkin, *Life Begins at Forty*, p. 3.

110 *Life Begins at 40*, Fox Film Corporation (1935), www.imdb.com, accessed 5 March 2019.

111 Sophie Tucker, *Some of These Days: An Autobiography* (London, 1951), p. 95.

112 Stanley Brandes, *Forty: The Age and the Symbol* (Knoxville, TN, 1985).

113 Alva Myrdal and Viola Klein, *Women's Two Roles: Home and Work* [1956] (London, 1968), p. 17. Publications similar to Pitkin's include Boris Sokoloff, *Middle Age Is What You Make It* (New York, 1938); Martin Gumpert, *You Are Younger than You Think* (New York, 1944); Dame Annis Gillie, *Do Something About That Middle Age* (London, 1969).

114 Myrdal and Viola, *Women's Two Roles*, p. 17.
115 Sinclair Lewis, *Babbitt* (Leipzig, 1922), p. 288.
116 Pitkin, *Life Begins at Forty*, p. 7.
117 Ibid., p. 24.
118 Mark Abrams, 'British Standards of Living', *Current Affairs*, 63
     (18 September 1948); Denys Thompson, 'The Importance of Leisure',
     Current Affairs, 72 (22 January 1949); Mass-Observation, 'A Report
     on Work and Leisure', File Report 3067 (November 1948).
119 Pitkin, *Life Begins at Forty*, p. 107.
120 Ibid.
121 Jan Struther, *Mrs Miniver* (London, 1939), p. 4.
122 Pitkin, *Life Begins at Forty*, p. 86.
123 Ibid., p. 149.
124 Ibid., pp. 49, 107.
125 Heidi Marie Rimke, 'Governing Citizens through Self-help Literature',
     Cultural Studies, 14 (2000), pp. 61–78.
126 Walter Pitkin Jr, *Life Begins at Fifty* (New York, 1965), pp. 21–2. Italics in
     original.
127 Sue Currell, 'Depression and Recovery: Self-help and America in the 1930s',
     in *Historicizing Lifestyle: Mediating Taste, Consumption and Identity from
     the 1900s to 1970s*, ed. David Bell and Joanne Hollows (Aldershot, 2006),
     pp. 131–44.
128 Edmund Jacobson, *You Must Relax: A Practical Method of Reducing the
     Strains of Modern Living* (New York, 1934); Grace Loucks Elliott, *Women
     After Forty: The Meaning of the Last Half of Life* (New York, 1936);
     Sokoloff, *Middle Age Is What You Make It*; Hauser, *Look Younger, Live
     Longer*; Maxine Davis, *Get the Most Out of Your Best Years* (New York,
     1960); Desmond Dunne, *Yoga for Everyman: How to Have Long Life and
     Happiness* (London, 1951). On relaxation therapies, see Ayesha Nathoo,
     'Initiating Therapeutic Relaxation in Britain: A Twentieth-century Strategy
     for Health and Wellbeing', *Palgrave Communications* (2016), www.nature.
     com, accessed 25 February 2019. On self-help literature for the stressed,
     see Jill Kirby, *Feeling the Strain: A Cultural History of Stress in Twentieth-
     century Britain* (Manchester, 2019).
129 Neil Brierley, *Relaxation for Men: Tension in Modern Living*
     (London, 1965), p. 7.
130 E. J. Boome and M. A. Richardson, *Relaxation in Everyday Life*
     (London, 1938), pp. 1, 99.
131 Nancy Phelan and Michael Volin, *Yoga over Forty* (New York, 1965), p. 48.
132 Hauser, *Look Younger, Live Longer*, pp. 188–97.
133 Ibid., p. 188.
134 Nadina R. Kavinoky, 'A Balanced Life for Mental Health', *Marriage and
     Family Living*, 6 (1944), pp. 41–2, 58, 64.
135 Tizard and Guntrip, *Middle Age*, pp. 60–61; Sir Heneage Ogilvie, 'In Praise
     of Idleness', *British Medical Journal* (16 April 1949), pp. 645–51.
136 Tom Lutz, '"Sweat or die": The Hedonization of the Work Ethic in the
     1920s', *American Literary History*, 8 (1996), pp. 259–83.
137 Frederick Cooper, 'Medical Feminism, Working Mothers, and the
     Limits of Home: Finding a Balance between Self-care and Other-care in

Cross-cultural Debates about Health and Lifestyle, 1952–1956', *Palgrave Communications*, www.nature.com, 12 July 2016.

138 Pitkin, *Life Begins at Forty*, pp. 112, 115. Pitkin's son also recognized the specific problems of middle-aged women: Pitkin Jr, *Life Begins at Fifty*, pp. 16, 211–13.

139 Pitkin, *Life Begins at Forty*, p. 112.

140 On Hilliard's views, see Kaitlynn Mendes, 'Reading *Chatelaine*: Dr Marion Hilliard and 1950s Women's Health Advice', *Canadian Journal of Communication*, 35 (2010), pp. 515–31. On the popularity and significance of *Chatelaine* magazine in the post-war decades, see Valerie Korinek, *Roughing It in the Suburbs: Reading Chatelaine Magazine in the Fifties and Sixties* (Toronto, 2000).

141 Marion Hilliard, *Women and Fatigue* (London, 1963), p. 82.

142 Marion Hilliard, 'Stop Being Just a Housewife', *Chatelaine* (September 1956), pp. 11, 90–95.

143 Martin Roth, 'Psychiatric Aspects of Middle Age', in Report on the Hazards of Middle Age, *Journal of the Royal College of General Practitioners*, Supplement I to vol. VIII (1964), pp. 27–52, at p. 27.

144 Sarah Churchwell, *Behold, America: A History of America First and the American Dream* (London, 2018), pp. 15–16.

145 Adams, *The Epic of America*, p. 415. For detailed discussion of Adams's interpretation of the dream, see Churchwell, *Behold, America*, pp. 169–82.

146 Adams, *The Epic of America*, pp. 416–17.

147 James Truslow Adams, *Our Business Civilization: Some Aspects of American Culture* (New York, 1929), pp. 289–306, at p. 299.

148 Adams, *The Epic of America*, p. 424; Pitkin, *Life Begins at Forty*, p. 95.

149 Edward P. J. Corbett, 'Life at the Top', *America* (27 October 1962), pp. 961–2.

150 Sloan Wilson, *The Man in the Gray Flannel Suit* [1955] (Cambridge, MA, 2002); Sloan Wilson, *The Man in the Gray Flannel Suit II* (New York, 1984).

151 Gregory Peck in the trailer for *The Man in the Gray Flannel Suit* (1956), www.imdb.com, accessed 11 April 2019.

152 Norman Mailer, *An American Dream* (London, 1965). See the review of the book in Conrad Knickerbocker, 'A Man Desperate for a New Life', *New York Times* (14 March 1965), BR, pp. 1, 36, 38, 39.

153 Beauvoir, *The Woman Destroyed*, p. 214. In Doris Lessing's *The Summer Before the Dark* (London, 1973), Kate Brown's growing discontent with her life and marriage and her relationship with a younger man are precipitated by her husband's absences for work and his multiple infidelities.

154 Beauvoir, *The Woman Destroyed*, pp. 183–4.

155 Barbara Fried, *The Middle-age Crisis* (New York, 1967), p. 6.

156 Titmuss, *Essays on 'The Welfare State'*, p. 101.

3 SCENES FROM A MARRIAGE

1 Margaret Mead, *Male and Female* [1949] (Harmondsworth, 1962), p. 325.

2 Rupert Cross, 'Final Report of the Committee on Procedure in Matrimonial Causes (The Denning Committee)', *Modern Law Review*, 10 (April 1947), pp. 184–92, at p. 187.

3 Marie Carmichael Stopes, *Enduring Passion* [1929] (London, 1936), pp. 9–10.

4 Ibid., p. 24. On love and marriage in this period, see Timothy Willem Jones and Alana Harris, 'Introduction: Historicizing "Modern" Love and Romance', in *Love and Romance in Britain, 1918–1970*, ed. Alana Harris and Timothy Jones (Basingstoke, 2014), pp. 1–19; Marcus Collins, *Modern Love: An Intimate History of Men and Women in Twentieth-century Britain* (London, 2003).

5 Penrose Halson, *The Marriage Bureau: The True Story of how Two Matchmakers Arranged Love in Wartime London* (New York, 2017).

6 Office of National Statistics, 'Number of Marriages, Marriage Rates and Periods of Occurrence', www.ons.gov.uk, accessed 1 August 2019.

7 On companionate marriage as an ideal, see John R. Gillis, *For Better, For Worse: British Marriages, 1600 to the Present* (Oxford, 1985); Collins, *Modern Love*; Claire Langhamer, 'Love, Selfhood and Authenticity in Post-war Britain', *Cultural and Social History*, 9 (2012), pp. 277–97; Claire Langhamer, *The English in Love: The Intimate Story of an Emotional Revolution* (Oxford, 2013).

8 Margaret Mead, 'Modern Marriages', *The Nation*, www.thenation.com, 31 October 1953.

9 Marital Studies Advisory Panel, 'Expectations of Marriage', Wellcome Library, SA/TCC/A/3/5: Box 6, p. 6.

10 Gillis, *For Better, For Worse*, p. 5.

11 Richard Titmuss, *Essays on 'The Welfare State'* [1958] (London, 1963), p. 98.

12 Janet Finch and Penny Summerfield, 'Social Reconstruction and the Emergence of the Companionate Marriage, 1945–59', in *Marriage, Domestic Life and Social Change: Writings for Jacqueline Burgoyne (1944–88)*, ed. David Clark (London, 1991), pp. 6–27, at p. 17.

13 Angela Davis and Laura King, 'Gendered Perspectives on Men's Changing Familial Roles in Postwar Britain, *c.* 1950–1990', *Gender and History*, 30 (2018), pp. 70–92.

14 Peter Berger and Hansfried Kellner, 'Marriage and the Construction of Reality', *Diogenes*, 12 (1964), pp. 1–24, at p. 16; Elizabeth Bott, *Family and Social Networks: Roles, Norms, and External Relationships in Ordinary Urban Families* (London, 1957), pp. 52–96; Isabel B. P. Menzies, 'Factors Affecting Family Breakdown in Urban Communities', Wellcome Library, SA/TCC/A/1/1: Box 1. Hannah Gavron compared the roles of extended families in both working-class and middle-class communities: Hannah Gavron, *The Captive Wife: Conflicts of Housebound Mothers* [1966] (London, 1968), pp. 95–105.

15 Cross, 'Final Report', p. 187.

16 'Panorama: Divorce', www.bbc.co.uk, 11 March 1963, 3 minutes 30 seconds. On moves towards no-fault divorce from the 1960s, see Roderick Phillips, *Putting Asunder: A History of Divorce in Western Society* (Cambridge, 1988), pp. 561–72.

17 The programmes were broadcast between 16 September and 14 October 1964: 'Marriage Today: A Social Institution', www.bbc.co.uk/archive/marriage/10507.shtml; 'Marriage Today: Intimate Union', www.bbc.co.uk/archive/marriage/10508.shtml; 'Marriage Today: An Excellent Mystery', www.bbc.co.uk/archive/marriage/10509.shtml, all accessed 8 March 2019.

18 'Marriage Today: An Excellent Mystery'. Mead's views on marriage and

family were influential. From the 1940s to the '70s, she was a prominent figure in public discussions about marriage and divorce, contributing regularly to newspaper articles, influencing television debates and helping to shape Geoffrey Gorer's anthropological survey of English character published in 1955, as well his later analysis of sex and marriage in England – see Peter Mandler, 'Being His Own Rabbit: Geoffrey Gorer and English Culture', in *Classes, Cultures, and Politics: Essays on British History of Ross McKibben*, ed. Clare V. J. Griffiths, James J. Nott and William Whyte (Oxford, 2011), pp. 192–216. The curve of Mead's life, punctuated at the age of 43 by her divorce from the anthropologist Gregory Bateson and her adoption of new ways of working, also provided a reference point for Gail Sheehy's later work on the midlife crisis: Gail Sheehy, *Passages: Predictable Crises of Adult Life* (New York, 1974), pp. 16, 268–76.

19 Mead, *Male and Female*, p. 325.

20 Mead's views and those of science fiction writers are considered in William F. Kenkel, 'Marriage and the Modern Family', *Journal of Marriage and the Family*, 31 (1969), pp. 6–14.

21 Mass-Observation, Spring 1998 Directive, 'Having an Affair', Respondent A.883, Sheet 12.

22 See the report by the Archbishop of Canterbury, *Putting Asunder: A Divorce Law for Contemporary Society* (London, 1966).

23 'Marriage under Stress: 1: Children Made a Difference', www.bbc.co.uk/archive/marriage/10512.shtml; 'Marriage under Stress: 2: Breaking Point', www.bbc.co.uk/archive/marriage/10513.shtml; 'Marriage under Stress: 3: Put Asunder', www.bbc.co.uk/archive/marriage/10514.shtml, all accessed 8 March 2019.

24 'Breaking Point', at 20 minutes 50 seconds (20:50).

25 'Put Asunder', at 7:22. For examples of men pretending to be single in order to have affairs, see Joanne Klein, 'Irregular Marriages: Unorthodox Working-class Domestic Life in Liverpool, Birmingham, and Manchester, 1900–1939', *Journal of Family History*, 30 (2005), pp. 210–29, at p. 216.

26 'Put Asunder', from 5:16 to 9:14. The clubs were brought together by Mercia Emerson under the umbrella of the National Federation of Clubs for the Divorced and Separated. On other 'singles groups', see Marjorie Fiske Lowenthal and Lawrence Weiss, 'Intimacy and Crises in Adulthood', *Counseling Psychologist*, 6 (1976), pp. 10–15, at p. 12.

27 Reuben Hill, *Families Under Stress* (New York, 1949), p. ix.

28 The honeymoon was rarely investigated as a component of marriage, even though it also opened up opportunities for couples to be dissatisfied with conflicts between expectations and reality – Rhona Rapoport and Robert Rapoport, 'New Light on the Honeymoon', *Human Relations*, 17 (1964), pp. 33–56.

29 Between October and November 1967, a BBC One television series explored the topic of marriage within the specific context of middle age. Contributions to the series, which included Elliott Jaques speaking about the midlife crisis and the psychiatrist Doris Odlum exploring marriage and the family during the middle years, were subsequently published in Roger Owen, ed., *Middle Age* (London, 1967).

30 Macpherson Lawrie, *Love, Marriage and Divorce* (London, 1937), pp. 185–8.

31 Mass-Observation, 'The State of Matrimony' (June 1947), File Report 2495, p. 3, www.massobservation.amdigital.co.uk, accessed 11 March 2019.

32 Robert Lee and Marjorie Casebier, *The Spouse Gap* (London, 1973).

33 George R. Bach and Peter Wyden, *The Intimate Enemy: How to Fight Fair in Love and Marriage* (New York, 1969).

34 Barbara Gordon, 'You, Your Husband and the Younger Woman', *Chatelaine*, 61 (September 1988), pp. 88–93.

35 Mead, *Male and Female*, p. 325.

36 Steven Ruggles, 'The Rise of Divorce and Separation in the United States, 1880–1990', *Demography*, 34 (1997), pp. 455–66.

37 Roberto Rossellini, *Journey to Italy* (1953), released on DVD by the British Film Institute. Rossellini and Bergman were married until 1957.

38 *The Seven Year Itch* (Charles K. Feldman Productions, 1955). The play by George Axelrod was first performed on 20 November 1952.

39 *The Seven Year Itch*, at 56 minutes 9 seconds.

40 Sherman first plays Rachmaninov's Piano Concerto No. 2 on the gramophone at 26 minutes 30 seconds. *Spring in a Small Town* (1948), a Chinese film based on a short story by Li Tianji, also explores a loveless marriage and nostalgia for youthful romance. More recent films on midlife are discussed in: Julie Levinson, *The American Success Myth on Film* (Basingstoke, 2012); Margaret Gatling, Jane Mills and David Lindsay, 'Representations of Middle Age in Comedy Film: A Critical Discourse Analysis', *The Qualitative Report*, 19 (2014), pp. 1–15.

41 Eric Berne, *Games People Play: The Psychology of Human Relationships* (London, 1964), p. 80.

42 Ibid., pp. 80–95.

43 Berger and Kellner, 'Marriage and the Construction of Reality', p. 5.

44 Ibid.

45 Marital Studies Advisory Panel, 'Expectations of Marriage', pp. 6–8.

46 Ulrich Beck and Elisabeth Beck-Gernsheim, *The Normal Chaos of Love* (London, 1995), pp. 45, 68, 66.

47 Richard E. Gordon, Katherine K. Gordon and Max Gunther, *The Split-level Trap* (New York, 1961), p. 110.

48 Alvin Toffler, *Future Shock* (London, 1970), pp. 211–30.

49 Beck and Beck-Gernsheim, *The Normal Chaos of Love*, pp. 66–7, 72. On romance as a 'means to self-actualization', see Jones and Harris, 'Introduction', p. 8.

50 Mass-Observation, 'The State of Matrimony', p. 1. According to the report, the divorce rate per 10,000 population was 1 in England, 4.5 in Sweden and 13.9 in the USA.

51 Lawrie, *Love, Marriage and Divorce*, p. 152.

52 Ibid.

53 O. R. McGregor, *Divorce in England: A Centenary Study* (London, 1957); Lawrence Stone, *Road to Divorce: England, 1530–1987* (Oxford, 1990).

54 Mass-Observation, 'The State of Matrimony', p. 2.

55 Anon., 'Services Divorce Delays', *The Times*, 27 March 1946, p. 8. See also: Anon., 'Broken Marriages', *The Times*, 17 July 1945, p. 5; Anon., 'Divorce in the Services: Effects of Long Absence', *The Times*, 2 April 1946, p. 5.

56 Anon., 'Broken Marriages'.

57 Adam Curle, 'Transitional Communities and Social Re-connection: Part I', *Human Relations*, 1 (1947), pp. 42–68; Adam Curle and E. L. Trist, 'Transitional Communities and Social Re-connection: Part II', *Human Relations*, 1 (1947), pp. 240–66.

58 Sloan Wilson, *The Man in the Gray Flannel Suit* (New York, 1955).

59 Angela Reed, *The Woman on the Verge of Divorce* (London, 1970); Gerald Sanctuary and Constance Whitehead, *Divorce – and After* (London, 1970).

60 Office of National Statistics, 'Vital Statistics: Population and Health Reference Tables', www.ons.gov.uk. The 1969 Act was the product of a Law Commission on 'Reform of the Grounds of Divorce', which had been set up in 1965 and reported in 1966 – see Stephen Cretney, *Family Law in the Twentieth Century: A History* (Oxford, 2003), pp. 319–93. Objections to the use of 'matrimonial offence' included the fact that it implied fault and often required evidence from the use of private investigators or receipts from hotels to prove adultery if it was not admitted by the respondent.

61 'Breaking Point', at 2 minutes 20 seconds.

62 'Address of Dr. Sidney E. Goldstein on the Need of a White House Conference on Family', *Living*, 1 (1939), pp. 13–14.

63 'The National Conference on Family Relations', *Living*, 1 (1939), p. 31.

64 Alexander A. Plateris, *100 Years of Marriage and Divorce Statistics, United States, 1867–1967* (Rockville, MD, 1973), www.cdc.gov, accessed 15 April 2019; U.S. Census Bureau, *Births, Deaths, Marriages and Divorces* (Statistical Abstract of the United States, 2011), p. 96.

65 Ruggles, 'The Rise of Divorce and Separation', p. 464.

66 David R. Mace, 'Marriage Breakdown or Matrimonial Offense: A Clinical or Legal Approach to Divorce?', *American University Law Review*, 14 (1965), pp. 178–88.

67 Harald Fuess, *Divorce in Japan: Family, Gender, and the State, 1600–2000* (Stanford, CA, 2004), pp. 119–43, 152–61.

68 'Statistics Canada, Table 39-10-0008-01: Vital Statistics, Divorces', www150.statcan.gc.ca, accessed 3 September 2019; Josie McLellan, *Love in the Time of Communism: Intimacy and Sexuality in the GDR* (Cambridge, 2011), pp. 77–8.

69 David Fitzpatrick, 'Divorce and Separation in Modern Irish History', *Past and Present*, 114 (1987), pp. 172–96; Natalia Pushkareva, 'Marriage in Twentieth Century Russia: Traditional Precepts and Innovative Experiments', www.iisg.nl/womhist/pushkareva.doc, accessed 15 December 2020.

70 M. F. Ashley Montagu, ed., *Marriage: Past and Present: A Debate Between Robert Briffault and Bronislaw Malinowski* (Boston, MA, 1956), p. 21.

71 *Final Report of the Denning Committee on Procedure in Matrimonial Causes* (Cmd. 7024, London, HMSO, 1946), cited in Cross, 'Final Report', pp. 184–92. The ratio of women to men petitioning for divorce across the post-war years can be seen in Office of National Statistics, 'Vital Statistics', Table 1. Financial support for divorce was made available by the Legal Aid and Advice Act of 1949 – see Carol Smart, 'Good Wives and Moral Lives: Marriage and Divorce, 1937–51', in *Nationalising Femininity: Culture, Sexuality and British Cinema in the Second World War*, ed. Christine Gledhill and Gillian Swanson (Manchester, 1996), pp. 91–105.

72 Benita Eisler, *Private Lives: Men and Women of the Fifties* (New York, 1986), p. 300.

73 *Report of the Royal Commission on Marriage and Divorce* (Cmd. 9678, London, HMSO, 1956), cited in O. Kahn-Freund, 'Divorce Law Reform?', *Modern Law Review*, 19 (1956), pp. 573–600, at p. 577.

74 A.T.M. Wilson, 'Some Reflections and Suggestions on the Prevention and Treatment of Marital Problems', *Human Relations*, 2 (1949), pp. 233–52.

75 *Report of the Royal Commission on Marriage and Divorce*, pp. 7–8, cited in Carol Smart, 'Divorce in England 1950–2000: A Moral Tale', CAVA Workshop Paper, 1999, p. 2, www.leeds.ac.uk, accessed 16 April 2019.

76 McGregor, *Divorce in England*, pp. 126, 152, 158. McGregor was quoting the Morton Commission, but was himself critical of many of these arguments. Griselda Rowntree also challenged assumptions being made about marriage, separation and divorce: Griselda Rowntree, 'Some Aspects of Marriage Breakdown in Britain during the Last Thirty Years', *Population Studies*, 18 (1964), pp. 147–63.

77 Philip Gibbs, *The Eighth Year: A Vital Problem of Married Life* (London, 1913), p. 100.

78 Anon., 'The Divorce Picture', *Marriage and Family Living*, 19 (1957), p. 381.

79 U.S. Department of Health, Education and Welfare, *100 Years of Marriage and Divorce Statistics*, p. 14. In 1972 a report for the Bureau of the Census also asserted that the 'median duration of marriage before divorce has been about seven years for the last half century', cited in Sheehy, *Passages*, p. 17.

80 Fuess, *Divorce in Japan*, pp. 153–4.

81 Rowntree, 'Some Aspects of Marriage Breakdown'.

82 Ronald Fletcher, *The Family and Marriage in Britain* (London, 1973), p. 155. The same was still true in the early 1980s: Ronald Fletcher, *The Shaking of the Foundations: Family and Society* (London, 1988), pp. 58–60.

83 Jack Dominian, *Marital Breakdown* (London, 1968), pp. 18–19. This was also an argument made in Marie Carmichael Stopes, *Married Love or Love in Marriage* (New York, 1918); Stopes, *Enduring Passion*. On the success of *Married Love*, see Alexander C. T. Geppert, 'Divine Sex, Happy Marriage, Regenerated Nation: Marie Stopes' Marital Manual *Married Love* and the Making of a Best-seller, 1918–1955', *Journal of the History of Sexuality*, 8 (1998), pp. 389–433.

84 Clifford Kirkpatrick, 'Factors in Marital Adjustment', *American Journal of Sociology*, 43 (1937), pp. 270–83; Ernest W. Burgess, 'Predictive Factors in the Success or Failure of Marriage', *Living* (1939), pp. 1–3; Dr Pauline Park Wilson, 'A Plan for Successful Marriage', *Living*, 1 (1939), p. 8; Boyd C. Rollins and Harold Feldman, 'Marital Satisfaction over the Family Life Cycle', *Journal of Marriage and the Family*, 32 (1970), pp. 20–28.

85 James H. S. Bossard and Eleanor Stoker Boll, 'Marital Unhappiness in the Life Cycle', *Marriage and Family Living*, 17 (1955), pp. 10–14, at p. 14. See also Wesley R. Burr, 'Satisfaction with Various Aspects of Marriage over the Life Cycle: A Random Middle Class Sample', *Journal of Marriage and the Family*, 32 (1970), pp. 29–37.

86 Rosalie Macrae, 'Middle-age is Danger Time for Marriages', *Daily Mail*, 14 June 1965, p. 5.

87 Kenneth Soddy and Mary C. Kidson, *Men in Middle Life* (London, 1967), p. 56.

88 Stopes, *Enduring Passion*, pp. 12–29.

89 Geoffrey Gorer, *Exploring English Character* (London, 1955), pp. 125–6, 138–9, 145. Gorer was sometimes referred to as the 'British Margaret Mead', see Jeremy MacClancy, *Anthropology in the Public Arena: Historical and Contemporary Contexts* (London, 2013), pp. 81–109.

90 Gorer, *Exploring English Character*, pp. 148–9.

91 Ibid., p. 148.

92 J. H. Wallis, *The Challenge of Middle Age* (London, 1962), p. 110.

93 Jane Lewis, *The End of Marriage? Individualism and Intimate Relations* (Cheltenham, 2001), pp. 108–13.

94 C. G. Jung, 'Marriage as a Psychological Relationship', in C. G. Jung, *The Development of Personality*, trans. R.F.C. Hull (London, 1964), pp. 189–201, at p. 192.

95 Oswald Schwarz, 'Sex and Personality: (3) On Marriage', *World Review* (1947), pp. 47–52, at p. 52. On Schwarz, see H. J. Berberich, D. Schultheiss and B. Kieser, 'Oswald Schwartz: Ein Pionier der Psychosomatischen Urologie und Sexualmedizin', *Urologe*, 54 (2015), pp. 88–96.

96 Lowenthal and Weiss, 'Intimacy and Crises in Adulthood', pp. 10, 14.

97 Schwarz, 'Sex and Personality', pp. 47, 52. Schwarz's opinions were not uncommon in Britain. In 1958 C. P. Blacker's analysis of marriage problems seen in patients at the Maudsley Hospital in London similarly stressed the impact of personality and psychiatric disorders and suggested the need to consider eugenic approaches to marriage and family life: C. P. Blacker, 'Disruption of Marriage: Some Possibilities of Prevention', *Lancet* (15 March 1958), pp. 578–81. In 1952, Blacker hosted a meeting of the Eugenics Society in London, at which a lecture on 'The Stability of Marriage' was presented by A. J. Brayshaw, General Secretary of the National Marriage Guidance Council – details of the event and correspondence between Blacker and Brayshaw are in the Eugenics Society Archive at the Wellcome Library, SAEUG/D/141, https://wellcomelibrary.org, accessed 21 May 2019.

98 Germaine Greer, *The Female Eunuch* [1970] (London, 1999), pp. 213–68. On the social and cultural factors that shaped aspirations for marriage, see also Marital Studies Advisory Panel, 'Expectations of Marriage', pp. 4–5.

99 Alva Myrdal and Viola Klein, *Women's Two Roles: Home and Work* [1956] (London, 1968), pp. 22–5.

100 Titmuss, *Essays on 'The Welfare State'*, p. 98.

101 Michael Young and Peter Willmott, *The Symmetrical Family* [1973] (London, 1975), pp. 31–2.

102 Klein, 'Irregular Marriages'.

103 Schwarz, 'Sex and Personality', pp. 51–2.

104 Beata Bishop, 'Women in a Man's World', *Punch*, 3 January 1968, p. 34.

105 Elizabeth Wilson, *Women and the Welfare State* (London, 1977), p. 60.

106 Jack Dominian, 'Families in Divorce', in *Families in Britain*, ed. Peter Laslett (London, 1982), pp. 263–85, at p. 282.

107 Marion Hilliard, *A Woman Doctor Looks at Love and Life* (London, 1958), p. 70.

108 Jane Pearce and Saul Newton, *The Conditions of Human Growth* (New York, 1963), p. 133.
109 Hilliard, *A Woman Doctor,* pp. 70–71.
110 Kenneth C. Hutchin, *How Not to Kill Your Husband* (London, 1962), pp. 12, 118–20, 132. See also Kenneth C. Hutchin, *How Not to Kill Your Wife* (London, 1965); Kenneth C. Hutchin, *How Not to Kill Your Children* (London, 1968); Kenneth C. Hutchin, *How Not to Kill Yourself* (London, 1973).
111 Greer, *The Female Eunuch*, pp. 307, 315–16.
112 Mary Macaulay, *The Art of Marriage* [1952] (London, 1956), pp. 73, 97.
113 Eliot Slater and Moya Woodside, *Patterns of Marriage: A Study of Marriage Relationships in the Urban Working Classes* (London, 1951), p. 138.
114 Barbara Fried, *The Middle-age Crisis* (New York, 1967), p. 108.
115 Leslie J. Tizard and Harry J. S. Guntrip, *Middle Age* (London, 1959), pp. 81–9.
116 Lee and Casebier, *The Spouse Gap*, p. 153.
117 Josephine Klein, *Samples from English Culture* (London, 1965), pp. 291, 195.
118 Mass-Observation, 'The State of Matrimony', p. 3.
119 Fried, *The Middle-age Crisis*, p. 105.
120 Lee and Casebier, *The Spouse Gap*, p. 130.
121 Edmund Bergler, *The Revolt of the Middle-aged Man* (London, 1958), p. 103.
122 Ibid., p. 6.
123 Greer, *The Female Eunuch*, p. 189.
124 Bergler, *The Revolt of the Middle-aged Man*, pp. 75–6.
125 Ibid., p. 266.
126 Edmund Bergler, *Divorce Won't Help* (New York, 1948).
127 Bergler, *The Revolt of the Middle-aged Man*, pp. 179–80. David Mace also believed that middle-aged men and women should consult marriage counsellors rather than lawyers: Mace, 'Marriage Breakdown'.
128 Anon., 'Lax Views on Adultery', *The Times*, 3 May 1954, p. 2.
129 Alfred C. Kinsey et al., *Sexual Behavior in the Human Male* (Bloomington, IN, 1948), pp. 587–8.
130 Alfred C. Kinsey et al., *Sexual Behavior in the Human Female* (Philadelphia, PA, 1953), pp. 416, 436–8.
131 Harald Fuess, 'Adultery and Gender Equality in Modern Japan, 1868–1948', in *Gender and Law in the Japanese Imperium*, ed. Susan L. Burns and Barbara J. Brooks (Honolulu, HI, 2014), pp. 109–35.
132 Albert Deutsch, 'The Sex Habits of American Men: Some of the Findings of the Kinsey Report', *Harper's Magazine* (December, 1947), pp. 490–97; Marjorie Binford Woods, 'Sex Preparation for Marriage', *Modern Bride* (Fall 1949), pp. 32–3, 111; 'All about Eve: Kinsey Reports on American Women', *Newsweek* (24 August 1953), pp. 68–71. Over 25,000 media responses to the Kinsey reports, as well as Kinsey's papers, are in the archives of the Kinsey Institute at Indiana University, https://kinseyinstitute.org, accessed 9 May 2019.
133 'Second Interim Report of the Committee on Procedure in Matrimonial Causes (Cmd. 6945/46)', *Modern Law Review*, 10 (January 1947), pp. 58–62; the British *Man Alive* television series on marriages under stress aired in 1967.

134 As Lee and Casebier pointed out, infidelity itself could be 'expensive and time-consuming': Lee and Casebier, *The Spouse Gap*, p. 157.

135 Hannah Charnock, '"A Million Little Bonds": Infidelity, Divorce and the Emotional Worlds of Marriage in British Women's magazines of the 1930s', *Cultural and Social History*, 14 (2017), pp. 363–79.

136 Claire Langhamer, 'Adultery in Post-war England', *History Workshop Journal*, 62 (2006), pp. 87–115.

137 Wallis, *The Challenge of Middle Age*, pp. 74–92. For related works by Wallis, see J. H. Wallis, *Thinking about Marriage* (London, 1963); J. H. Wallis, *Sexual Harmony in Marriage* (London, 1964); J. H. Wallis, *Thinking about Retirement* (Oxford, 1975); J. H. Wallis, *Jung and the Quaker Way* (London, 1988), p. 128.

138 Wallis, *The Challenge of Middle Age*, pp. 89–90.

139 Mass-Observation, Spring 1998 Directive, 'Having an Affair', Respondent A.883, Sheet 11.

140 Simone de Beauvoir, *The Woman Destroyed* [1967] (New York, 1979), p. 177.

141 Sylvia Plath letter to Dr Beuscher, 22 September 1962, in *The Letters of Sylvia Plath*, vol. II: *1956–63*, ed. Peter K. Steinberg and Karen V. Kukil (London, 2018), pp. 827–32.

142 Ibid., p. 832.

143 Gail Sheehy, *Lovesounds* (New York, 1970), p. 20.

144 Wallis, *The Challenge of Middle Age*, pp. 90–91, 93–111.

145 Cross, 'Final Report of the Denning Committee', p. 185.

146 'Marriage Advice Centres', *The Times*, 17 July 1945, p. 2.

147 Mary Macaulay, 'Problems of Love and Marriage', in *Healthy Minds and Bodies*, ed. T. Traherne (London, 1956), pp. 209–24, at pp. 218, 224.

148 Jane Lewis, 'Public Institution and Private Relationship: Marriage and Marriage Guidance, 1920–1968', *Twentieth Century British History*, 1 (1990), pp. 233–63; Alana Harris, 'Love Divine and Love Sublime: The Catholic Marriage Advisory Council, the Marriage Guidance Movement and the State', in *Love and Romance in Britain*, ed. Harris and Jones, pp. 188–224.

149 David R. Mace, *Marriage Crisis* (London, 1948), p. 14. The term had previously been used in the interwar years: Ernest R. Groves, *The Marriage Crisis* (London, 1928).

150 J. H. Wallis, *Someone to Turn To* (London, 1961), p. 100.

151 The Council's First Annual Report 1938/39 is in Wellcome Library, SA/FPA/A13/69: Box 345. Subsequent reports from the 1960s are in Wellcome Library, SA/MWF/F.24: Box 63.

152 Wallis, *Someone to Turn To*, p. 99.

153 Mace, *Marriage Crisis*, p. 111.

154 See the constitution of the Conference (later Council) in *Living*, 1 (January 1939), pp. 31–2.

155 David Mace, 'What Is Counselling?', *Marriage Guidance* (1951), pp. 1–3. See also David Clark, 'Guidance, Counselling, Therapy: Responses to "Marital Problems" 1950–90', *Sociological Review*, 39 (1991), pp. 765–98.

156 Ruth Penny, David Epston, and Margaret Agee, 'A History of Marriage Guidance in New Zealand', *New Zealand Journal of Counselling*, 28 (2008), pp. 1–9; McLellan, *Love in the Time of Communism*, pp. 77–81.

157 Stopes, *Enduring Passion*, p. 1. See also Richard Overy, *The Morbid Age: Britain between the Wars* (London, 2009).

158 Macaulay, *The Art of Marriage*, pp. 96–7.

159 William Brown, *Psychological Methods of Healing: An Introduction to Psychotherapy* (London, 1938), pp. 158–60.

160 Wallis, *Someone to Turn To*, p. 100.

161 Gerald I. Manus, 'Marriage Counseling: A Technique in Search of a Theory', *Journal of Marriage and the Family*, 28 (1966), pp. 449–53.

162 Wallis, *The Challenge of Middle Age*, p. 70.

163 J. H. Wallis and H. S. Booker, *Marriage Counselling: A Description and Analysis of the Remedial Work of the National Marriage Guidance Council* (London, 1958), pp. 39, 92.

164 Ibid., p. 136.

165 Ibid., pp. 177–86.

166 Ibid., pp. 147, 186–90.

167 Ibid., pp. 125–66. The result was unknown in 33 per cent of cases.

168 Ibid., pp. 270–74.

169 Teri Chettiar, '"More than a Contract": The Emergence of a State-supported Marriage Welfare Service and the Politics of Emotional Life in Post–1945 Britain', *Journal of British Studies*, 55 (2016), pp. 566–91.

170 Kathleen Bannister et al., *Social Casework in Marital Problems: The Development of a Psychodynamic Approach* (London, 1955), p. 28. For a history of the clinic, see Henry V. Dicks, *Fifty Years of the Tavistock Clinic* (London, 1970); Enid Eicholz, 'The Development of the Family Discussion Bureaux Work', *Social Work*, 8 (1951), pp. 495–500.

171 Bannister et al., *Social Casework*, p. 8.

172 Douglas Woodhouse, 'Non-marital Therapy: The Growth of the Marital Studies Institute', in *The Social Engagement of Social Science*, vol. I: *A Tavistock Anthology: The Socio-psychological Perspective,* ed. Eric Trist, Hugh Murray and Beulah Trist (Philadelphia, PA, 1990), pp. 299–322.

173 Bannister et al., *Social Casework*, pp. 67–78, at p. 78.

174 Henry V. Dicks, *Marital Tensions: Clinical Studies towards a Psychological Theory of Interaction* (London, 1967), pp. 1–2, 42.

175 Henry V. Dicks, 'Clinical Studies in Marriage and the Family: A Symposium on Methods', *British Journal of Medical Psychology*, 26 (1953), pp. 181–96.

176 Dicks, *Marital Tensions*, pp. 236–53. On the novelty of Dick's approach, see Geoffrey Gorer, 'Book Review', *International Journal of Psycho-analysis*, 49 (1968), pp. 107–9.

177 Dicks, 'Clinical Studies in Marriage and the Family'.

178 Dicks, *Marital Tensions*, p. 165.

179 Dicks, 'Clinical Studies in Marriage and the Family', p. 195.

180 Hilliard, *A Woman Doctor*, pp. 106–7, 112, 146. On Hilliard, see Kaitlynn Mendes, 'Reading *Chatelaine*: Dr. Marion Hilliard and 1950s Women's Health Advice', *Canadian Journal of Communication*, 35 (2010), pp. 515–31.

181 Dicks, 'Clinical Studies in Marriage and the Family', p. 195.

182 See reviews in Anon., *Proceedings of the Royal Society of Medicine*, 48 (1955), p. 751; A. M. de Field, *Probation Journal* (1 March 1956), p. 14; Ernestina Alexander, *Social Service Review*, 30 (1956), pp. 476–7; Rosalind

Chambers, *British Journal of Sociology*, 8 (1957), pp. 92–3; *British Journal of Social Work*, 1 (1971), pp. 126–7.

183 Gorer, 'Book Review'; Robert Shields, 'Marriage à la Mode', *The Observer* (4 February 1968); E. A. Bennet, 'Psychopathology of Disturbed Marriages', *British Medical Journal* (23 March 1968), pp. 757; Glin Bennet, *British Journal of Medical Psychology*, 42 (April 1969), pp. 83–4; *Journal of the Royal Society of Health*, 88 (1 May 1968), p. 168; R. D. Laing, 'Preventing Dissolution', *New Society* (2 November 1967); LeRoy J. Cordrey in *Marriage Counseling Quarterly* (August 1968), pp. 65–7. Copies of reviews of Dicks's work are in the papers of Henry V. Dicks, PP/HVD/D/2, Wellcome Archives and Manuscripts. Dicks referred to the personal significance of *Marital Tensions* in a letter to B. B. Mitchell of the Family Welfare Association on 29 September 1969, in the same collection.

184 Catherine Lisette Peters, 'More than the Sum of 1 and 1', *Times Literary Supplement*, 3447 (21 March 1968), p. 294.

185 Dicks, *Marital Tensions*, p. 225. Jaques's work featured in the three-volume series on the writings of the Tavistock edited by one of the Institute's founders Eric Trist – see Trist's correspondence with Jaques in Eric Trist Fonds, F0681, S00726-2016-004/13(56), Clara Thomas Archives, York University, Canada.

186 Dicks, *Marital Tensions*, pp. 224–5.

187 Clifford Odets, *Rocket to the Moon*, in *Six Plays of Clifford Odets* (New York, 1979), pp. 323–419, at p. 333.

188 Sheridan Morley, 'Theatre Guide', *Punch*, 6419 (17 November 1982), p. 844.

189 Ellen Goodman, 'The 40 Year Itch', *Daily Mail* (4 September 1975), p. 10.

4 BIOLOGICAL CLOCKS

1 Simone de Beauvoir, *The Second Sex* [1949] (London, 1997), p. 593.

2 Curt P. Richter, 'Animal Behavior and Internal Drives', *Quarterly Review of Biology*, 2 (1927), pp. 307–43. On Richter, see Jay Schulkin, Paul Rozin and Eliot Stellar, 'Curt P. Richter, 1894–1988: A Biographical Memoir', *National Academy of Sciences* (Washington, DC, 1994), pp. 311–20; Paul R. McHugh, 'Curt Richter and Johns Hopkins: A Union of Assets', *American Journal of Physiology: Regulatory, Integrative and Comparative Physiology*, 256 (2000), R, pp. 1169–70; Timothy H. Moran and Jay Schulkin, 'Curt Richter and Regulatory Physiology', *American Journal of Physiology: Regulatory, Integrative and Comparative Physiology*, 279 (2000), R, pp. 357–63; Nori Geary, 'Curt Richter and the Female Rat', *Appetite*, 49 (2007), pp. 376–87; Edmund Ramsden, 'Rats, Stress and the Built Environment', *History of the Human Sciences*, 25 (2012), pp. 123–47.

3 Curt P. Richter, 'Biological Clocks in Medicine and Psychiatry: Shock-phase Hypothesis', *Proceedings of the National Academy of Sciences*, 46 (1960), pp. 1506–30.

4 Curt Paul Richter, *Biological Clocks in Medicine and Psychiatry* (Springfield, IL, 1965), pp. 88–9.

5 Arne Sollberger, 'General Properties of Biological Rhythms', *Annals of the New York Academy of Sciences*, 98 (1962), pp. 757–94; Erwin Bünning, *The*

Physiological Clock (Heidelberg, 1964); Anne Sollberger, *Biological Rhythm Research* (New York, 1965); Jürgen Aschoff, 'Circadian Rhythms in Man', *Science*, 148 (1965), pp. 1427–32.

6 Jürgen Aschoff, ed., *Circadian Clocks: Proceedings of the Feldafing Summer School, 7–18 September 1964* (Amsterdam, 1965); Jürgen Aschoff, 'On the Dilatability of Subjective Time', *Perspectives in Biology and Medicine*, 35 (1992), pp. 276–80.

7 Aschoff, 'Circadian Rhythms in Man', p. 1431. In his classic study of adaptation published in 1965, René Dubos also reviewed the evidence about internal and external clocks: René Dubos, *Man Adapting* [1965] (New Haven, CT, 1980), pp. 42–55.

8 G. Pincus, ed., *Recent Progress in Hormone Research: Proceedings of the Laurentian Hormone Conference, 1956* (New York, 1957).

9 Arthur Chovnik, ed., *Biological Clocks: Cold Spring Harbor Symposia on Quantitative Biology*, 25 (1960). Richter presented a paper and chaired a session at the symposium.

10 For evolutionary biologists, senescence was often linked to the cessation of women's reproductive capacity. See Hyung Wook Park, *Old Age, New Science: Gerontologists and their Biosocial Visions, 1900–1960* (Pittsburgh, PA, 2016), pp. 183–90. During the 1950s and '60s, ageing constituted one of the unsolved problems of biology, as Peter Medawar put it in 1952: P. B. Medawar, *An Unsolved Problem of Biology* (London, 1952).

11 Jürgen Aschoff, 'Exogenous and Endogenous Components in Circadian Rhythms', in *Biological Clocks*, ed. Chovnik, pp. 11–28.

12 Andrew Scull and Jay Schulkin, 'Psychobiology, Psychiatry, and Psychoanalysis: The Intersecting Careers of Adolf Meyer, Phyllis Greenacre, and Curt Richter', *Medical History*, 53 (2009), pp. 5–36.

13 Helene Deutsch, *The Psychology of Women*, vol. II (London, 1947), p. 405; Helene Deutsch, 'The Menopause', *International Journal of Psycho-analysis*, 65 (1984), pp. 55–62.

14 Richard Cohen, 'The Clock Is Ticking for the Career Woman', *Washington Post* (16 March 1978). For discussion of Cohen's argument, see Moira Weigel, *Labor of Love: The Invention of Dating* (New York, 2016), pp. 218–25; Molly McKaughan, *The Biological Clock: Balancing Marriage, Motherhood, and Career* (London, 1987).

15 Beauvoir, *The Second Sex*; Betty Friedan, *The Feminine Mystique* (New York, 1963); Hannah Gavron, *The Captive Wife: Conflicts of Housebound Mothers* [1966] (London, 1968); Germaine Greer, *The Female Eunuch* [1970] (London, 1999); Ann Oakley, *Woman's Work: The Housewife Past and Present* (New York, 1974); Marilyn French, *The Women's Room* (New York, 1977).

16 French, *The Women's Room*, p. 60.

17 Elliott Jaques, 'Death and the Midlife Crisis', reproduced in Elliott Jaques, *Work, Creativity, and Social Justice* (London, 1970), pp. 38–63, at p. 38.

18 For references to the timing of menopause, see Joan Malleson, *Change of Life: Facts and Fallacies of Middle Age* [1949] (London, 1963), p. 14; Kenneth C. Hutchin, *The Change of Life* (London, 1963), p. 60; R. H. Gray, 'The Menopause – Epidemiological and Demographic Considerations', in *The Menopause: A Guide to Current Research and Practice*, ed. R. J. Beard (Lancaster, 1976), pp. 25–40.

19 On Deutsch's approach, see Janet Sayers, *Mothering Psychoanalysis: Helene Deutsch, Karen Horney, Anna Freud and Melanie Klein* (London, 1992), pp. 25–81.

20 Deutsch, 'The Menopause', p. 57.

21 Beauvoir, *The Second Sex*, pp. 587–90. For further reference to women's hypomanic defence mechanisms to cope with ageing, see also Deutsch, *The Psychology of Women*, pp. 407–8.

22 On late nineteenth-century understandings of menopausal and post-menopausal women, see Kay Heath, *Aging by the Book: The Emergence of Midlife in Victorian Britain* (New York, 2009), pp. 73–89.

23 Mary Ann Dacomb Scharlieb, *The Seven Ages of Woman: A Consideration of the Successive Phases of Woman's Life* (London, 1915), pp. 264–70.

24 Ibid., p. 269.

25 Gregorio Marañón, *The Climacteric (The Critical Age)* (London, 1929), pp. 17–18.

26 Ibid., pp. 78–9.

27 Susan E. Bell, 'Changing Ideas: The Medicalization of Menopause', *Social Science and Medicine*, 24 (1987), pp. 535–42.

28 Marañón, *The Climacteric*, pp. 107–8.

29 See reviews in *Archives of Internal Medicine*, 44 (1929), pp. 153–4; *American Journal of Sociology*, 35 (1929), pp. 521–2.

30 Marcha Flint, 'The Menopause: Reward or Punishment?', *Psychosomatics*, 16 (1975), pp. 161–3.

31 Bernice L. Neugarten and Ruth J. Kraines, '"Menopausal Symptoms" in Women of Various Ages', *Psychosomatic Medicine*, 27 (1965), pp. 266–73; Louis Parrish, *No Pause at All: Living through the Middle Years – A Guide to the Male and Female Climacteric* (London, 1976).

32 Margaret Lock, *Encounters with Aging: Mythologies of the Menopause in Japan and North America* (Berkeley, CA, 1993); Margaret Lock, 'Ambiguities of Aging: Japanese Experience and Perceptions of Menopause', *Culture, Medicine and Psychiatry*, 10 (1986), pp. 23–46; Margaret Lock, 'Deconstructing the Change: Female Maturation in Japan and North America', in *Welcome to Middle Age! (And Other Cultural Fictions)*, ed. Richard A. Shweder (Chicago, IL, 1998), pp. 45–74; Margaret Lock and Patricia Kaufert, 'Menopause, Local Biologies, and Cultures of Aging', *American Journal of Human Biology*, 13 (2001), pp. 494–504.

33 Margaret Morganroth Gullette, *Declining to Decline: Cultural Combat and the Politics of the Midlife* (Charlottesville, VA, 1997); Margaret Morganroth Gullette, *Aged by Culture* (Chicago, IL, 2004).

34 Marie Carmichael Stopes, *Change of Life in Men and Women* (London, 1936), p. 19.

35 Marie Carmichael Stopes, *Enduring Passion* [1928] (London, 1936), pp. 150–51, 160–64.

36 Ibid., pp. 183, 199–204.

37 Stopes, *Change of Life*, pp. 7, 11. The 'harmony of the hormones' was a phrase that Stopes used in *Enduring Passion*, p. 152.

38 George Riddoch, 'Nervous and Mental Manifestations of the Climacteric', *British Medical Journal* (13 December 1930), pp. 987–90.

39 'An Investigation of the Menopause in One Thousand Women', *The Lancet*

(14 January 1933), pp. 106–8. American studies could be similarly positive about menopausal changes. In 1941 the gynaecologist Robert T. Frank
believed that many of the anticipated features of menopause, including
'flabbiness', hirsutism and the perceived loss of sexual allure, had been
unnecessarily exaggerated by family doctors – Robert T. Frank, 'Treatment
of Disorders of the Menopause', *Bulletin of the New York Academy of
Medicine*, 17 (1941), pp. 854–63.

40 Julie-Marie Strange, 'In Full Possession of her Powers: Researching and
Rethinking Menopause in Early Twentieth-century England and Scotland',
Social History of Medicine, 25 (2012), pp. 685–700.

41 Anon., 'The Menopause and After', *The Lancet* (23 October 1943),
pp. 511–12.

42 See Barbara Brookes, *Abortion in England, 1900–1967* (London, 1988).

43 Joan Malleson, 'An Endocrine Factor in Certain Affective Disorders', *Lancet*
(25 July 1953), pp. 158–64; Miss M. E. Landau, 'Looking Happily Ahead',
Family Doctor, 12 (1962), pp. 346–7. On the medicalization of menopause
in the twentieth century, see Louise Foxcroft, *Hot Flushes, Cold Science:
A History of the Modern Menopause* (London, 2009); Judith A. Houck,
Hot and Bothered: Women, Medicine, and Menopause in Modern America
(Cambridge, MA, 2006).

44 Malleson, 'An Endocrine Factor', pp. 159, 161.

45 Joan Malleson, 'Climacteric Stress: Its Empirical Management', *British
Medical Journal* (15 December 1956), pp. 1422–5, at p. 1423.

46 Malleson, *Change of Life*, pp. 59, 69.

47 Ibid., pp. 69, 76–81.

48 Ibid., p. 79. Malleson was on the Advisory Board of the Marriage Guidance
Council – see the First Annual Report of the Council, 1938/9, in Wellcome
Library, SA/TCC/A/13/69: Box 345, p. 2.

49 Ada P. Kahn and Linda Hughey Holt, *Midlife Health: Every Woman's Guide
to Feeling Good* (New York, 1987); Landau, 'Looking Happily Ahead'.

50 Mrs O. van Andel-Ripke, 'Mother and Housewife in the Climacteric',
in Medical Women's International Association, *La Menopause/The
Menopause* (Edizioni Minerva Medica, 1954), pp. 93–8. For more on the
Association's work, see Frederick Cooper, 'Medical Feminism, Working
Mothers, and the Limits of Home: Finding a Balance between Self-care
and Other-care in Cross-cultural Debates about Health and Lifestyle,
1952–1956', *Palgrave Communications*, www.nature.com, 12 July 2016.

51 Mary Macaulay, *The Art of Marriage* (London, 1952), pp. 93, 97.

52 James H. S. Bossard and Eleanor Stoker Boll, 'Marital Unhappiness
in the Life Cycle', *Marriage and Family Living*, 17 (1955), pp. 10–14.

53 Hutchin, *The Change of Life*, pp. 67–9.

54 Bernice L. Neugarten, 'Adaptation and the Life Cycle', *Counselling
Psychologist*, 6 (1976), pp. 16–20, at p. 20; Neugarten and Kraines,
'"Menopausal Symptoms"'.

55 Houck, *Hot and Bothered*, pp. 114, 89–113, 117–20.

56 Ibid., p. 101.

57 Marion Hilliard, *A Woman Doctor Looks at Love and Life* (London, 1958),
pp. 148, 161–2.

58 Flint, 'The Menopause', p. 163.

59 Beauvoir, *The Second Sex*, p. 587.
60 Ibid., pp. 593–5.
61 Ibid., p. 588.
62 Jean Baudrillard, *Cool Memories*, trans. Chris Turner [1987] (London, 1990), p. 14.
63 French, *The Women's Room*, p. 239.
64 Ibid., pp. 476, 510.
65 Patricia Cohen, *In Our Prime: The Invention of Middle Age* (New York, 2012).
66 C. M. Durrant, 'On the Commencing Climacteric in the Male', *British Medical Journal* (2 September 1865), pp. 233–5. See also: Michael Stolberg, 'From the "Climacteric Disease" to the "Male Climacteric": The Historical Origins of a Modern Concept', *Maturitas*, 58 (2007), pp. 111–16; Hans-Georg Hofer, 'Medizin, Altern, Männlichkeit: Zur Kulturgeschichte des Männlichen Klimakteriums', *Medizinhistorisches Journal*, 42 (2007), pp. 210–46.
67 Marañón, *The Climacteric*, p. 350.
68 Ibid., pp. 349–76, at p. 367.
69 Stopes, *Change of Life*.
70 Havelock Ellis, *Psychology of Sex* (London, 1934), p. 274.
71 Ibid., p. 273.
72 Kenneth Walker, 'The Male Climacteric', *Post-graduate Medical Journal* (April 1938), pp. 120–23; M. Prados and Lieut. B. Ruddick, 'Depression and Anxiety States of the Middle-aged Man', *Psychiatric Quarterly*, 21 (1947), pp. 410–30; Anon., 'The Middle-aged Man', *British Medical Journal* (9 May 1953), pp. 1039–40.
73 Otto Billig and Robert Adams, 'Emotional Problems of the Middle-aged Man', *Psychiatric Quarterly*, 28 (1954), pp. 442–52.
74 Barbara Fried, *The Middle-age Crisis* (New York, 1967), pp. 41–2.
75 Ibid., p. 48.
76 Edmund Bergler, *The Revolt of the Middle-aged Man* (London, 1958), p. 3. On the coincidence of factors leading to midlife distress, also see Orville G. Brim, 'Theories of the Male Mid-life Crisis', *Counseling Psychologist*, 6 (March 1976), pp. 2–9.
77 Bergler, *The Revolt of the Middle-aged Man*, p. 203.
78 Ibid., p. 205.
79 Ibid.
80 *The Seven Year Itch* (Charles K. Feldman Productions, 1955).
81 Bergler, *The Revolt of the Middle-aged Man*, pp. 213–14.
82 Elizabeth Siegel Watkins, 'The Medicalisation of Male Menopause in America', *Social History of Medicine*, 20 (2007), pp. 369–88.
83 Nancy Mayer, *The Male Mid-life Crisis: Fresh Starts After Forty* (New York, 1978), p. 28.
84 Joan Cook, 'The Male Menopause', *New York Times* (5 April 1971), p. 28.
85 Joanna Bourke, *Dismembering the Male: Men's Bodies, Britain and the Great War* (London, 1996); Joanna Bourke, 'Effeminacy, Ethnicity and the End of Trauma: The Sufferings of "Shell-shocked" Men in Great Britain and Ireland, 1914–39', *Journal of Contemporary History*, 35 (2000), pp. 57–69. On male fears of creeping emotionalism and effeminacy, see Foxcroft, *Hot Flushes, Cold Science*, pp. 213–14.

86 Roy R. Grinker and John P. Spiegel, *Men Under Stress* (Philadelphia, PA, 1945), p. 188. For further discussion on the history of stress, see Mark Jackson, *The Age of Stress: Science and the Search for Stability* (Oxford, 2013). On the post-war crisis in masculinity, see Benita Eisler, *Private Lives: Men and Women of the Fifties* (New York, 1986), pp. 39–42.

87 Jessamyn Neuhaus, 'The Importance of Being Orgasmic: Sexuality, Gender, and Marital Sex Manuals in the United States, 1920–1963', *Journal of the History of Sexuality*, 9 (2000), pp. 447–73.

88 Arthur Schlesinger, Jr, 'The Crisis of American Masculinity', *Esquire* (1 November 1958). See also James Gilbert, *Men in the Middle: Searching for Masculinity in the 1950s* (Chicago, IL, 2005).

89 Allen Wheelis, *The Seeker* (New York, 1960), p. 10.

90 Mayer, *The Male Mid-life Crisis*, p. 29.

91 Esther Godfrey, *The January–May Marriage in Nineteenth-century British Literature* (Basingstoke, 2009). See also Margaret Morganroth Gullette, 'The Puzzling Case of the Deceased Wife's Sister: Nineteenth-century England Deals with a Second-chance Plot', *Representations*, 31 (Summer 1990), pp. 142–66.

92 This conclusion was supported by sociobiological studies of animal mating practices: Robert Trivers, 'Parental Investment and Sexual Selection', in *Sexual Selection and the Descent of Man*, ed. Bernard Campbell (Chicago, IL, 1972), pp. 136–79.

93 G. Stanley Hall, *Senescence: The Last Half of Life* (London, 1922), pp. 390–92.

94 Martha Weinman Lear, 'Is There a Male Menopause?', *New York Times* (28 January 1973), pp. 10, 57–8, 61, 64–5.

95 Ibid., p. 64.

96 Ibid., p. 61.

97 Ibid., p. 65.

98 Thomas C. Desmond, 'America's Unknown Middle-agers', *New York Times* (29 July 1956), pp. 5, 42–3.

99 Ibid., p. 43.

100 Kenneth Soddy and Mary C. Kidson, *Men in Middle Life* (London, 1967), pp. 56–7, 63–70, 95–8.

101 Wheelis, *The Seeker*, p. 13.

102 Anon., 'The Problem of an Ageing Population', *British Medical Journal* (31 July 1954), pp. 296–8; John Fry, 'Care of the Elderly in General Practice', *British Medical Journal* (21 September 1957), pp. 666–70; 'Old Age', *British Medical Journal* (27 May 1961), pp. 1516–17. On growing medical interest in midlife health, see 'Report on the Hazards of Middle Age', *Journal of the Royal College of General Practitioners*, Supplement 1 to Volume VII (1964); Roger Owen, ed., *Middle Age* (London, 1967).

103 'Old Age', UNESCO *International Social Science Journal*, 15 (1963), pp. 339–47.

104 Mark Jackson and Martin D. Moore, eds, *Balancing the Self: Medicine, Politics and the Regulation of Health in the Twentieth Century* (Manchester, 2020).

105 John Roper, 'Over-45 Health Bill £1,000m', *The Times* (31 July 1969), p. 4.

106 Dr. T. Traherne, 'Good Health is Your Birthright', in *Healthy Minds and Bodies*, ed. T. Traherne (London, 1956), pp. 9–21, at p. 18.

107 Ibid., pp. 18–19.

108 Sander L. Gilman, *Obesity: The Biography* (Oxford, 2010), pp. 80–112.

109 Anon., 'Promotion of Health', *British Medical Journal* (6 January 1968),
     pp. 64–5. See also John Benson, *Prime Time: A History of the Middle Aged
     in Twentieth-century Britain* (London, 1997), pp. 47–8. On how under-
     standings of the life course shaped debates about women's exercise, see:
     Eilidh Macrae, *Exercise in the Female Life-cycle in Britain, 1930–1970*
     (Basingstoke, 2016).

110 Jessica Parr and Nicolas Rasmussen, 'Making Addicts of the Fat: Obesity,
     Psychiatry and the "Fatties Anonymous" Model of Self-help Weight Loss in
     the Post-war United States', in *Critical Perspectives on Addiction: Advances
     in Medical Sociology*, vol. XIV, ed. Julie Netherland (Emerald Group
     Publishing, 2012); Jessica M. Parr, 'Obesity and the Emergence of Mutual
     Aid Groups for Weight Loss in the Post-war United States', *Social History
     of Medicine*, 27 (2014), pp. 768–88.

111 A. H. Douthwaite, 'Obesity', *British Medical Journal* (10 February 1951),
     pp. 291–3.

112 Evelyn Forbes, 'Health and Beauty', in *Healthy Minds and Bodies*, ed.
     Traherne, pp. 225–49.

113 Gayelord Hauser, *Look Younger, Live Longer* (London, 1950), pp. 92–102,
     105–10.

114 Ibid., p. 102.

115 Marion Hilliard, *Women and Fatigue* (London, 1960), p. 82.

116 Dame Annis Gillie, *Do Something About That Middle Age* (London, 1969),
     p. 63.

117 Kenneth Hutchin, *How Not to Kill Your Wife* (London, 1965), pp. 143–53.

118 Alfred Torrie, *The Middle-aged Man* (London, 1960), pp. 6–7.

119 Sinclair Lewis, *Babbitt* (Leipzig, 1922), pp. 143–4.

120 F. A. Hornibrook, *The Culture of the Abdomen* [1924] (London, 1957),
     p. 80.

121 Jane Hand, 'Marketing Health Education: Advertising Margarine and
     Visualising Health in Britain from 1964–c. 2000', *Contemporary British
     History* (2017), pp. 477–500.

122 Kenneth Hutchin, *How Not to Kill Your Husband* (London, 1962), p. 73.

123 Hornibrook, *The Culture of the Abdomen*; Leonard Williams, *Obesity*
     (Oxford, 1926), p. 36; Leonard Williams, *Middle Age and Old Age* (London,
     1925). For further discussion, see Ina Zweiniger-Bargielowska, '*The Culture
     of the Abdomen*: Obesity and Reducing in Britain, circa 1900–1939', *Journal
     of British Studies*, 44 (2005), pp. 239–73.

124 Harold G. Wolff, 'Life Stress and Cardiovascular Disorders', *Circulation*,
     1 (1950), pp. 187–203; I. McD. G. Stewart, 'Coronary Disease and Modern
     Stress', *Lancet* (23 December 1950), pp. 867–70; Harold G. Wolff, *Stress
     and Disease* (Chicago, IL, 1952); Meyer Friedman and Ray H. Rosenman,
     'Association of Specific Overt Behavior Pattern with Blood and
     Cardiovascular Findings', *Journal of the American Medical Association*, 168
     (1959), pp. 1286–96; Fred Kerner, *Stress and Your Heart* (New York, 1961);
     Neil Brierley, *Relaxation for Men: Tension in Modern Living* (London,
     1965); Meyer Friedman and Ray H. Rosenman, *Type A Behavior and Your
     Heart* (New York, 1974).

125 Stewart, 'Coronary Disease'; Hutchin, *How Not to Kill Your Husband*, pp. 15–17, 65–86; Anon., 'Problem of Heart Disease', *Times* (14 June 1963), p. 3.

126 On heart disease in younger men and women, see Wolff, 'Life Stress and Cardiovascular Disease', pp. 191–3; Rhona Churchill, 'Heart Attacks', *Daily Mail* (13 April 1966), p. 8.

127 Hutchin, *How Not to Kill your Husband*, p. 11. See also Rima Apple, 'Constructing Mothers: Scientific Motherhood in the Nineteenth and Twentieth Centuries', *Social History of Medicine*, 8 (1995), pp. 161–78.

128 A. T. Welford, 'Problems of Middle Age', *Health Education Journal* (1 December 1951), pp. 167–71.

129 Sr Dolores Kane, 'Wanted: TLC for the Middle-aged', *AORN Journal* (December 1970), pp. 58–61.

130 Lawrence Greenleigh, 'Facing the Challenge of Change in Middle Age', *Geriatrics*, 29 (1974), pp. 61–8.

131 Nicholas Coleridge, 'What Ever Happened to the Angry Young Man?', *Punch*, 7150 (12 October 1977); Jeff Nuttall, *Bomb Culture* (London, 1968).

132 Coleridge, 'What Ever Happened'.

133 Cyril Connolly, *Enemies of Promise* (London, 1938), p. 116. Connolly's words were used by a male correspondent to the Mass-Observation directive on the pace of life in 1992 to explain the obstacles to his own productivity earlier in his life – Mass-Observation, Spring 1992 Directive, 'The Pace of Life', Respondent G.2199, Sheet 12, p. 2.

134 Margaret Morganroth Gullette, 'Inventing the "Postmaternal" Woman, 1898–1927: Idle, Unwanted, and Out of a Job', *Feminist Studies*, 21 (1995), pp. 221–53; Margaret Morganroth Gullette, 'Wicked Powerful: The Postmaternal in Contemporary Film and Psychoanalytical Theory', *Gender and Psychoanalysis*, 4 (2000), pp. 107–39; Margaret Morganroth Gullette, 'Valuing "Postmaternity" as a Revolutionary Feminist Concept', *Feminist Studies*, 28 (2002), pp. 553–72.

135 Marjorie Fiske Lowenthal and David Chiriboga, 'Transition to the Empty Nest: Crisis, Challenge, or Relief?', *Archives of General Psychiatry*, 26 (1972), pp. 8–14. See also Howard P. Chudacoff and Tamara K. Hareven, 'From the Empty Nest to Family Dissolution: Life Course Transitions into Old Age', *Journal of Family History* (1979), pp. 69–83.

136 Dorothy Canfield Fisher, *Mothers and Children* (London, 1915), p. 252.

137 Ibid., pp. 247, 282–3.

138 Charlotte Perkins Gilman, *Herland* [1915] (London, 1979), p. 95.

139 Lee and Casebier, *The Spouse Gap*, p. 134.

140 Lowenthal and Chiriboga, 'Transition to the Empty Nest', p. 8.

141 Cynthia Bell, 'Why Middle Age Isn't the End', *New York Times* (29 July 1979), WC14.

142 Although the empty nest was sometimes dismissed as a myth – Jana L. Raup and Jane E. Myers, 'The Empty Nest Syndrome: Myth or Reality?', *Journal of Counseling and Development*, 68 (1989), pp. 180–83.

5 FAMILIES UNDER STRESS

1 Reuben Hill, *Families Under Stress: Adjustment to the Crises of War Separation and Reunion* [1949] (Westport, CT, 1971), pp. 10–11.

2 Sarah Hayes, 'Industrial Automation and Stress, *c.* 1945–79', in *Stress in Postwar Britain, 1945–85*, ed. Mark Jackson (London, 2015), pp. 75–93, 211–15.

3 Joseph Heller, *Catch-22* (New York, 1961); Joseph Heller, *Something Happened* [1974] (London, 1988); Joseph Heller, *Good as Gold* [1976] (New York, 2004).

4 Heller, *Something Happened*, p. 72.

5 Ibid., p. 509.

6 Alvin Toffler, *Future Shock* (London, 1970), pp. 221–2, 224.

7 Heller, *Good as Gold*, p. 49.

8 Ibid., p. 162.

9 C. W. Topping, 'The Happy Family', *Marriage and Family Living*, 7 (1945), p. 57.

10 For reviews of Hill's work, see: E. L. Koos, *American Journal of Sociology*, 56 (1950), pp. 90–91; Ruth Shonle Cavan, *Social Forces*, 29 (October 1950-May 1951), pp. 102–4. For further work in this area, some of which cited Hill, see John F. Cuber, 'Readjustment of Veterans', *Marriage and Family Living*, 7 (1945), pp. 28–30; Evelyn Millis Duvall, 'Soldier Come Home', *Marriage and Family Living*, 7 (1945), pp. 61–3, 72; Evelyn Millis Duvall, 'Loneliness and the Serviceman's Wife', *Marriage and Family Living*, 7 (1945), pp. 77–81; Elise Boulding, 'Family Adjustments to War Separation and Reunion', *Annals of the American Academy of Political and Social Science*, 272 (1950), pp. 59–67.

11 Hill, *Families Under Stress*, pp. 11–12.

12 Robin M. Williams, Jr, *American Society: A Sociological Interpretation* (New York, 1955), pp. 75–7.

13 E. E. LeMasters, 'Parenthood as Crises', *Marriage and Family Living*, 19 (1957), pp. 352–5.

14 Thomas C. Desmond, 'America's Unknown Middle-agers', *New York Times*, 29 July 1956, pp. 5, 42–3.

15 David R. Mace, *Marriage Crisis* (London, 1948), p. 136.

16 Henry V. Dicks, 'The Predicament of the Family in the Modern World', *Lancet* (5 February 1955), pp. 295–7.

17 Henry V. Dicks, 'Strains within the Family', in National Association for Mental Hygiene, *Strain and Stress in Modern Living: Special Opportunities and Responsibilities of Public Authorities: Proceedings of a Conference Held at Friends House, London, NW1, 25th to 26th March, 1954* (London, 1954), pp. 28–37, in Wellcome Library, PP HVD/D/1/9.

18 Ibid.

19 Harry S. Truman, 'Remarks at the National Conference on Family Life' (6 May 1948), www.presidency.ucsb.edu/documents/remarks-the-national-conference-family-life, accessed 17 March 2020; *Highlights of the National Conference on Family Life* (New York, National Conference on Family Life, 1948), https://history.ncfr.org/wp-content/uploads/2013/01/1948-Natl-Conf-on-Family-Life-highlights.pdf, accessed 17 May 2020. For renewed emphasis on family life, see Steven Mintz and Susan Kellogg, *Domestic*

Revolutions: A Social History of American Family Life (New York, 1988), pp. 179–82.

20 Paul C. Glick, 'The Life Cycle of the Family', *Marriage and Family Living*, 17 (1955), pp. 3–9; Paul C. Glick, *American Families* (New York, 1957); Paul C. Glick and Robert Parke Jr, 'New Approaches in Studying the Life Cycle of the Family', *Demography*, 2 (March 1965), pp. 187–202; Margaret Mead and Ken Heyman, *Family* (New York, 1965); Boyd C. Rollins and Harold Feldman, 'Marital Satisfaction over the Family Life Cycle', *Journal of Marriage and the Family*, 32 (1970), pp. 20–28.

21 Toffler, *Future Shock*, pp. 214–15.

22 Ibid.

23 Michael Young and Paul Willmott, *The Symmetrical Family* (London, 1973). On the history of the family in America, see Mintz and Kellogg, *Domestic Revolutions*.

24 Robert F. Winch, 'Permanence and Change in the History of American Family and some Speculations as to its Future', *Journal of Marriage and the Family*, 32 (1970), pp. 6–15.

25 Diversity and heterogeneity, rather than uniformity, in family structure across the twentieth century, with major differences visible between nations and cultures, have been emphasized by Steven Ruggles, 'The Transformation of American Family Structure', *American Historical Review*, 99 (1994), pp. 103–28; Josie McLellan, *Love in the Time of Communism: Intimacy and Sexuality in the GDR* (Cambridge, 2011), pp. 53–82.

26 Lord Horder, 'Introduction', in *Rebuilding Family Life in the Post-war World*, ed. Sir James Marchant (London, 1948), p. 5.

27 Sir Arthur S. MacNalty, 'Influence of War on Family Life', in *Rebuilding Family Life*, ed. Marchant, p. 136.

28 'Address by Sidney E. Goldstein', *Living*, 1 (1939), pp. 13–14.

29 *Highlights of the National Conference on Family Life.*

30 Grace Reeves, 'The New Family in the Postwar World', *Marriage and Family Living*, 7 (1945), pp. 73–6, 89.

31 'Introduction to Family Process', *Family Process*, 1 (1962), pp. 1–4; Joseph Kirk Folsom, *The Family and Democratic Society* (London, 1948); Elizabeth Bott, *Family and Social Network* (London, 1957); Peter Townsend, *The Family Life of Old People* [1957] (London, 1963); Ronald Fletcher, *Britain in the Sixties: Family and Marriage* (London, 1962); Young and Willmott, *The Symmetrical Family*.

32 Chris Steve Maltezos, 'The Return of the 1950s Nuclear Family in Films of the 1980s' (2011), Graduate Theses and Dissertations, http://scholarcommons.usf.edu/etd/3230.

33 Denys Thompson, 'The Importance of Leisure', *Current Affairs*, 72 (22 January 1949). See also Jane Hand, 'Marketing Health Education: Advertising Margarine and Visualising Health in Britain from 1964–c.2000', *Contemporary British History* (2017), pp. 477–500.

34 Mass-Observation, 'A Survey of the Ideal Family', File Report 3107 (April 1949).

35 Robert S. Lynd and Helen Merrell Lynd, *Middletown: A Study in American Culture* (New York, 1929), pp. 131–52, 522; Folsom, *The Family*, pp. 345–50.

36 'What's happening to the American family: interview with Dr. Margaret Mead, noted anthropologist', *u.s. News and World Report* (20 May 1963), reproduced online on 16 May 2008, www.usnews.com, accessed 21 September 2019.

37 O. R. McGregor, *Divorce in England: A Centenary Study* (London, 1957), pp. 98–9.

38 Edmund Leach, *A Runaway World? The Reith Lectures 1967* (London, 1968), p. 44.

39 Ibid., p. 46.

40 Ronald Fletcher, *The Family and Marriage in Britain* (London, 1973); Ronald Fletcher, *The Abolitionists: The Family and Marriage under Attack* (London, 1988); Ronald Fletcher, *The Shaking of the Foundations: Family and Society* (London, 1988).

41 The feminist perspective was contested by studies that suggested that the status of women was improved by family life – Colin Rosser and Christopher Harris, *Family and Social Change: A Study of Family and Kinship in a South Wales Town* (London, 1965), p. 205. See also the discussion in Elizabeth Wilson, *Women and the Welfare State* (London, 1977), pp. 59–72.

42 Tamara K. Hareven, 'The Last Stage: Historical Adulthood and Old Age', in *Adulthood*, ed. Erik H. Erikson (New York, 1976), pp. 201–15.

43 Florence Mitchell, 'Marriage Counselling in a Family Casework Agency', *Social Work*, 14 (1957), pp. 309–12. The Association was the professional body for British social workers.

44 Fletcher, *The Shaking of the Foundations*, pp. 160–86.

45 Jack Dominian, *Marital Breakdown* (London, 1968), pp. 13–14.

46 Thomas H. Holmes and Richard H. Rahe, 'The Social Readjustment Rating Scale', *Journal of Psychosomatic Research*, 11 (1967), pp. 213–18, at pp. 216–17.

47 Fletcher, *The Shaking of the Foundations*, pp. 89, 192–3.

48 Christopher Lasch, *Haven in a Heartless World: The Family Besieged* (New York, 1977).

49 Leo Tolstoy, *Anna Karenina*, trans. Constance Garnett (London, 1901), p. 1.

50 Cathy Porter, trans., *The Diaries of Sofia Tolstoy* (Richmond, 2010), p. 517.

51 Ibid., p. 89.

52 Ibid., pp. 171–2.

53 Carola H. Mann, 'Mid-life and the Family: Strains, Challenges and Options of the Middle Years', in *Mid-life: Developmental and Clinical Issues*, ed. William H. Norman and Thomas J. Scaramella (New York, 1980), pp. 128–48.

54 Alice S. Rossi, 'A Biosocial Perspective on Parenting', *Daedalus*, 106 (1977), pp. 1–31, 13.

55 Anon, 'Failure as a Family', *Lancet* (27 December 1947), p. 967; Anon., 'Casualties of Family Life', *Health Education Journal*, 9 (1951), p. 1; J. Louise Despert, *Children of Divorce* (New York, 1962).

56 Deborah Weinstein, *The Pathological Family: Postwar America and the Rise of Family Therapy* (Ithaca, 2013).

57 Kathleen Bannister et al., *Social Casework in Marital Problems: The Development of a Psychodynamic Approach* (London, 1955), p. 159.

58 John P. Spiegel, 'The Resolution of Role Conflict within the Family', *Psychiatry*, 20 (1957), pp. 1–16, at p. 3.

59 See Glin Bennet's criticism of Henry Dicks in a review of *Marital Tensions* in *British Journal of Medical Psychology*, 42 (1969), pp. 83–4.

60 Michael Fordham, 'Clinical Studies in Marriage and the Family: A Symposium on Methods. II. A Child Guidance Approach to Marriage', *British Journal of Medical Psychology*, 26 (1953), pp. 197–203. On the development of child guidance clinics, see: John Stewart, '"I thought you would want to come and see his home": Child Guidance and Psychiatric Social Work in Inter-war Britain', in *Health and the Modern Home*, ed. Mark Jackson (New York, 2007), pp. 111–27; Sarah Hayes, 'Rabbits and Rebels: The Medicalization of Maladjusted Children in Mid-twentieth-century Britain', in *Health and the Modern Home*, ed. Jackson, pp. 128–52. For discussion of these issues within the context of debates about 'problem families' and 'problem mothers', see: John Welshman, 'Troubles and the Family: Changes and Continuities since 1943', *Social Policy and Society*, 16 (2017), pp. 109–17. On the presumed impact of poor mothering on child health, see Mark Jackson, '"Allergy con Amore": Psychosomatic Medicine and the "Asthmogenic Home" in the Mid-twentieth Century', in *Health and the Modern Home*, ed. Jackson, pp. 153–74.

61 Ali Haggett, *Desperate Housewives, Neuroses and the Domestic Environment, 1945–1970* (London, 2012).

62 Robert Lee and Marjorie Casebier, *The Spouse Gap* (London, 1973), pp. 156–7.

63 LeMasters, 'Parenthood as Crisis'; Everett D. Dyer, 'Parenthood as Crisis: A Re-study', *Marriage and Family Living*, 25 (1963), pp. 196–201; Daniel F. Hobbs, 'Parenthood as Crisis: A Third Study', *Journal of Marriage and the Family*, 27 (1965), pp. 367–72. For studies of the children of divorced parents, see Despert, *Children of Divorce*; Frank F. Furstenberg et al., 'The Life Course of Children of Divorce: Marital Disruption and Parental Contact', *American Sociological Review*, 48 (1983), pp. 656–68; Judith S. Wallerstein, 'Children of Divorce: Preliminary Report of a Ten-year Follow-up of Older Children and Adolescents', *Journal of the American Academy of Child Psychiatry*, 24 (1985), pp. 545–53.

64 Heller, *Something Happened*, p. 75.

65 Ibid., p. 133.

66 Charles W. Hobart, 'Commitment, Value Conflict and the Future of the American Family', *Marriage and Family Living*, 25 (1963), pp. 405–14, at p. 409.

67 Ibid., pp. 409–10.

68 Jessie Bernard, 'Factors in the Distribution of Success in Marriage', *American Journal of Sociology*, 40 (1934), pp. 49–60. Bernard believed that marriage benefited men more than women.

69 Wesley R. Burr, 'Satisfaction with Various Aspects of Marriage over the Life Cycle: A Random Middle Class Sample', *Journal of Marriage and the Family*, 32 (1970), pp. 29–37, at p. 36; Eleanore Braun Luckey and Joyce Koym Bain, 'Children: A Factor in Marital Satisfaction', *Journal of Marriage and the Family*, 32 (1970), pp. 43–4.

70 Mass-Observation Directive, 'The Pace of Life' (1998), Respondent H.2269, p. 3.

71   George Carstairs, 'Lecture 3: Vicissitudes of adolescence', *This Island Now*, BBC Home Service, Reith Lectures, 25 November 1962.

72   John Demos and Virginia Demos, 'Adolescence in Historical Perspective', *Journal of Marriage and the Family*, 31 (1969), pp. 632–8; John Modell, Frank F. Furstenberg, Jr, and Theodore Hershberg, 'Social Change and Transitions to Adulthood in Historical Perspective', *Journal of Family History*, 1 (1976), pp. 7–32. One clear example of contemporary interest in adolescence is G. Stanley Hall, *Adolescence* (New York, 1904).

73   Anon., 'Casualties of Family Life', *Health Education Journal*, 9 (1951), p. 1; Anon., 'The Adolescent Delinquent Boy', *British Medical Journal* (2 June 1951), pp. 1256–60.

74   Isabel E. P. Menzies, 'Factors Affecting Family Breakdown in Urban Communities', *Human Relations*, 2 (1949), pp. 363–74.

75   Lynd and Lynd, *Middletown*, p. 142. See also their later study: Robert S. Lynd and Helen Merrell Lynd, *Middletown in Transition: A Study in Cultural Conflicts* (New York, 1937). For further discussion of parent-child conflicts, see Folsom, *The Family*, pp. 326–64. On parenting in the twentieth century, see Steven Mintz, *The Prime of Life: A History of Modern Adulthood* (Cambridge, MA, 2015), pp. 187–249.

76   Karl Mannheim, 'The Problem of Generations', in *Karl Mannheim: Essays*, ed. Paul Kecskemeti (London, 1952), pp. 276–322, at p. 287.

77   Bruno Bettelheim, 'The Problem of Generations', *Daedalus*, 91 (1962), pp. 68–96; Kenneth Keniston, 'Social Change and Youth in America', *Daedalus*, 91 (1962), pp. 145–71.

78   Difficulties adjusting to ageing often appeared first in middle, rather than old, age. See Hans Thomae, 'Ageing and Problems of Adjustment', *International Social Science Journal*, 15 (1963), pp. 366–76; Lawrence Greenleigh, 'Facing the Challenge of Change in Middle Age', *Geriatrics*, 29 (1974), pp. 61–8.

79   Margaret Mead, 'Broken Homes', *The Nation*, 128 (27 February 1929), pp. 253–5.

80   Mass-Observation Directive, 'Having an Affair' (1998), Respondents B.1180, B.2605, C.2570.

81   Wilson, *Women and the Welfare State*, p. 9. As James Gilbert has argued, between the 1940s and '60s, families were often viewed with both 'optimism and despair' – James Gilbert, *Another Chance: Postwar America, 1945–68* (Philadelphia, PA, 1981), p. 55.

82   John Benson, *Prime Time: A History of the Middle Aged in Twentieth-century Britain* (London, 1997), pp. 114–24.

83   Anonymous, 'An Exhausted Parent Speaks', *Harper's Monthly Magazine* (1 June 1936), pp. 120–26.

84   Kingsley Davis, 'The Sociology of Parent-youth Conflict', *American Sociological Review*, 5 (1940), pp. 523–35.

85   F. Scott Fitzgerald, *The Crack-up and Other Pieces and Stories* (Harmondsworth, 1965), pp. 39–56, at p. 42. See also Michel Mok's interview with Fitzgerald, first published in the *New York Post* on 25 September 1936 and reproduced in *The Guardian* on 18 September 2007, www.theguardian.com, accessed 1 October 2019.

86   Fitzgerald, *The Crack-up*, pp. 50, 52–3, 55–6.

87 Heller, *Something Happened*, pp. 518–19.
88 Edmund Bergler, *The Revolt of the Middle-aged Man* (London, 1958), p. vii. The term 'rat race' was first used in the mid-1950s by Daniel Lang, 'A Farewell to String and Sealing Wax', *New Yorker* (7 November 1953), p. 47. The following year, it appeared in a novelette by Philip K. Dick, *The Last of the Masters*, first published in an issue of *Orbit Science Fiction*, 5 (November/December 1954).
89 On the pace of life, stress and disease, see Mark Jackson, *The Age of Stress: Science and the Search for Stability* (Oxford, 2013).
90 Leslie J. Tizard and Harry J. S. Guntrip, *Middle Age* (London, 1959), pp. 60–71, 45.
91 Kenneth Hutchin, *How Not to Kill Your Husband* (London, 1962), pp. 11–14, 78.
92 Ivor H. Mills, 'The Disease of Failure of Coping', *Practitioner*, 217 (1976), pp. 529–38, at p. 536.
93 David Riesman, *The Lonely Crowd: A Study of American Character* [1950] (New Haven, CT, 1963), pp. xliv–xlv – the preface was written in 1960.
94 Ibid.
95 The 'career clock' is discussed in Douglas C. Kimmel, *Adulthood and Aging: An Interdisciplinary, Developmental View* (New York, 1974), pp. 253–4.
96 Riesman, *The Lonely Crowd*, pp. xxvi, xv.
97 William H. Whyte, *The Organization Man* (New York, 1956).
98 Joseph Nocera, 'Foreword', in William H. Whyte, *The Organization Man* (Philadelphia, PA, 2002), p. x. On the fulfilment of the American Dream, see Whyte, *The Organization Man*, p. 5.
99 Hobart, 'Commitment, Value Conflict and the Future of the American Family', p. 407.
100 Mass-Observation, 'The Pace of Life', Respondent C.110, pp. 18–19.
101 Ibid., pp. 19–20.
102 Herbert Marcuse, *One-dimensional Man* [1964] (London, 2002), p. xxxix.
103 Ibid., pp. xlv–xlvi.
104 Jessica Field Cohen, 'Male Roles in Mid-life', *Family Coordinator*, 28 (1979), pp. 465–71. For wider discussion of the effects of corporate life on men's health, see Martin Halliwell, *Therapeutic Revolutions: Medicine, Psychiatry, and American Culture, 1945–1970* (New Brunswick, CT, 2013), pp. 107–65.
105 See, for example, Jerome Steiner, 'What Price Success?', *Harvard Business Review* (March–April 1972), pp. 69–74; Sudhir Kakar, 'Middle Age and Organizational Role', *Vikalpa*, 1 (1976), pp. 31–8.
106 Whyte, *The Organization Man*, p. 267.
107 A. C. Spectorsky, *The Exurbanites* (Philadelphia, PA, 1955).
108 Ibid., pp. 10–12.
109 Richard E. Gordon, Katherine K. Gordon and Max Gunther, *The Split-level Trap* (New York, 1961), inside front cover.
110 Mass-Observation, 'The Pace of Life', Respondent H.2269, p. 5.
111 Richard Yates, *Revolutionary Road* [1961] (London, 2007), p. 68.
112 Whyte, *The Organization Man*, p. 269.
113 Ibid., p. 281.
114 Ibid., pp. 312, 393.

115 Ibid., p. 356.
116 Scott Donaldson, *The Suburban Myth* (New York, 1969), p. 59.
117 See, for example, Barbara Snell Dohrenwend and Bruce P. Dohrenwend, *Stressful Life Events: Their Nature and Effects* (New York, 1974).
118 Young and Willmott, *The Symmetrical Family*, p. 156.
119 F. Le Gros Clark, 'The Middle-aged Wage-worker', in *Middle Age*, ed. Roger Owen (London, 1967), pp. 115–23, at p. 121.
120 Ibid., p. 118.
121 Mass-Observation, 'The Pace of Life', Respondent w.768, p. 1.
122 Ibid., p. 2.
123 Ibid., pp. 3–4.
124 Angela Reed, *The Woman on the Verge of Divorce* (London, 1970), pp. 48–9.
125 Marilyn French, *The Women's Room* [1978] (London, 1997), p. 372.
126 Ibid., p. 376.
127 John Keats, *The Crack in the Picture Window* (New York, 1956), p. xi.
128 Ibid.
129 Ibid., pp. xi–xii.
130 Donaldson, *The Suburban Myth*. The song 'Little Boxes' was written and composed by Malvina Reynolds in 1962 and recorded the following year by Pete Seeger.
131 Yates, *Revolutionary Road*, p. 30.
132 Gordon, Gordon and Gunther, *The Split-level Trap*, pp. 198–9.
133 Andrew M. Greeley, 'Cuckoos in Suburbia', *America* (25 March 1961), pp. 832–3. See also Irving Tallman, 'Working-class Wives in Suburbia: Fulfilment or Crisis?, *Journal of Marriage and Family*, 31 (1969), pp. 65–72.
134 Betty Friedan, *The Feminine Mystique* [1963] (London, 2010); Hannah Gavron, *The Captive Wife: Conflicts of Housebound Mothers* (London, 1966); Germaine Greer, *The Female Eunuch* (London, 1970). See also Horace Gray, 'The Trapped Housewife', *Marriage and Family Living*, 24 (1962), pp. 179–82.
135 George Carstairs, 'Lecture 4: The Changing Role of Women', *This Island Now*, BBC Home Service, Reith Lectures, 3 December 1962.
136 'The Relaxed Wife' (On Film Inc., 1957), https://archive.org/details/Relaxedw1957, accessed 9 October 2019; Haggett, *Desperate Housewives*, pp. 129–69.
137 Friedan, *The Feminist Mystique*, p. 20.
138 Spectorsky, *The Exurbanites*, p. 228.
139 Friedan, *The Feminist Mystique*, pp. 210–27.
140 Ibid., p. 308.
141 Pearl Jephcott, *Married Women Working* (London, 1962), p. 19.
142 Helen McCarthy, 'Social Science and Married Women's Employment in Post-war Britain', *Past and Present*, 233 (2016), pp. 269–305; Helen McCarthy, 'Women, Marriage and Paid Work in Post-war Britain', *Women's History Review*, 26 (2017), pp. 46–61; Frederick Cooper, 'Health, Balance, and Women's "Dual Role" in Britain, 1945–1963' (PhD dissertation, University of Exeter, 2018).
143 Frederick Le Gros Clark, *The Economic Rights of Women* (Liverpool, 1963), p. 8.

144 See contributions to a special issue of *Marriage Guidance*, 1 (April 1955). On the percentage of women working across time and across the life course, see Louise A. Tilly and Joan W. Scott, *Women, Work, and Family* [1978] (New York, 1989), pp. 219–25.

145 Roland G. Tharp, 'Dimensions of Marriage Roles', *Marriage and Family Living*, 25 (1963), pp. 389–403, at p. 395.

146 Jephcott, *Married Women Working*, pp. 29, 95–8.

147 Alva Myrdal and Viola Klein, *Women's Two Roles: Home and Work* [1956] (London, 1968), p. 192.

148 Ibid., p. xvi.

149 Robert Rapoport and Rhona Rapoport, 'Work and Family in Contemporary Society', *American Sociological Review*, 30 (1965), pp. 381–94.

150 Rhona Rapoport and Robert N. Rapoport, 'The Dual Career Family: A Variant Pattern and Social Change', *Human Relations*, 22 (1969), pp. 3–30; Rhona Rapoport and Robert N. Rapoport, *Dual-career Families* (London, 1971).

151 Joseph H. Pleck, 'The Work-family Role System', *Social Problems*, 24 (1977), pp. 417–27, at p. 425.

152 Eugène Ionesco, *The Bald Soprano* [1954] (New York, 1965).

153 Rosemary Anastasio Segalla, *Departure from Traditional Roles: Midlife Women Break the Daisy Chains* (Ann Arbor, MI, 1979). The title was inspired by Charlotte M. Yonge, *The Daisy Chain; or, Aspirations: A Family Chronicle* (Leipzig, 1856).

154 F. Scott Fitzgerald, *My Lost City: Personal Essays, 1920–1940* (Cambridge, 2005), pp. 106–29, at p. 114.

155 Yates, *Revolutionary Road*, p. 130.

156 David Ely, *Seconds* (New York, 1963), p. 21. The film, directed by John Frankenheimer, supposedly triggered the breakdown of Brian Wilson, founder of the Beach Boys.

157 Ibid., p. 47.

158 Ibid., p. 108.

159 Ibid., p. 146.

160 Ibid., pp. 149, 164.

161 Anthony Storr, 'A New Life in Middle Age', in *Middle Age*, ed. Owen, pp. 37–43, at p. 37.

162 Ibid.

163 Ibid., pp. 38–42.

164 Ibid., p. 43.

165 Kenneth Keniston, 'Alienation and the Decline of Utopia', *American Scholar*, 29 (1960), pp. 161–200, at p. 161.

6 IN SEARCH OF A SOUL

1 Carl Jung, *Modern Man in Search of a Soul* [1933] (London, 1945), p. 120.

2 For an overview of Dante's life, see Robert M. Durling, ed., *The Divine Comedy of Dante Alighieri*, vol. 1: *Inferno* (New York, 1996), pp. 3–24.

3 Ibid., p. 27.

4 Ibid., Canto 34, p. 541.

5 Elliott Jaques, *The Life and Behavior of Living Organisms: A General Theory* (Westport, CT, 2002), p. 3; Elliott Jaques, 'Death and the Midlife Crisis', *International Journal of Psychoanalysis*, 46 (1965), reproduced in Elliott Jaques, *Work, Creativity, and Social Justice* (London, 1970), pp. 38–63.

6 C. G. Jung, *Memories, Dreams, Reflections* [1961] (London, 1983), pp. 203–5, 220.

7 Murray Stein, *In Midlife* (Putnam, CT, 1983) – references to Dante are on pp. 23–4.

8 James Hollis, *The Middle Passage: From Misery to Meaning in Midlife* (Toronto, 1993) – Dante is cited in the epigraph and at p. 80. For other references to Dante, see J. H. Wallis, *The Challenge of Middle Age* (London, 1962), p. ix; Orville Brim, 'Theories of the Mid-life Crisis', *Counseling Psychologist* (1976), pp. 2–9, at p. 4; Gail Sheehy, *Passages: Predictable Crises of Adult Life* (New York, 1976), pp. 297–8; Henry Still, *Surviving the Male Mid-life Crisis* (New York, 1977), epigraph; Stanley Brandes, *Forty: The Age and the Symbol* (Knoxville, TN, 1987), p. 3; Daryl Sharp, *The Survival Papers: Anatomy of a Midlife Crisis* (Toronto, 1988), p. 65.

9 T. S. Eliot, 'What Dante Means to Me', in T. S. Eliot, *To Criticize the Critic and Other Writings* (New York, 1965). For reference to the absence of a 'secure foothold' in the 'dark wood', see T. S. Eliot, 'East Coker', in *The Four Quartets* (New York, 1943).

10 Osip Mandelstam, 'Conversation about Dante', in *The Poets' Dante*, ed. Peter S. Hawkins and Rachel Jacoff (New York, 2002), pp. 40–93, at p. 55.

11 Caroline Bergvall, *Fig* (Cambridge, 2005), pp. 63–71.

12 Mary Jo Bang, *Inferno* (Minneapolis, MN, 2012).

13 Will Levington Comfort, *Midstream: A Chronicle at Halfway* (New York, 1914), p. 306.

14 Jung, *Modern Man in Search of a Soul*, pp. 122–8.

15 James Hilton, *Lost Horizon* (London, 1933), p. 138.

16 Daniel J. Levinson et al., *The Seasons of a Man's Life* (New York, 1979), p. 91. For reference to Levinson having 'christened' the male midlife crisis, see Linda Wolfe, 'A Time of Change', *New York Magazine* (5 June 1972), pp. 68–9.

17 Levinson et al., *The Seasons of a Man's Life*, p. 90.

18 Ibid., p. 109.

19 Ibid., p. 111.

20 Erik H. Erikson, *Childhood and Society* [1950] (New York, 1963), pp. 269–74.

21 Jung, *Memories, Dreams, Reflections*, pp. 194–225.

22 Walter B. Pitkin, *Life Begins at Forty* (New York, 1932).

23 Carl G. Jung, *The Integration of the Personality* (London, 1940).

24 Erikson, *Childhood and Society*, pp. 17, 23–5.

25 Ibid., pp. 247–63.

26 Erik H. Erikson, *Identity and the Life Cycle* (New York, 1980), p. 13. The articles in the volume had been first published in *Psychological Issues* in 1959. For discussion of community and its meanings in post-war England, see Jon Lawrence, *Me, Me, Me? The Search for Community in Post-war England* (Oxford, 2019).

27 Erikson, *Childhood and Society*, pp. 263–6.
28 Ibid., p. 266.
29 Ibid., pp. 267–8.
30 Ibid., pp. 268–9. Erikson noted elsewhere that ageing resulted in a sense of 'narrowing space-time' – Erik H. Erikson, *Insight and Responsibility: Lectures on the Ethical Implications of Psychoanalytic Insight* (London, 1964), p. 134.
31 Erikson, *Childhood and Society*, pp. 270–71.
32 Ibid., pp. 271–2.
33 On the variable crises of middle-aged men and women, see Jane Pearce and Saul Newton, *The Conditions of Human Growth* (New York, 1963), pp. 131–5.
34 Erikson, *Childhood and Society*, pp. 270, 274.
35 Erikson, *Identity and the Life Cycle*, pp. 177–8.
36 C. H. Waddington, 'The Epigenotype', *Endeavour*, 1 (1942), pp. 18–20. Erikson referred to Waddington's work in Erikson, *Insight and Responsibility*, pp. 142, 224, 227.
37 Adolf Meyer, 'The Life-chart', in *The Commonsense Psychiatry of Dr Adolf Meyer: Fifty-two Selected Papers*, ed. Alfred Lief (New York, 1948), pp. 418–22. See also Ruth Leys, 'Types of One: Adolf Meyer's Life Chart and the Representation of Individuality', *Representations*, 34 (1991), pp. 1–28.
38 George Draper, *Disease and the Man* (London, 1930), p. 243.
39 James L. Halliday, *Psychosocial Medicine: A Study of the Sick Society* (London, 1948).
40 James L. Halliday, 'The Rising Incidence of Psychosomatic Illness', *British Medical Journal* (2 July 1938), pp. 11–14.
41 Mark Jackson, *The Age of Stress: Science and the Search for Stability* (Oxford, 2013).
42 Thomas H. Holmes and Richard H. Rahe, 'The Social Readjustment Rating Scale', *Journal of Psychosomatic Research*, 11 (1967), pp. 213–18.
43 Erikson, *Childhood and Society*, pp. 412–13.
44 Erikson, *Insight and Responsibility*, p. 125.
45 Erik H. Erikson, 'Youth: Fidelity and Diversity', *Daedalus*, 91 (1962), pp. 5–27. This paper was reprinted in Erik H. Erikson, ed., *Youth: Change and Challenge* (New York, 1963), pp. 1–23.
46 Erikson, 'Youth: Fidelity and Diversity', p. 15.
47 Ibid.
48 Erikson, *Identity and the Life Cycle*, p. 174 – a discussion in which Erikson referenced the work of David Riesman on the lonely crowd.
49 Erikson, 'Youth: Fidelity and Diversity', p. 25.
50 Ibid., p. 26.
51 Erikson, *Identity and the Life Cycle*, p. 150.
52 Erikson's impact is evident in: Judd Marmor, 'The Crisis of Middle Age', *Psychiatry Digest*, 25 (1968), pp. 17–21; Bernice L. Neugarten, ed., *Middle Age and Aging: A Reader in Social Psychology* (Chicago, IL, 1968); Roger L. Gould, 'The Phases of Adult Life: A Study in Developmental Psychology', *American Journal of Psychiatry*, 129 (1972), pp. 33–43; Douglas C. Kimmel, *Adulthood and Aging: An Interdisciplinary Developmental*

View (New York, 1974); Daniel J. Levinson et al., 'Periods in the Adult Development of Men: Ages 18–45', *Counseling Psychologist*, 6 (1976), pp. 21–5; Marjorie Fiske and Lawrence Weiss, 'Intimacy and Crises in Adulthood', *Counseling Psychologist*, 6 (1976), pp. 10–15; Marjorie Fiske Lowenthal, Majda Thurnher and David Chiriboga, *Four Stages of Life: A Comparative Study of Women and Men Facing Transitions* (San Francisco, CA, 1976).

53 Erik H. Erikson, ed., *Adulthood* (New York, 1976).

54 Janet Zollinger Giele, 'Adulthood as Transcendence of Age and Sex', in *Themes of Work and Love in Adulthood*, ed. Erik H. Erikson and Neil J. Smelser (Cambridge, 1980), pp. 151–73.

55 Ibid., p. 162.

56 Ibid. See also Marjorie Fiske, 'Changing Hierarchies of Commitment in Adulthood', in *Themes of Work and Love*, ed. Erikson and Smelser, pp. 238–64.

57 Giele, 'Adulthood as Transcendence', pp. 156, 169.

58 Ann Swidler, 'Love and Adulthood in American Culture', in *Themes of Work and Love*, ed. Erikson and Smelser, pp. 120–47, at pp. 126–7.

59 Ibid., p. 131.

60 Ibid., pp. 130–32, 142.

61 Ibid., p. 135. See also Edmund Bergler, *The Revolt of the Middle-aged Man* (London, 1958).

62 Levinson et al., 'Periods in the Adult Development of Men'.

63 Daniel Levinson, 'The Mid-life Transition: A Period in Adult Psychosocial Development', *Psychiatry*, 40 (1977), pp. 99–112, at pp. 107–8.

64 Ibid., p. 110.

65 Ibid.

66 Initial findings were reported in George E. Vaillant, *Adaptation to Life* (Cambridge, MA, 1977).

67 Sheehy, *Passages*, p. 6.

68 Ibid., pp. 32–3.

69 Ibid., pp. 33–5.

70 Ibid., pp. 10, 285–96.

71 Ibid., pp. 308–14, 320–34.

72 Ibid., p. 21.

73 Gail Sheehy, *Daring: My Passages* (New York, 2014), pp. 218–20; Anon., 'Book Ends', *New York Times* (30 May 1976), p. 16.

74 Michael S. Kimmel, 'Review of *Passages: Predictable Crisis of Adult Life* by Gail Sheehy', *Contemporary Sociology*, 6 (1977), pp. 490–93, at p. 493.

75 Herbert Mitgang, 'Behind the Best Sellers: Gail Sheehy', *New York Times* (12 June 1977), p. 237.

76 Anatole Broyard, 'Books of the Times: Clearing our Passages', *New York Times* (16 August 1976), p. 60.

77 Susanne Schmidt, 'The Anti-feminist Reconstruction of the Midlife Crisis: Popular Psychology, Journalism and Social Science in 1970s USA', *Gender and History*, 30 (2018), pp. 153–76; Susanne Schmidt, *Midlife Crisis: The Feminist Origins of a Chauvinist Cliché* (Chicago, IL, 2020).

78 References to these ideas in turn are in Sheehy, *Passages*, pp. 288, 32, 290–91, 287, 297–8. For Neugarten's reference to punctuation marks in the life

course, see Bernice L. Neugarten, 'Dynamics of Transition of Middle Age to Old Age: Adaptation and the Life Cycle', *Journal of Geriatric Psychiatry*, 4 (1970), pp. 71–87.

79 Sheehy, *Passages*, p. 27.

80 Sheehy, *Passages*, pp. 19, 26. See also Gail Sheehy, *The Silent Passage: Menopause* (New York, 1992); Gail Sheehy, *Understanding Men's Passages: Discovering the New Map of Men's Lives* (New York, 1998); Sheehy, *Daring: My Passages*.

81 Gail Sheehy, 'What Do Men Want?', *New York Times* (19 March 1978), BR4.

82 Mark Jackson, 'Men and Women under Stress: Neuropsychiatric Models of Resilience during and after the Second World War', in *Stress in Post-war Britain, 1945–85*, ed. Mark Jackson (London, 2015), pp. 111–29, 219–26.

83 Sheehy, *Passages*, p. 107. Sheehy was reinforcing Beata Bishop's lament about the challenges faced by women in a man's world – Beata Bishop, 'Women in a Man's World', *Punch* (3 January 1968), p. 34.

84 Sheehy, *Daring*, pp. 215–16.

85 Gail Sheehy, *Lovesounds* (New York, 1970), p. 213.

86 Sheehy, *Daring*, pp. 229, 234. See also Michele Landsberg, 'How Women should Plan their Lives', *Chatelaine*, 50 (June 1977), pp. 53, 105–9; Evelyne Michaels, 'Family Passages', *Chatelaine*, 59 (November 1986), pp. 64–5, 102–3.

87 Angela Reed, *The Woman on the Verge of Divorce* (London, 1970); Gerald Sanctuary and Constance Whitehead, *Divorce – And After* (London, 1970).

88 Vaillant, *Adaptation to Life*; Roger L. Gould, *Transformations: Growth and Change in Adult Life* (New York, 1978); Levinson et al., *The Seasons of a Man's Life*.

89 Lillian B. Rubin, *Women of a Certain Age: The Midlife Search for Self* (New York, 1979).

90 Ibid., pp. 5, 13.

91 Rosemary Anastasio Segalla, *Departure from Traditional Roles: Mid-life Women Break the Daisy Chains* (Ann Arbor, MI, 1979); Grace Baruch and Jeanne Brooks-Gunn, *Women in Midlife* (New York, 1984); Amia Lieblich, 'Successful Career Women at Midlife: Crises and Transitions', *International Journal of Aging and Human Development*, 23 (1986), pp. 301–12; Michèle Thiriet and Suzanne Képès, *Women at Fifty* (New York, 1987); Ada Kahn and Linda Hughey Holt, *Midlife Health: Every Woman's Guide to Feeling Good* (New York, 1987).

92 Marilyn French, *The Women's Room* [1978] (London, 1997); Doris Lessing, *The Summer Before the Dark* [1973] (London, 2002); Doris Lessing, 'To Room Nineteen', in Doris Lessing, *To Room Nineteen: Collected Stories*, vol. I (London, 1994), pp. 352–86.

93 Schmidt, 'The Anti-feminist Reconstruction of the Midlife Crisis'.

94 For a confessional and largely exculpatory account, see William A. Nolen, *Crisis Time: Love, Marriage, and the Male at Mid-life* (New York, 1984).

95 Sheila Gormley, 'How to Survive your Husband's Menopause', *Chatelaine*, 50 (January 1977) pp. 34–5, 72–3; William A. Nolen, 'Male Midlife Crisis', *Chatelaine*, 58 (1985), pp. 70–71, 91–4; Melissa Sands, 'The Double Standard of Male Intimacy', *Chatelaine*, 61 (October 1988), pp. 78–81;

Melissa Sands, 'The Hidden Crises in Men's Lives', *Chatelaine*, 63 (February 1990), pp. 66–8.

96 As Kimmel pointed out in 1974, there was very little research on single 'heterosexual' or 'homosexual' men and women – Kimmel, *Adulthood and Aging*, pp. 230–37.

97 For a comparison between Levinson's discussions of men and women, see Dancy Kittrell, 'A Comparison of the Evolution of Men's and Women's Dreams in Daniel Levinson's Theory of Adult Development', *Journal of Adult Development*, 5 (1998), pp. 105–15.

98 Levinson et al., *The Seasons of a Man's Life*, p. 200.

99 Ibid.

100 Jung, *The Integration of the Personality*, pp. 3, 29.

101 Carl G. Jung, 'Marriage as a Psychological Relationship', in *The Collected Works of C. G. Jung*, ed. Herbert Read, Michael Fordham and Gerhard Adler, vol. XVII (London, 1954), pp. 189–201.

102 See his discussion of 'the spiritual problems of modern man', in Jung, *Modern Man in Search of a Soul*, pp. 226–54.

103 See Jung's essay on 'psychology and literature', ibid., pp. 175–99.

104 Erikson, *Identity and the Life Cycle*, pp. 103, 110–18.

105 Jaques, 'Death and the Midlife Crisis', pp. 62–3.

106 This pattern of midlife behaviour became known as the 'Gauguin syndrome', captured in fictional works based partly on Gauguin's life: W. Somerset Maugham, *The Moon and Sixpence* (London, 1919); Mario Vargas Llosa, *The Way to Paradise* (London, 2003).

107 Notes by Helen Lucas, 1982, in York University Libraries, Clara Thomas Archives & Special Collections, Helen Lucas Fonds F0100, 1994-040/011(03).

108 Ibid. For Lucas's thoughts on the politics of creativity and survival, see her notes for a book that was never written, entitled *The Fine Art of Survival: An Illustrated Guide to Liberation and Feminine Independence*, in Helen Lucas Fonds F0100, 1994-040/011(04).

109 'The Diary Drawings', in Helen Lucas Fonds F0100, 1994-040/001.

110 *Helen Lucas: Her Journey – Our Journey* (Davey Productions, 1996), copy available in York University Libraries, Donna Davey Fonds, F0506, 2006-052/001.

111 Pearce and Newton, *The Conditions of Human Growth*, pp. 131–3.

112 Robert N. Butler, 'Looking Forward to What? The Life Review, Legacy, and Excessive Identity versus Change', *American Behavioral Scientist*, 14 (1970), pp. 121–8.

113 Wallis, *The Challenge of Middle Age*, p. 93.

114 Richard Yates, *Revolutionary Road* [1961] (London, 2007), p. 112.

115 Wallis encouraged those struggling at midlife to gain inspiration from introspective diaries and autobiographies, such as W.N.P. Barbellion, *The Journal of a Disappointed Man* (London, 1919) – Wallis, *The Challenge of Middle Age*, p. 147.

116 William Brown, *Psychological Methods of Healing: An Introduction to Psychotherapy* (London, 1938), pp. 163–6.

117 Bergler, *The Revolt of the Middle-aged Man*, pp. 75–6.

118 Rollo May, *Man's Search for Himself* [1953] (New York, 2009), pp. 192–200.

119 Otto F. Kernberg, 'Mature Love: Prerequisites and Characteristics', *Journal of the American Psychoanalytical Association*, 22 (1974), pp. 743–68.
120 Tom Wolfe, 'The "Me" Decade and the Third Great Awakening', *New York Magazine*, 23 August 1976, http://nymag.com.
121 Ibid.
122 Christopher Lasch, *The Culture of Narcissism: American Life in an Age of Diminishing Expectations* (New York, 1978).
123 Barbara Ehrenreich, *The Hearts of Men: American Dreams and the Flight from Commitment* (New York, 1984).
124 Lasch, *The Culture of Narcissism*, pp. xvi–xvii.
125 Ibid., p. xviii.
126 Ibid., p. 26.
127 Ulrich Beck and Elisabeth Beck-Gernsheim, *The Normal Chaos of Love*, trans. Mark Ritter and Jane Wiebel (Cambridge, 1995), pp. 4, 6.
128 Alvin Toffler, *Future Shock* (London, 1970), pp. 47–161.
129 Beck and Beck-Gernsheim, *The Normal Chaos of Love*, p. 11.
130 Ibid., p. 69.
131 John Updike, *Rabbit, Run* (New York, 1960), p. 111.
132 John Updike, *A Month of Sundays* [1974] (London, 2007), p. 43.
133 Ibid., p. 46.
134 Ibid., p. 138.
135 Ibid., p. 192.
136 Erikson, ed., *Youth: Change and Challenge*, p. 22.
137 Lessing, 'To Room Nineteen', p. 360.
138 Ibid., p. 371.
139 Ibid., p. 386.
140 Doris Lessing, 'The Temptation of Jack Orkney', in Doris Lessing, *The Temptation of Jack Orkney: Collected Stories*, vol. II (London, 1994), pp. 237–302, at p. 264.
141 Ibid., pp. 258–9.
142 J. G. Ballard, 'The Overloaded Man', in J. G. Ballard, *The Voices of Time* [1974] (London, 1992), pp. 79–92, at p. 92.
143 Lessing, 'The Temptation of Jack Orkney', p. 302.

POSTSCRIPT

1 David Nobbs, *I Didn't Get Where I Am Today: An Autobiography* (London, 2004), p. 263.
2 Ibid., pp. 264, 272.
3 Ibid., p. 284.
4 Ibid., p. 291.
5 Sloan Wilson, *The Man in the Gray Flannel Suit II* (New York, 1984), p. 72.
6 Nobbs, *I Didn't Get Where I am Today*, p. 266.
7 Chris Fox, 'The Emancipatory Strategies of Reginald Perrin', in Jonathan Bignell, Stephen Lacey and Madeleine Macmurrough-Kavanagh, *British Television Drama: Past, Present and Future* (Basingstoke, 2000), pp. 122–32. For more light-hearted reflections, see Richard Webber, *The Life and Legacy of Reginald Perrin: A Celebration* (London, 1996);

Jonathan Freedland, 'Reggie Perrin – A Suburban Everyman Who Captured the Essence of His Era', *Guardian*, www.theguardian.com, 14 August 2015; Jonathan Coe, 'The Fall and Rise of Reginald Perrin Is a Modern Classic', *The Guardian*, www.theguardian.com, 23 February 2018.

SELECT BIBLIOGRAPHY

ARCHIVAL SOURCES

Clara Thomas Archives, York University, Canada
    Helen Lucas Fonds, F0100, 1994–040/001–0041
    University Women's Club of North York Fonds, F0160, 1998–009/007
    Donna Davey Fonds, F0506, 2006–052/001
    Eric Trist Fonds, F0681, 2016–004/12/1–76; 2016–004/13/1–74
Mass-Observation Archive, The Keep, University of Sussex Library
    'The Pace of Life', Spring 1992 Directive, SXMOA2/1/36/2/1–3
    'Having an Affair', Spring 1998 Directive, SXMOA2/1/54/2/1
    'Midlife Transitions', Winter 2009 Directive, SXMOA2/1/87/1/1
Wellcome Archives and Manuscripts
    Henry Dicks papers, PP/HVD/D/1/9; PP/HVD/D/2
    Family Discussion Bureau, SA/TCC/C/3/2, Box 17; SA/TCC/A/4/10, Box 8;
        SA/TCC/4/6, Box 7; SA/TCC/A/1/1, Box 1; SA/TCC/A/1/3, Box 1;
        SA/TCC/B-F
    Marriage Guidance Council, SA/TCC/A/3/1/7, Box 3; SA/MWF/F.24, Box 63;
        SA/FPA/A13/96, Box 345
    Tavistock Institute of Human Relations, SA/TCC/A/1/5
    Tavistock Institute of Marital Studies, SA/TCC/A/3/5, Box 6; SA/TIH/A/5/2

PRIMARY PUBLISHED SOURCES

Adams, James Truslow, *The Epic of America* (Boston, MA, 1935)
Bannister, Kathleen, et al., *Social Casework in Marital Problems:
    The Development of a Psychodynamic Approach* (London, 1955)
Baruch, Grace, and Jeanne Brooks-Gunn, eds, *Women in Midlife*
    (New York, 1983)
Beauvoir, Simone de, *The Second Sex* [1949] (London, 1997)
Bergler, Edmund, *Divorce Won't Help* (New York, 1948)
——, *The Revolt of the Middle-aged Man* (London, 1958)
Billig, Otto, and Robert Adams, 'Emotional Problems of the Middle-aged Man',
    Psychiatric Quarterly, 28 (1954), pp. 442–52
Bott, Elizabeth, *Family and Social Networks: Roles, Norms, and External
    Relationships in Ordinary Urban Families* (London, 1957)

Brim, Orville G., 'Theories of the Male Mid-life Crisis', *Counseling Psychologist*,
    6 (March, 1976), pp. 2–9
Bühler, Charlotte, 'The Curve of Life as Studied in Biographies', *Journal*
    of Applied Psychology, 18 (1935), pp. 405–9
——, 'The Human Course of Life in its Goal Aspects', *Journal of Humanistic*
    Psychology, 4 (1964), pp. 1–18
Cohen, Richard, 'The Clock Is Ticking for the Career Woman', *Washington Post*
    (16 March 1978)
Conway, Jim, and Sally Conway, *Women in Midlife Crisis* (Wheaton, IL, 1983)
Despert, J. Louise, *Children of Divorce* (New York, 1962)
Dicks, Henry V., 'The Predicament of the Family in the Modern World', *Lancet*
    (5 February 1955), pp. 295–7
Dicks, Henry V., *Marital Tensions: Clinical Studies towards a Psychological*
    Theory of Interaction (London, 1967)
Dominian, Jack, *Marital Breakdown* (London, 1968)
Donaldson, Scott, *The Suburban Myth* (New York, 1969)
Erikson, H. Erik, *Childhood and Society* [1950] (New York, 1963)
——, *Identity and the Life Cycle* [1959] (New York, 1980)
——, *Youth: Change and Challenge* (New York, 1963)
——, *Insight and Responsibility: Lectures on the Ethical Implications*
    of Psychoanalytic Insight (London, 1964)
——, ed., *Adulthood* (New York, 1976)
Fletcher, Ronald, *The Family and Marriage in Britain* (London, 1973)
——, *The Abolitionists: The Family and Marriage under Attack* (London, 1988)
——, *The Shaking of the Foundations: Family and Society* (London, 1988)
Fried, Barbara, *The Middle-age Crisis* (New York, 1967)
Friedan, Betty, *The Feminine Mystique* (New York, 1963)
Gavron, Hannah, *The Captive Wife: Conflicts of Housebound Mothers* [1966]
    (London, 1968)
Gillie, Dame Annis, *Do Something About That Middle Age* (London, 1969)
Glick, Paul C., *American Families* (New York, 1957)
Gordon, Richard E., Katherine K. Gordon and Max Gunther, *The Split-level*
    Trap (New York, 1961)
Gorer, Geoffrey, *Exploring English Character* (London, 1955)
Gould, Roger L., 'The Phases of Adult Life: A Study in Developmental
    Psychology', *American Journal of Psychiatry*, 129 (1972), pp. 33–43
——, *Transformations: Growth and Change in Adult Life* (New York, 1978)
Greer, Germaine, *The Female Eunuch* [1970] (London, 1999)
Hall, G. Stanley, 'The Dangerous Age', *Pedagogical Seminary*, 28 (1921),
    pp. 275–94
——, *Senescence: The Last Half of Life* (New York, 1922)
Hauser, Gayelord, *Look Younger, Live Longer* (London, 1950)
Hill, Reuben, *Families Under Stress: Adjustment to the Crises of War Separation*
    and Reunion [1949] (Westport, CT, 1971)
Hilliard, Marion, *Women and Fatigue* (London, 1960)
——, *A Woman Doctor Looks at Love and Life* (London, 1958)
Hobart, Charles W., 'Commitment, Value Conflict and the Future of the
    American Family', *Marriage and Family Living*, 25 (1963), pp. 405–14
Hutchin, Kenneth C., *How Not to Kill Your Husband* (London, 1962)

——, *The Change of Life* (London, 1963)

——, *How Not to Kill Your Wife* (London, 1965)

Jaques, Elliott, 'Death and the Mid-life Crisis', *International Journal of Psychoanalysis*, 46 (1965), in Elliott Jaques, *Work, Creativity, and Social Justice* (London, 1970), pp. 38–63

——, *The Form of Time* (London, 1982)

Jephcott, Pearl, *Married Women Working* (London, 1962)

Jung, C. G., *Modern Man in Search of a Soul* (London, 1933)

——, *The Integration of the Personality* (London, 1940)

Keats, John, *The Crack in the Picture Window* (New York, 1956)

Klein, Josephine, *Samples from English Culture* (London, 1965)

Lawrie, Macpherson, *Love, Marriage and Divorce* (London, 1937)

Lawson, Annette, *Adultery: An Analysis of Love and Betrayal* (New York, 1988)

Leach, Edmund, *A Runaway World? The Reith Lectures 1967* (London, 1968)

Lee, Robert, and Marjorie Casebier, *The Spouse Gap* (London, 1973)

Levinson, Daniel J., 'The Mid-life Transition: A Period in Adult Psychosocial Development', *Psychiatry*, 40 (1977), pp. 99–112

——, *The Seasons of a Woman's Life* (New York, 1996)

——, et al., 'Periods in the Adult Development of Men: Ages 18–45', *Counseling Psychologist*, 6 (1976), pp. 21–5

——, *The Seasons of a Man's Life* (New York, 1979)

Lowenthal, Marjorie Fiske, and David Chiriboga, 'Transition to the Empty Nest: Crisis, Challenge, or Relief?', *Archives of General Psychiatry*, 26 (1972), pp. 8–14

——, Majda Thurnher and David Chiriboga, eds, *Four Stages of Life: A Comparative Study of Women and Men Facing Transitions* (San Francisco, CA, 1976)

——, and Lawrence Weiss, 'Intimacy and Crises in Adulthood', *Counseling Psychologist*, 6 (1976), pp. 10–15

Lynd, Robert S., and Helen M. Lynd, *Middletown: A Study in American Culture* [1929] (New York, 1956)

——, *Middletown in Transition: A Study in Cultural Conflicts* (New York, 1937)

Macaulay, Mary, *The Art of Marriage* [1952] (London, 1956)

Mace, David R., *Marriage Crisis* (London, 1948)

Macrae, Rosalie, 'Middle-age is Danger Time for Marriages', *Daily Mail*, 14 June 1965, p. 5

Malleson, Joan, *Change of Life: Facts and Fallacies of Middle Age* [1949] (London, 1963)

Marañón, Gregorio, *The Climacteric (The Critical Age)* (London, 1929)

Marcuse, Herbert, *One-dimensional Man* [1964] (London, 2002)

Mayer, Nancy, *The Male Mid-life Crisis: Fresh Starts After Forty* (New York, 1978)

Mead, Margaret, *Male and Female* [1949] (Harmondsworth, 1962)

Myrdal, Alva, and Viola Klein, *Women's Two Roles: Home and Work* [1956] (London, 1968)

Neugarten, Bernice L., ed., *Middle Age and Aging: A Reader in Social Psychology* (Chicago, IL, 1968)

——, 'Continuities and Discontinuities of Psychological Issues into Adult Life', *Human Development*, 12 (1969), pp. 121–30

——, 'Dynamics of Transition of Middle Age to Old Age: Adaptation and the Life Cycle', *Journal of Geriatric Psychiatry*, 4 (1970), pp. 71–87

——, and Ruth J. Kraines, '"Menopausal Symptoms" in Women of Various Ages', *Psychosomatic Medicine*, 27 (1965), pp. 266–73

Nolen, William A., *Crisis Time: Love, Marriage, and the Male at Mid-life* (New York, 1984)

Oakley, Ann, *Woman's Work: The Housewife Past and Present* (New York, 1974)

Owen, Roger, ed., *Middle Age* (London, 1967)

Pearce, Jane, and Saul Newton, *The Conditions of Human Growth* (New York, 1963)

Pitkin, Walter B., *Life Begins at Forty* (New York, 1932)

Pitkin, Walter Jr, *Life Begins at Fifty* (New York, 1965)

Rapoport, Robert N., and Rhona Rapoport, 'Work and Family in Contemporary Society', *American Sociological Review*, 30 (1965), pp. 381–94

Rapoport, Rhona, and Robert N. Rapoport, *Dual-career Families* (London, 1971)

Reed, Angela, *The Woman on the Verge of Divorce* (London, 1970)

Richter, Curt Paul, *Biological Clocks in Medicine and Psychiatry* (Springfield, IL, 1965)

Riesman, David, *The Lonely Crowd: A Study of American Character* [1950] (New Haven, CT, 1963)

Rowntree, Griselda, 'Some Aspects of Marriage Breakdown in Britain during the Last Thirty Years', *Population Studies*, 18 (1964), pp. 147–63

Rubin, Lillian B., *Women of a Certain Age: The Midlife Search for Self* (New York, 1979)

Scharlieb, Mary, *The Seven Ages of Woman: A Consideration of the Successive Phases of Woman's Life* (London, 1915)

Sheehy, Gail, *Lovesounds* (New York, 1970)

——, *Passages: Predictable Crises of Adult Life* (New York, 1974)

Slater, Eliot, and Moya Woodside, *Patterns of Marriage: A Study of Marriage Relationships in the Urban Working Classes* (London, 1951)

Soddy, Kenneth, and Mary C. Kidson, *Men in Middle Life* (London, 1967)

Sokoloff, Boris, *Middle Age Is What You Make It* (New York, 1938)

Spectorsky, A. C., *The Exurbanites* (Philadelphia, PA, 1955)

Still, Henry, *Surviving the Male Mid-Life Crisis* (New York, 1977)

Stopes, Marie Carmichael, *Enduring Passion* [1928] (London, 1936)

——, *Change of Life in Men and Women* (London, 1936)

Thiriet, Michèle, and Suzanne Képès, *Women at Fifty* (New York, 1987)

Tizard, Leslie J., and Harry J. S. Guntrip, *Middle Age* (London, 1959)

Torrie, Alfred, *The Middle-aged Man* (London, 1960)

Vaillant, George E., *Adaptation to Life* (Cambridge, MA, 1977)

Wallis, J. H., *Someone to Turn To* (London, 1961)

——, *The Challenge of Middle Age* (London, 1962)

——, and H. S. Booker, *Marriage Counselling: A Description and Analysis of the Remedial Work of the National Marriage Guidance Council* (London, 1958)

Welford, A. T., 'Problems of Middle Age', *Health Education Journal* (1 December 1951), pp. 167–71

Whyte, William H., *The Organization Man* (New York, 1956)
Williams, Leonard, *Middle Age and Old Age* (London, 1925)
Young, Michael, and Paul Willmott, *The Symmetrical Family* (London, 1973)

SECONDARY SOURCES

Anderson, Michael, 'The Emergence of the Modern Life Cycle in Britain',
    Social History, 10 (1985), pp. 69–87
Bauman, Zygmunt, *The Individualized Society* (Cambridge, 2001)
——, *Liquid Love: On the Frailty of Human Bonds* (Cambridge, 2003)
Beck, Ulrich, and Elisabeth Beck-Gernsheim, *The Normal Chaos of Love*,
    trans. Mark Ritter and Jane Wiebel (Cambridge, 1995)
Benson, John, *Prime Time: A History of the Middle Aged in Twentieth-century
    Britain* (London, 1997)
Brandes, Stanley, *Forty: The Age and the Symbol* (Knoxville, TN, 1985)
Charnock, Hannah, '"A Million Little Bonds": Infidelity, Divorce and the
    Emotional Worlds of Marriage in British Women's Magazines of the 1930s',
    Cultural and Social History, 14 (2017), pp. 363–79
Chettiar, Teri, '"More than a Contract": The Emergence of a State-supported
    Marriage Welfare Service and the Politics of Emotional Life in Post-1945
    Britain', *Journal of British Studies*, 55 (2016), pp. 566–91
Chudacoff, Howard P., *How Old Are You? Age Consciousness in American
    Culture* (Princeton, NJ, 1989)
——, and Tamara K. Hareven, 'From the Empty Nest to Family Dissolution:
    Life Course Transitions into Old Age', *Journal of Family History* (1979),
    pp. 69–83
Churchwell, Sarah, *Behold, America: A History of America First and the
    American Dream* (London, 2018)
Clark, David, 'Guidance, Counselling, Therapy: Responses to "Marital
    Problems" 1950–90', *Sociological Review*, 39 (1991), pp. 765–98
Cohen, Patricia, *In Our Prime: The Invention of Middle Age* (New York, 2012)
Cole, Thomas R., *The Journey of Life: A Cultural History of Aging in America*
    (Cambridge, 1992)
Collins, Marcus, *Modern Love: An Intimate History of Men and Women
    in Twentieth-century Britain* (London, 2003)
Cooper, Frederick, 'Health, Balance, and Women's "Dual Role" in Britain,
    1945–1963' (PhD dissertation, University of Exeter, 2018)
Coupland, Justine, 'Time, the Body and the Reversibility of Ageing:
    Commodifying the Decade', *Ageing and Society*, 29 (2009), pp. 953–76
Davis, Angela, and Laura King, 'Gendered Perspectives on Men's Changing
    Familial Roles in Postwar Britain, c. 1950–1990', *Gender and History*,
    30 (2018), pp. 70–92
Ehrenreich, Barbara, *The Hearts of Men: American Dreams and the Flight
    from Commitment* (New York, 1984)
Eisler, Benita, *Private Lives: Men and Women of the Fifties* (New York, 1986)
Finch, Janet, and Penny Summerfield, 'Social Reconstruction and the
    Emergence of the Companionate Marriage, 1945–59', in *Marriage, Domestic
    Life and Social Change: Writings for Jacqueline Burgoyne (1944–88)*,
    ed. David Clark (London, 1991), pp. 6–27

Foxcroft, Louise, *Hot Flushes, Cold Science: A History of the Menopause* (London, 2009)

Fuess, Harald, *Divorce in Japan: Family, Gender, and the State, 1600–2000* (Stanford, CA, 2004)

Gilbert, James, *Men in the Middle: Searching for Masculinity in the 1950s* (Chicago, IL, 2005)

Gillis, John R., *For Better, For Worse: British Marriages, 1600–the Present* (Oxford, 1985)

Gullette, Margaret Morganroth, *Safe at Last in the Middle Years: The Invention of the Midlife Progress Novel* (Berkeley, CA, 1988)

——, *Declining to Decline: Cultural Combat and the Politics of the Midlife* (Charlottesville, VA, 1997)

——, *Aged by Culture* (Chicago, IL, 2004)

Hareven, Tamara K., 'Aging and Generational Relations: A Historical and Life Course Perspective', *Annual Review of Sociology*, 20 (1994), pp. 437–61

Harris, Alana, and Timothy Jones, eds, *Love and Romance in Britain, 1918–1970* (Basingstoke, 2014)

Heath, Kay, *Aging by the Book: The Emergence of Midlife in Victorian Britain* (New York, 2009)

Houck, Judith A., *Hot and Bothered: Women, Medicine, and Menopause in Modern America* (Cambridge, MA, 2006)

Hutchinson, Ben, *The Midlife Mind: Literature and the Art of Ageing* (London, 2020)

Jackson, Mark, *The Age of Stress: Science and the Search for Stability* (Oxford, 2013)

——, and Martin Moore, eds, *Balancing the Self: Medicine, Politics and the Regulation of Health in the Twentieth Century* (Manchester, 2020)

Kearl, Michael C., and Lisbeth J. Hoag, 'The Social Construction of the Midlife Crisis: A Case Study in the Temporalities of Identity', *Sociological Inquiry*, 54 (1984), pp. 279–300

Langhamer, Claire, 'The Meanings of Home in Postwar Britain', *Journal of Contemporary History*, 40 (2005), pp. 341–62

——, 'Adultery in Post-war England', *History Workshop Journal*, 62 (2006), pp. 87–115

——, *The English in Love: The Intimate Story of an Emotional Revolution* (Oxford, 2013)

Lasch, Christopher, *The Culture of Narcissism: American Life in an Age of Diminishing Expectations* (New York, 1978)

Lawrence, Jon, *Me, Me, Me? The Search for Community in Post-war England* (Oxford, 2019)

Levinson, Julie, *The American Success Myth on Film* (Basingstoke, 2012)

Lewis, Jane, 'Public Institution and Private Relationship: Marriage and Marriage Guidance, 1920–1968', *Twentieth Century British History*, 1 (1990), pp. 233–63

——, *The End of Marriage? Individualism and Intimate Relations* (Cheltenham, 2001)

Lock, Margaret, *Encounters with Aging: Mythologies of the Menopause in Japan and North America* (Berkeley, CA, 1993)

McCarthy, Helen, 'Women, Marriage and Paid Work in Post-war Britain',
    Women's History Review, 26 (2017), pp. 46–61
McKaughan, Molly, *The Biological Clock: Balancing Marriage, Motherhood,
    and Career* (London, 1987)
Mintz, Steven, *The Prime of Life: A History of Modern Adulthood*
    (Cambridge, MA, 2015)
——, and Susan Kellogg, *Domestic Revolutions: A Social History of American
    Family Life* (New York, 1988)
Park, Hyung Wook, *Old Age, New Science: Gerontologists and their Biosocial
    Visions, 1900–1960* (Pittsburgh, PA, 2016)
Phillips, Roderick, *Putting Asunder: A History of Divorce in Western Society*
    (Cambridge, 1988)
Port, Cynthia, '"Ages are the Stuff!": The Traffic in Ages in Interwar Britain',
    NWSA *Journal*, 18 (2006), pp. 138–61
Ruggles, Steven, 'The Transformation of American Family Structure',
    American Historical Review, 99 (1994), pp. 103–28
——, 'The Rise of Divorce and Separation in the United States, 1880–1990',
    Demography, 34 (1997), pp. 455–66
Schmidt, Susanne, 'The Feminist Origins of the Midlife Crisis', *Historical
    Journal*, 61 (2018), pp. 503–23
——, 'The Anti-Feminist Reconstruction of the Midlife Crisis: Popular
    Psychology, Journalism and Social Science in 1970s USA', *Gender and
    History*, 30 (2018), pp. 153–76
——, *Midlife Crisis: The Feminist Origins of a Chauvinist Cliché*
    (Chicago, IL, 2020)
Shweder, Richard A., ed., *Welcome to Middle Age! (And Other Cultural Fictions)*
    (Chicago, IL, 1998)
Stark, James F., *The Cult of Youth: Anti-ageing in Modern Britain*
    (Cambridge, 2020)
Stone, Lawrence, *Road to Divorce: England, 1530–1987* (Oxford, 1990)
Strange, Julie-Marie, 'In Full Possession of Her Powers: Researching and
    Rethinking Menopause in Early Twentieth-century England and Scotland',
    Social History of Medicine, 25 (2012), pp. 685–700
Watkins, Elizabeth Siegel, 'The Medicalisation of the Male Menopause
    in America', *Social History of Medicine*, 20 (2007), pp. 369–88
Weinstein, Deborah, *The Pathological Family: Postwar America and the Rise
    of Family Therapy* (Ithaca, NY, 2013)
Wethington, Elaine, 'Expecting Stress: Americans and the "Midlife Crisis"',
    Motivation and Emotion, 24 (2000), pp. 85–103
Winch, Robert F., 'Permanence and Change in the History of American Family
    and some Speculations as to its Future', *Journal of Marriage and the Family*,
    32 (1970), pp. 6–15

ACKNOWLEDGEMENTS

This book is about time. About how time changes us and how we change time. About the acceleration – and eventual cessation – of time across the life course. About the refusal or denial of time. About our reluctance to appreciate the time remaining before, or extending beyond, the grave. About a time of life that sits indistinctly between youth and old age, between birth and death. About conjunctions and conflicts between social, cultural, historical and biological time, between individual and collective time, between clock time and emotional time. About the manner in which contested notions of ageing, crisis and identity have been employed to rationalize, but also disrupt, relationships with ourselves and others across time. About how to balance – and survive – the pleasures and demands of love and work throughout the life course. About how changing patterns of marriage, infidelity, separation and divorce, as well as the mechanisms for regulating the breakdown of relationships, have shaped and reshaped families, communities and societies. About the extent to which a critical moment – or decade – can define a life, a family, a century.

Successfully mastering the combined stresses and strains of research and middle age requires accomplices – beyond regular measures of Writers Tears, the incomparable champagne of Irish whiskey. Development of the research ideas over the last few years has been facilitated by colleagues, archivists and librarians who have generously shared their expertise and resources. I am indebted to Fred Cooper, Natasha Feiner and Nicole-Kerstin Baur for identifying relevant archival and published sources; to Martin Moore, Ali Haggett and Nicos Kefalas, as well as Fred and Natasha, for their energetic contributions to the collaborative project on notions of balance in modern medicine, from which this book emerged; to colleagues in the Wellcome Centre for Cultures and Environments of Health; to Nils Fietje and his team at WHO Europe for their commitment to addressing the challenge of linking research in the humanities with public health policy; to audiences at conferences, workshops and seminars in cities and countries around the world for listening patiently to my nascent reflections on the meanings and manifestations of midlife; and to librarians and archivists at the Wellcome Library, the Clara Thomas Archives at York University in Toronto, the Mass-Observation Archive at The Keep, University of Sussex, and the Royal College of General Practitioners, London.

I am grateful to Michael Leaman and Ben Hayes at Reaktion, who were reassuringly enthusiastic about the project when I first discussed it with them. Michael's astute comments on the first draft were especially helpful in clarifying the evidence and refining the arguments. I would also like to thank Phoebe Colley for carefully coordinating the editorial and production process, and Linda Smith for her attentive proofreading. At the University of Exeter, I have been generously supported by Steve Smith, Janice Kay and Andrew Thorpe, who have always tolerated and trusted my aspirations to build research capacity in medical humanities. None of the work presented in this book would have been possible without the support of the Wellcome Trust, which funded the Senior Investigator Award (Grant No.100601/z/12/z) that provided time and resources necessary to pursue research that has become progressively significant to me, personally and professionally.

Loyal companions through midlife – or indeed across the longer curve of life – are difficult to find. Against all odds, I am deeply fortunate to have loved, and been loved by, Siobhán, an intimate friend, accomplice and lover of incomparable beauty and fidelity, who has sustained me through the multiple crises that have threatened to capsize us over the last three decades: parenthood; work-related stress; ill health; grief; and the fear, loneliness and loss of life generated by a devastating pandemic. Together with our mercurial children, Ciara, Riordan and Conall, it is Siobhán who has made possible my safe passage through the physical, emotional, family and occupational challenges of middle age and enabled me to reconcile myself to the realization that eventually – as Eugene O'Neill put it rather bleakly in 1939 – 'the iceman cometh' to us all.

PHOTO ACKNOWLEDGEMENTS

The author and publishers wish to express their thanks to the following sources of illustrative material and/or permission to reproduce it:

The Advertising Archives, London: pp. 109, 126, 160; photo courtesy British Cartoon Archive, Templeman Library, University of Kent, Canterbury: p. 78; from George Draper, *Human Constitution: Its Significance in Medicine and How It May Be Studied* (Baltimore, MD, 1928): p. 183; from Alexander A. Plateris, *100 Years of Marriage and Divorce Statistics, United States, 1867–1967* (Rockville, MD, 1973), photo courtesy Stephen B. Thacker CDC Library Collection: p. 75; Punch Cartoon Library/TopFoto: p. 94; Wellcome Library, London: p. 143.

INDEX

Page numbers in *italics* indicate illustrations